The Complete Poetry and Translations

CLARK ASHTON SMITH

The Complete Poetry and Translations

Volume 1: *The Abyss Triumphant*

Edited by S. T. Joshi and David E. Schultz

Hippocampus Press

New York

Cover Design by Barbara Briggs Silbert.
Hippocampus Press logo designed by Anastasia Damianakos.

Published by Hippocampus Press
P.O. Box 641, New York, NY 10156
www.hippocampuspress.com

The Library of Congress has cataloged the hardcover edition as follows:

Smith, Clark Ashton, 1893-1961.
[Poems]
The complete poetry and translations / Clark Ashton Smith ; edited by S. T. Joshi and David E. Schultz. -- 1st ed.
p. cm.
Includes bibliographical references and index.
ISBN-13: 978-0-9771734-0-2 (v. 3)
I. Joshi, S. T., 1958- II. Schultz, David E., 1952- III. Title.
PS3537.M335A6 2007
811'.52--dc22

2006039390

First Paperback Edition, 2012
1 3 5 7 9 8 6 4 2

ISBN 978-1-61498-045-2 (Volume 1)
ISBN 978-1-61498-048-3 (3 Volume Set)

Contents

Volume 1

Volume 2

Introduction

Clark Ashton Smith (1893–1961) has long been recognized as a pioneering writer of fantasy, horror, and supernatural fiction; but his earliest literary work, and the work for which he first attained celebrity, was poetry. Even before his first volume, *The Star-Treader and Other Poems* (1912), was published, he was being hailed as a modern-day Keats or Swinburne, and poetry remained his primary mode of literary creation for most of his fifty-year career as a writer.

This is not the place for a critical analysis or evaluation of Smith's poetry.[1] Instead, this introduction seeks to provide a broad overview of the progression of Smith's poetic work and to elucidate the principles governing the preparation and arrangement of this edition.

Smith's first "poem," a three-line bit of doggerel about his mother, probably dates to the age of seven or eight, but Smith himself declared that he was inspired to write poetry when he read Edgar Allan Poe's verse at the age of thirteen.[2] Smith appears to suggest that, during the next four or five years, he wrote not only "long adventure novels dealing with Oriental life" (such as *The Black Diamonds*) but also "much mediocre verse."[3] An examination of his extant poetic juvenilia indicates that the dominant influence on this work was not Poe but the Persian poet Omar Khayyam (as filtered through the translation of Edward FitzGerald). Smith had, at any rate, absorbed much information about the Middle East, India, and other exotic realms either from the *Arabian Nights* or from reference works. His non-Arabian juvenilia tends to be somewhat conventionally moralistic and didactic—a curious feature from a writer who, in adulthood, vigorously rejected didacticism and pursued the ideal of "pure poetry."

In 1907 Smith discovered the work of a living writer who would exercise the greatest influence on his poetry, early and late: George Sterling. Sterling had published a volume, *The Testimony of the Suns and Other Poems* (1903), that had attracted wide attention in his native California and elsewhere. But Smith apparently first read Sterling only when the long poem, "A Wine of Wizardry," appeared in *Cosmopolitan* (September 1907), prefaced by a lengthy encomium of it by Ambrose Bierce. Smith speaks eloquently of his initial reaction to the poem:

1. Valuable work on the interpretation of Smith's poetry has been done in such items as *Nyctalops* No. 7 (August 1972 [special Clark Ashton Smith memorial issue]), Donald Sidney-Fryer's *The Last of the Great Romantic Poets* (Albuquerque, NM: Silver Scarab Press, 1973), and *The Freedom of Fantastic Things*, ed. Scott Connors (New York: Hippocampus Press, 2006), among others.
2. See "George Sterling—An Appreciation" (*SU* 294). For abbreviations used in this introduction and elsewhere, see Vol. 2, pp. 653–55.
3. "An Autobiography of Clark Ashton Smith" (*PD* 42).

> The poem, with its necromantic music, and splendours as of sunset on jewels and cathedral windows, was veritably all that its title implied; and—to pile marvel upon enchantment—there was the knowledge that it had been written in my own time, by someone who lived little more than a hundred miles away. In the ruck of magazine verse it was a fire-opal of the Titans in a potato-bin; and, after finding it, I ransacked all available contemporary periodicals, for verse by George Sterling, to be rewarded, not too frequently, with some marmoreal sonnet or "molten golden" lyric. (*SU* 294)

It would appear, then, that the work of Sterling turned Smith definitively into the direction of writing primarily *fantastic* verse, something that had not been notably evident in his juvenilia. As with Poe, the influence of Sterling is not easily detectable in Smith's very early juvenilia, but it begins to manifest itself in the work that he appears to have done in the period around 1910. It was at this time that a distinctively "cosmic" vein—inspired in part by Sterling's long "star-poem," *The Testimony of the Suns*—becomes apparent. Of course, Smith would not have been so taken with this phase of Sterling's work had he not been independently inclined toward it.

Smith appears to have written a great deal of poetry in the 1910–11 period. He notes that, in 1911, he showed his work to an English teacher at the Auburn High School, Emily J. Hamilton, who took the initiative of sending some of it, along with a cover letter, to Sterling himself, then residing in Carmel. Sterling was immediately taken with the work and, as Bierce had done for him a decade earlier, he wrote back, encouraging Smith to continue and acting as his mentor. Smith had actually published two poems in 1910—"Moonlight" in the *Overland Monthly* and "The Sierras" in *Munsey's*—but these relatively conventional poems soon gave way to the prodigiously original work that Smith produced in the 1911–12 period. It was during this time that Smith wrote the great bulk of the poems that constituted *The Star-Treader and Other Poems,* which Sterling arranged for publication with the San Francisco bookseller and publisher A. M. Robertson. In August 1912, as a result of public discussions of Smith's work by Sterling, Ambrose Bierce (who had read and appreciated Smith's "Ode to the Abyss"), and Boutwell Dunlap (who claimed to be Smith's "discoverer"), Smith experienced a flurry of attention in local newspapers, and his work even attained a flicker of national interest in such periodicals as *Current Literature.* That attention was augmented when *The Star-Treader* appeared in November 1912.

Over the next ten years, Smith began his career as a prose-poet and produced verse only sporadically. He would later declare that "My comparative non-productiveness during the ten years given to *E. & C.* [*Ebony and Crystal,*

1922] was due largely to ill-health."[4] Smith's maladies were of various sorts—both an apparent case of tuberculosis and a succession of nervous or psychological ailments, partially the result of living a lonely and isolated life in the small town of Auburn. Smith continued to show his work to Sterling, and, beginning around 1913, to a new correspondent, Samuel Loveman, and attempted to place his poems in both major national magazines such as the *Atlantic Monthly* and the *North American Review* (where he was uniformly rejected) and local magazines and newspapers. In 1912 he managed to have some poems published in the newly founded Chicago journal *Poetry,* but its subsequent devotion to avant-garde verse largely barred Smith from its pages. When Sterling's colleague H. L. Mencken became editor of the *Smart Set* in late 1914, Smith published several poems there—although usually through the mediation of Sterling. Sterling and Albert Bender—a wealthy San Francisco businessman who would become Smith's occasional patron—arranged for the publication of *Odes and Sonnets* (1918) by the prestigious Book Club of California; it contained 15 poems, of which 11 were previously uncollected.

As early as 1912, Sterling had encouraged Smith to go beyond his "cosmic" verse and seek new subjects for his poetic imagination. Smith eventually followed Sterling's advice and began to produce some elegiac and lyric poetry by the middle of the decade—possibly inspired by his various love affairs with women (several of them married) in Auburn. One woman in particular, Mamie Lowe Miller, inspired great affection from Smith, and her death in 1917 caused Smith to "go mad with grief and a guilty conscience" (*SU* 141), although he also produced the exquisite elegy "Requiescat in Pace" and other work to commemorate her passing. Sterling welcomed this expansion of Smith's poetic palette, since he had himself virtually abandoned the cosmicism of the *Testimony of the Suns* period. Smith's work was, by this time, being published somewhat more widely in national magazines—either in specialized poetry journals such as the *Sonnet* or in popular magazines such as *Live Stories* and *Ainslee's.*

Smith apparently completed the compilation of his next volume of poetry, *Ebony and Crystal,* as early as 1918. In 1920 he submitted the manuscript to Alfred A. Knopf (*SL* 54); possibly he thought that Mencken's influence with Knopf might work in his favor. But the volume was rejected, and since A. M. Robertson was now publishing only books by Sterling, Smith had to publish the volume himself, hiring the printer of the *Auburn Journal* for the job. It appeared in late 1922. At 152 pages, it would be Smith's largest poetry collection published in his lifetime (the last 25 pages consisted of prose-poems). But because the volume sold poorly, Smith had to work off his debt to

4. Letter to Donald Wandrei (4 July 1926); *Selected Letters of Clark Ashton Smith,* ed. David E. Schultz and Scott Connors (Sauk City, WI: Arkham House, 2003), p. 88. Hereafter cited in the text as *SL.*

the printer by becoming a columnist for the *Auburn Journal*. In his column, Smith published a substantial number of the poems he wrote during this period. By 1925 he felt he had written enough to assemble another, somewhat slimmer volume, *Sandalwood*. This also was published by the *Auburn Journal*, funded partly by Smith's new colleague and disciple, Donald Wandrei. *Sandalwood* contained not only original poems but also the first of Smith's translations of Baudelaire's *Les Fleurs du mal*—the result of Smith's having taught himself French in the early 1920s. (For Smith's translations of French and Spanish poetry, see Volume 3.)

Even before *Sandalwood* appeared in late 1925, Smith evidently had conceived his next volume of poetry: "I am planning a new book which will contain nothing but pure poetry, no sentimentalities, no philosophical aridities—nothing but the strange, the magical, and the gorgeous! *Incantations* might be a good title for this book . . . which, in all likelihood, I will have to print at my own expense" (*SL* 79). In 1928 Smith announced that the book was ready: "I haven't even tried anyone with *Incantations,* but may sometime muster up sufficient courage to send to Pascal Covici, of Chicago" (*SL* 102). In early 1929 Smith noted: "I have written a few poems . . . and have put my new volume of verse, which I have entitled *The Jasmine Girdle and Other Poems,* in the hands of a N. Y. literary agent who thinks he might inveigle some publisher into bringing it out" (*SL* 103). The long history of these two never-published volumes is difficult to disentangle, and the extant tables of contents (see Appendix) only appear to confuse the picture. Smith's letters from a much later period—the mid- to late 1930s—suggest that *The Jasmine Girdle* is merely a section of *Incantations,* as when he refers to "*The Jasmine Girdle,* or other material from *Incantations*" (*SL* 321). In early 1936, after R. H. Barlow offered to print *Incantations,* Smith sent him a typescript with the accompanying letter: "The typescript of *Incantations* goes forward to you by express. It includes 65 titles: 49 more or less lyric poems, 18 of which are grouped under the subtitle of The Jasmine Girdle; 3 renderings from Paul Verlaine, 9 from Baudelaire; and 4 of my prose pastels at the end" (*SL* 272). This description seems to correspond to the surviving table of contents (see Appendix, pp. 683–84), although it has 52 lyric poems rather than 49.[5] Meanwhile, two separate tables of contents for *The Jasmine Girdle* survive, one of which, paradoxically, contains a section of seven poems titled "Incantations"! Otherwise, this list contains a total of 35 original poems and 9 translations from Baudelaire; the other list contains only 17 poems, four of which are translations from Verlaine. None of the tables of contents matches the now distinct sections entitled "Incantations" and "The Jasmine Girdle" in *Selected Poems.*

George Sterling's death on November 17, 1926, certainly affected Smith strongly, but it did not have any immediately deleterious effects on his poetic

5. CAS had instructed Barlow to insert three additional poems in later correspondence.

output; indeed, in 1927 he wrote as many as 16 poems—a good yield as compared to several years of the 1913–22 period. His personal sense of loss was perhaps mitigated by the emergence of H. P. Lovecraft as a strong friend and colleague. Having first established epistolary contact in 1922, both writers witnessed the rise of the pulp magazine *Weird Tales* as a new outlet for fantastic fiction and poetry; and this and other markets in the fantasy and science fiction pulps, as well as Lovecraft's own example as a fiction writer, no doubt encouraged Smith to turn his attention to prose fiction and away from poetry as a creative and, preeminently, a remunerative outlet. From late 1929 to early 1935 Smith produced more than 100 tales of fantasy, horror, and science fiction, permanently establishing his reputation in these genres; during this same period, only 20 poems can be definitively identified, several of which are either Christmas greetings or epigraphs to his prose tales. In the spring of 1935 Smith at last resumed the writing of poetry, although his output was still quite low; only one poem ("Song of the Necromancer") can be clearly dated to the entire year 1936. Smith had been writing fiction chiefly to support his ailing parents, and the death of his mother on September 9, 1935, of his father on December 26, 1937, and of Lovecraft on March 15, 1937, must have had a considerable influence on his surcease of fiction writing, and perhaps of his literary productivity as a whole. Smith had, in any case, by this time turned to sculpture as a creative outlet.

Smith underwent a renewal of poetic inspiration in 1939, upon the development of his friendship with the poet Eric Barker and his wife, the dancer Madelynne Greene. It was during the years 1939–47 that Smith produced most of the poems that came to constitute the poetry cycle entitled *The Hill of Dionysus*. Although Smith claimed that he was doing more "living" than "writing" during the early part of this period, his incentive to renewed literary work—specifically to poetry—was inspired by his old friends August Derleth and Donald Wandrei, who in 1939 had founded Arkham House to publish the work of Lovecraft and other pulp writers. Recognizing the value of Smith's poetry, Derleth, and Wandrei especially, encouraged him to assemble a large volume of his *Selected Poems*. Smith began work on the project in 1944, and later that year he was writing optimistically that "Derleth and Wandrei hope to bring [it] out in 1945 or 1946" (*SL* 347). Of course, Smith himself would not even complete the assembly of the volume until 1949, and it would not appear until years after his death, in 1971. Most of the poetry volumes published by Arkham House were subsidized by their authors, but Derleth and Wandrei did not require Smith to fund the enormous undertaking. As a result, the money to cover the printing bills for what would probably prove to be a slow seller was never at hand.

Smith, for his part, worked diligently at not merely assembling but in extensively revising much of his poetry, especially his early work. In 1948 he wrote: "The heaviest revision, some of it including the partial or entire recasting of poems, has been on the *Star-Treader* group and certain unpublished pieces of the same or a slightly posterior date. . . . Revision of old work is a hellish task; but I hope that I have salvaged some poems which, in their original form, were too inferior or uneven" (*SL* 352–53). At the end of the whole process, Smith noted on December 1, 1949: "My *Selected Poems,* on which I have spent infinite labor, go forward to the publishers today" (*SL* 363). In the five-year period during which Smith worked on the volume, it perhaps took some turns that he did not expect. In the late 1940s, for example, as a result of helping Kenneth Yasuda in the translation of some Japanese haiku, Smith himself became intrigued by the possibilities of haiku as an English poetic form, producing more than 100 such poems and creating a section in *Selected Poems* for them.

Smith's poetic work did not by any means end with the compilation of *Selected Poems.* In 1949 he taught himself Spanish, just as he had taught himself French more than two decades earlier, and not only produced translations from Spanish poets but also began writing poems in Spanish. This work postdated his completion of *Selected Poems,* so that the Spanish poems are largely unpublished. In 1951, Derleth—who, as early as 1942, had taken over daily operations at Arkham House, especially when Donald Wandrei entered the army—perhaps mortified at the delay in issuing *Selected Poems,* decided to publish a slim, interim volume of Smith's poetry. The result was *The Dark Chateau* (1951), containing 18 poems taken from *Selected Poems* and 22 poems apparently written since its compilation. Seven years later, Derleth issued the equally slim *Spells and Philtres,* containing 60 poems, 52 of which were from *Selected Poems.* Smith wrote few poems following the publication of *Spells and Philtres,* and his last poem, "Cycles," was written on June 4, 1961, about two months before his death on August 14.

Smith's first literary executor, Roy A. Squires, clearly recognized the value of Smith's poetic work, and he issued a number of small-press volumes of selected bodies of this work—notably *The Hill of Dionysus: A Selection* (1962), in which Smith had a hand, followed by two separate series of "The Fugitive Poems of Clark Ashton Smith," the first (1970) consisting of four slim volumes (or "fascicles"), the second (1974–77) of six. Many of these volumes contained relatively early work, probably from the 1910–12 period. *Selected Poems,* finally issued in 1971, itself contained more than 500 poems, but as Smith's total poetic output extends to nearly 1000 poems (a figure that does not include his hundreds of translations), much remained uncollected or unpublished. A later literary executor, Richard Kuhn, donated Smith's papers—consisting of more than forty large and rather heterogeneous boxes of manuscripts, correspondence, and other material—to the John Hay Library of Brown University in 1979, where it was catalogued and made available for researchers around 1982. Many of Smith's poetry manuscripts have found their way into other institutions, and some remain in private hands.

The totality of Smith's poetic work is an achievement of impressive literary value. It is by no means an exaggeration to declare Smith not merely a great *fantastic* poet, although he is clearly preeminent in that narrow realm, but also one of the great American poets of the twentieth century. The fact that his poetry did not hew to the fashions of his time—especially the Modernist movement led by T. S. Eliot, William Carlos Williams, Hart Crane, and others—is no reflection on its merits, however much it may have hindered Smith's recognition in his own time. Although Smith adhered in general to formal poetic meters such as the sonnet, the quatrain, and the rhymed couplet, his early odes are a striking anticipation of free verse, while his late "satires and travesties" pungently mock the excesses that have made much modern poetry an unwitting parody of itself. His early emphasis on the poetry of the cosmos yielded to a wide imaginative scope, ranging from exquisite love poetry (including some vivid erotic verse) to philosophical, pastoral, and even political verse. But in even the most mundane of his poems, there was always a "touch of strange," and the "whisper of the worm" never seemed out of earshot. Smith's early readings of Poe, Keats, Swinburne, and Sterling led him to make extensive use of Greco-Roman myth, but it can be seen that he did so in a vital and not merely an academic or antiquarian manner; even in later verse, his allusions to the Greek gods or to forgotten locales such as Tyre or Ilium give them a new and vibrant reality. The publication of Clark Ashton Smith's complete poetry will, it is hoped, not merely encourage renewed study of his entire literary output but also grant him his rightful place in the canon of American and world literature.

—S. T. JOSHI
DAVID E. SCHULTZ

A Note on This Edition

This edition seeks to print the entirety of Clark Ashton Smith's extant poetry, published and unpublished, and including poems or poetic fragments found in letters, his *Black Book,* and elsewhere. The bulk of Smith's poetry has previously appeared in *Selected Poems* (1971), a volume that contained some 500 of his poems; but nearly as many poems remain uncollected or unpublished. While at first glance it may seem sensible to preserve not only Smith's textual preferences but also his methods of arrangement for *Selected Poems* in any subsequent edition of his poetry, we have come to feel that our edition—in essence an archival collection of Smith's *complete* poetry, rather than a mere selection, however extensive—should be governed by different principles, and that a strictly chronological scheme, insofar as it can be ascertained, presents a more accurate view of the scope and direction of Smith's poetic output, regardless of the collections that appeared (or, in the case of *Incantations* and *The*

Jasmine Girdle, did not appear) in his lifetime or posthumously. Thus, the editors have sought to print the poems in chronological sequence by date of original composition; but we have printed Smith's latest revisions to these poems, even if the revisions occurred decades later. Evidence for the date of writing of a substantial number of poems exists in many forms: many manuscripts or typescripts of poems are dated; Smith referred to his poems in correspondence, or his correspondents (especially George Sterling and Samuel Loveman) did so; date of publication in a magazine or collection establishes an end-date for composition; and so on. We have supplied information on dates of composition of many poems in our notes, especially when the manuscript is dated; we have not always supplied our source of information when we have found a mention of a poem in a letter.

Many poems have, however, been placed in a chronological sequence in the absence of a firm date of composition. In these cases, we have used our judgment, internal evidence, and other methods to establish an approximate date. Certain points in Smith's biography are relevant to this task. For example, he had essentially completed the assembly of *Ebony and Crystal* (1922) by the end of 1918, so that those poems from that volume that are otherwise undated have been placed at the end of 1918. Smith began composing poems in French only in the mid- to late 1920s, so that most of his poems in French date to the period 1925–35. Smith did not learn Spanish until the 1950s, so that his Spanish poems probably date to this decade. Most of his haiku probably date to the late 1940s, and therefore have been placed in one section in Volume 2. His satires appear to date, for the most part, to the 1940s and 1950s. Smith ceased to capitalize the initial letters of his poems in the 1950s, so that otherwise undated poems that feature this typographical element presumably date to this decade.

Smith's juvenile poems (probably written in the period 1905–09) have been placed in an appendix in Volume 1; the notes to these poems can be found after the notes to the poems of his mature period, followed by notes to the fragments (the texts of which are placed at the end of Volume 2). Poems that Smith deliberately subtitled as "Fragments," and published as such, are placed in the main body of the text.

In our notes, we have sought to identify the extant manuscripts of the poems and their publication (in newspapers, magazines, anthologies, and Smith's collections of poetry) within his lifetime (and, in some cases, in posthumous volumes). In cases where more than one source (either manuscript or printed) exists, we have indicated our copy-text with an asterisk. We have not in every case used an extant manuscript as our copy-text, as there are instances where, in our judgment, a printed text presents a superior or revised text. This is especially the case for the poems in *Selected Poems* (compiled 1944–49), which can be thought to embody Smith's final wishes in nearly every instance. There is, however, evidence that Smith consciously revised a number of poems from the *Selected Poems* manuscript when he assembled *The Dark Chateau* (1951) and *Spells and Philtres* (1958), and when he prepared a late transcript of *Sandalwood* (c. 1952) for Roy A. Squires, so that in some instances we have used the texts of these poems as our copy-text. In a few instances (especially in regard to early poems), Smith's revisions are so extensive that they constitute virtually new poems; in these cases, we have printed both the early version and the later version in their proper chronological sequences.

Our notes also contain elucidations of historical, literary, mythological, or other references in the poems; space restrictions have prevented us from being as exhaustive as we would have liked in this matter. In only a few instances have we included variant readings in our notes; Smith repeatedly revised his poems for each subsequent appearance, and the printing of such variants, while highly illuminating, would have expanded our commentary beyond reasonable bounds. We have sought to print Smith's texts as accurately, and as much in accordance with Smith's apparent wishes, as possible. In the case of his poems in French and Spanish, however, we have printed the titles in accordance with contemporary rules for capitalization of titles in the languages in question. It does not appear that Smith wished his poems with foreign titles to be printed in italics, so we have not done so.

It is the editors' privilege to thank the many individuals and institutions that have assisted us over the many years during which this edition was prepared. Preeminently, we are grateful to the staff of the John Hay Library of Brown University, especially Mark Brown, Barbara Filipac, Gerald Gaidmore, and Timothy Engels, for their courtesy in allowing us unprecedented access to the Clark Ashton Smith manuscripts in their possession. We are also grateful to the staff in the archives and special collections of the Wisconsin Historical Society; Susan Graham of the University of Maryland, Baltimore County; Wendy Wood of the Harrison Memorial Library, Carmel-by-the-Sea; and Susan M. Allison of the Bruce Pelz Fanzine Collection, UCR Special Collections, Rivera Library. Philippe Gindre and David Dunais supplied invaluable assistance in the editing of Smith's poems in French. Others who assisted us are Michael Abolafia, Douglas A. Anderson, Steve Behrends, Greg Belt, Scott Connors, Stefan Dziemianowicz, John D. Haefele, Mara Kirk Hart, Don Herron, Rah Hoffman, Derrick Hussey, Marc A. Michaud, Stuart David Schiff, Steve Sneyd, and Roy A. Squires. Special thanks are extended to Donald Sidney-Fryer who, in the early 1980s, shared much of his groundbreaking work, which served as the foundation to this volume.

The Voice of Silence

1910–1911

Cloudland

A faery land is this that far and high
And all suffused with tints of pearl and rose,
Above the crimson sunset hangs and glows,
By unseen hands upborne 'twixt earth and sky.
Vales long and broad and uppiled mountains lie,
Upon their pinnacles eternal snows
Within its bounds; a silv'ry river flows
Across yon plain within a lake to die.

Beside that lake a city great and fair
With opal walls and palaces doth stand,
Its minarets agleam with magic light.
How high and tapering they rear in air
O'er rounded domes where banners fanned
By phantom winds wave beautiful and bright!

The Fountain of Youth

Men sought a magic spring long years ago,
One draught of which would youth fore'er renew.
What need to seek afar? That fountain's flow
Runs ever Nature's dales and forests through.

The Road of Pain

A haggard scar across Life's verdant plain
Straight runs the Road of Pain,
The road of anguish, of despair and dread
Whereon all feet must tread.

Prince, merchant, mendicant, must all essay
That long and thorny way.
Through pitiless days each shall with gasping breath
Implore surcease or death.

At last shall come the long-with[h]eld release,
The Road shall lead to peace.

Reincarnation

When one who for a space has lived 'mong men
Some morn shall sudden pass beyond our ken,
Say not with sobs and tears that he is dead.
Say but that he to some new star is sped.

Lethe

Seekst thou that Lethe of whose depths profound
One drinking shall his sorrows all forget?
Not on this earth are Lethe's waters found:
That pool beyond the gates of Death is set.

A White Rose

Emblem of beauty thou shouldst be,
    That of all roses art most fair;
One day thou bloomest regally,
    Upon the morrow all is bare.

Death

Not as a tyrant cruel, hard and cold,
    A monarch unrelenting and severe,
    Think I of Death, whom all the many fear
And walk in daily terror of; I hold
The thought of one who doth the weary fold
    With gentle arms, and lays them on the bier
    Of earth, at rest and peace, as fall the sere
And withered autumn leaves. But from of old
Hath not the tree new leaves put forth? So may
The soul fresh forms assume another day;
    Thus testifies the miracle of spring,
Wherewith the leafless brumal world is rife.
    Who can the bare earth's time of blossoming
Behold, and say Death is the end of Life?

Companionship

The summit won at last, I stopped,
    And turned to trace, through wood and dale,

Where, robed in pine, the hill-side dropped,
    My devious, toilsome upward trail.

In air of midday, warm and still,
    Alone above the world I stood,
And held the silence of the hill,
    That reared in rugged solitude.

Yet not alone, for overhead
    An eagle rose and skyward flew,
With wings against the sun outspread—
    A climber of the hills of blue.

Illusion

Oft have I seen the sunset-fires
Illume the slumbering fen's extreme,
With splendour like the seraph's dream,
Or the fair light the soul desires.

In avenues of cypress-gloom,
The graveyard-loving moon forlorn
Has often seemed a ghostly morn—
Or cerements of a riven tomb.

The Call of the Wind

I hear the west wind's call through the window open flung:
"Oh, come ye forth the budding woods and fields among.
Your cares and worries fling like a worn-out cloak aside;
And come ye swiftly forth where the vernal day is wide;
Come ye out to the fields and the blue-pavilioned hills,
Where the wakened earth to the sun's warm kisses thrills;
And the songs of the birds are a rapturous paean of praise
To the joy and the beauty of Spring's first perfect days."
I hear the west wind's call, and I must arise and go
Out where the day is fair and the joyous breezes blow.

The Expanding Ideal

Up arduous slopes one shall attain, outworn,
    The peak he thought supreme, which shall reveal
    The loftier heights it served but to conceal.
Thus shall one win what seemed Achievement's bourne,

Crowned by his highest dream, and stand forlorn,
For from that place shall to his eyes appeal
A hitherto unglimpsed, more high Ideal
On nobler summits, lit by larger morn.

This is the Law. Upon the Upward Way,
With progress doth the inner sight expand:
The ends we strove to gain but yesterday,
At winning small and insufficient stand,
For from that vantage have our eyes descried
The greater ends the lesser served to hide.

Imagination

Imagination, to thine occult sight,
All things are crystal—earth, and sea, and sky,
The seen and the unseen, but limpid light;
Unvisioned stars shall not thy wings defy;
For thee the Future hath no secrecy:
Not with the senses dost thou share the chains
Of Time, and Space's prison; thou dost fly
At will the narrow bourne of their domains
For realms where never bruit of Time and Space attains.

All earth is empire of thy tireless quest:
Thy wings achieve the cloud-invested height,
Or down the distant sunset-flooded West,
Thou vanishest in long unerring flight,
That far outspeeds the swarthy plumes of Night.
Thou findest rest a space on sunset sands,
But soon a star, with Westward-sinking light,
Doth speak of more remote, untrodden strands,
And forth thou farest toward those undiscovered lands.

No realm nor place is secret from thy gaze.
The kingdoms of the bird and fish are thine:
Thy pinions try the eagle's lucid ways,
Then sink to search the foaming vasts of brine.
Thou soar'st to meet the morning's lucent shine,
Where Night and Day beneath thy feet are spread
In long insuperable battle-line;
Then in a breath thou front'st the sunset's red,
Or seekest midnight's realm of mystery and dread.

The ocean yields its secrets unto thee:
    Far down beneath the agitated wave,
Where winds stir not the anger of the sea,
    Thou plungest to some Nereid's emerald cave,
Whose floors the varied shells of ocean pave.
    Here wealth of pearls and strange sea-flowers is thine,
But soon, aweary grown, thy soul doth crave
    The noontide air, and where the breakers shine,
Thou soar'st to watch their furious cliff-assailing line.

And then thou questest dusks obscure and strange—
    Perpetual twilights—in some jungle's heart,
Where darkness comes, a scarcely-noted change.
    Here trees inweave, as if with conscious art,
O'er pools that of the gloom appear a part,
    Nor know the silver kiss of star or moon;
And birds strange-plumaged, unauthentic, dart
    Through shadows that affirm and then impugn
And leaves and flowers unfamiliar to the noon.

Now o'er a Winter land thou hoverest,
    Its sunlit snow to mark, on transient wing.
To trees, in glittering icy armour dressed,
    Mild Southern winds bear bruit of coming Spring,
And seek to rouse, with amorous whispering,
    The white-robed grass; the clouds austere and grey
That late were earth's dark-vaulted covering,
    In ranks disordered, dim, now flee away,
And skies of azure threaten Winter's waning sway.

Thy pinions find a desert drear, forlorn,
    Where purple Night fills all the fruitless land,
Deepest a little ere the East of morn
    Grows ominous. Her all-deleting hand
Seems promise that her reign awhile shall stand,
    When Day, with baleful Cyclopean eye,
Upleaps in flame, and of his sway the sand
    Grows ostent, swift. In gardens of the sky,
At his fell breath, the stars are withered utterly!

Of other worlds thy wings ambitious are:
    O'er airless gulfs that yawn past reach of Day—
Unfathomed voids of space 'twixt star and star,
    Unhesitatingly thou dost essay
Some world exclusive from the sun's wide sway.

Strange forms of life thine eyes thereon descry—
New, unfamiliar,—that yet tread a way,
Which, dim and difficult, like ours doth lie
Through dark and pain, toward goals that gleam in unity.

The outer barriers of our system past,
Thou stayst thy flight, to mark in awe and dread,
Some world that ruins down the darkling vast,
Or suns and asteroids, that hurtling red,
To cataclysmic vortices are fed,
And equallized in ruin. Then in gloom
Of planets derelict, long ages dead,
That whirl where never suns nor stars illume,
Thou 'light'st a space to muse upon their frozen doom.

Thy magic spells recall the Past to life,
Before thine eyes the pageant of the years
Doth move, with its reanimated strife,
Its record of forgotten hopes and fears;
Dead loves and hates, and buried joys, and tears
Long-fallen, to thy voice obedient,
Arise and live again; unto thine ears
Voices for ages still are eloquent,
And thou beholdest forms long years in darkness pent.

Once more the might of Rome and Babylon
Lies as a shadow over East and West;
Again Greece sheds a glory as of dawn,
Whose lambent splendour all the years attest;
Once more in empire's tidal, quick unrest,
Egypt and Tyre and Persia rise in state,
And Alexander's world-lust is addressed
Unto their humbling; thrones and nations great
Again are raised or levelled, as the Fates dictate.

'Mong peoples and through realms restored to light,
At will thou wanderest. Thou dost behold
Swart Egypt's gods, enthroned in templed might
Along the Nile, and 'fore thine eyes unfold
Their vanished pomps, with glare of gems and gold;
Thou look'st on Rome, when at its utmost height,
Her grandeur dazzled earth; the wars of old
Upflame and rage anew within thy sight,
With sanguine pageant of advance, retreat, and fight.

The Sunrise

Clear-cut the mountains tower high,
Against the paling eastern blue;
As snow-crowned kings they seem to lie,
Enwrapt in robes of purple hue.

Now suddenly upon the snow
Of yonder peak Day's lance-points gleam,
And tipped with flame, set it aglow—
A crimson beacon-pyre supreme

That signals the retreat of Night,
Whose sovereignty grows old and wan,
And who afar must wing her flight,
Before the banners of the Dawn.

In harness brave soon comes the Sun,
To enter on his ancient reign,
And sets his regal seal upon
The far expanse of his domain.

Night

The fires of sunset die reluctantly
As goes the kingly Day to seek his rest,
And Night, the sable queen, comes sombrely,
In dusky robes, with stars upon her breast.

Mistress of peace is she, who quiet brings,
And mystic balm of healing in her train,
Who drops Sleep's magic feather from her wings
To soothe a tired world's weariness and pain.

To a Yellow Pine

A giant tall, and arrow-straight
Alone upon a hilltop sate
O'erlooking from thy dizzy hold
A canyon deep, where far below
A mountain stream doth dashing flow
Thou art. For years and years untold
Thou there hast stood, in e'er green mail,
Defiant of the tempest's rage
Unbowed, unharmed, from age to age,
Through rain and sun a monarch hale.

* * *

How far, magnificent thy view
For higher than thy tufted head,
The eagle's flight alone is sped.
Up in the vast, unmeasured blue.
How far, how far the wooded hills
In wild and jumbled disarray,
Towards gentler lowlands stretch away,
With all their leaping streams and rills.
To east the blue Sierras lie
With heads half-hid by clouds that go
Across the sky like drifting snow
Before the southland's balmy sigh.
This is thy realm, O giant pine
Who doth watch calm the hurried years
Flee past with freight of hopes and fears
Though not for thee their fevered sign.
Thou standeth here, apart, alone,
A lord of splendid solitudes,
Where man his presence rare intrudes
And to his spoiling hand unknown.

A Sierran Sunrise

Look yonder, where the whitened orient skies
    Grow splendid with the radiance of the dawn,
O'er regal mountains that majestic rise
    With misty purple robes about them drawn.

The painting of the masterpiece behold
    That every morn, before our careless eye,
Nature portrays, in crimson and in gold,
    Upon the canvas of the earth and sky.

Mark what unequaled and supernal hues—
    Ever the artist's dream and his despair—
She doth, with art supreme, unrivaled use,
    To limn her vision wonderful and fair.

Long-sought, elusive Beauty here descends,
    And for a moment unto Nature's hand
Her star-caught skill and inspiration lends,
    Whence springs this dawn miraculous and grand.

The Sierras

Snow-topped, the far Sierras rise
In long and varied martial line,
Whose peaks first hold the dawn's surprise,
And catch the lingering sunset's sign.

Eternal sentinels they stand,
Supreme beside the Western shore;
Vast guarders of the golden land
That watch and wait forevermore.

The Wind and the Moon

Oh, list to the wind of the night, oh, hark,
How it shrieks as it goes on its hurrying quest!
Forever its voice is a voice of the dark,
Forever its voice is a voice of unrest.
Oh, list to the pines as they shiver and sway
'Neath the ceaseless beat of its myriad wings—
How they moan and they sob like living things
That cry in the darkness for light and day!
Now bend they low as the wind mounts higher,
And its eerie voice comes piercingly,
Like the plaint of humanity's misery,
And its burden of vain desire.
Now to a sad, tense whisper it fails,
Then wildly and madly it raves and it wails.

Oh, the night is filled with its sob and its shriek,
Its weird and its restless, yearning cry,
As it races adown the darkened sky,
With scurry of broken clouds that seek,
Borne on the wings of the hastening wind,
A place of rest that they never can find.
And around the face of the moon they cling,
Its fugitive face to veil they aspire;
But ever and ever it peereth out,
Rending the cloud-ranks that hem it about;
And it seemeth a lost and phantom thing,
Like a phantom of dead desire.

Moonlight

Ambitious of their solitary reign,
Whose many-pointed brilliance fills the sky,
The silver moon doth rise in majesty,
And with her splendour shares the stars' domain.
Now as she takes her lucent course on high,
Her light doth shroud all things in mystery
And subtle glamour. As of realms unknown
It seems—a radiance from worlds that lie
Beyond our ken, and glimpsed in dreams alone.
And in those rays is tender witchery,
Which softly doth erase the scars of day,
And with a pallid beauty touches all.
The Moon's light is a painter's brush, and she
An artist skilled who doth the world array,
In silence with a white, enchanted pall.

The Altars of Sunset

With crimson fires you mountains flame—
    Huge, lofty altars of the West—
As sunset, hesitating, stays
    To dip in light each slope and crest.

Each summit holds the vivid blaze
    Till all are burning in array,
As if some priesthood there had lit
    A sacrifice to passing Day.

To George Sterling

High priest of this our latter Song,
    Whose voice sustains her empery
    Far-fled beside the western sea,
With ocean-tones thy voice is strong.

And as the spirit of a height,
    Whose calm, majestic eyes behold
    The lower hills like waves outrolled,
And watch from vantages of light

The abysmal surge of heavenly wars,
 And know sidereal mirth and pain,
 Thou call'st to me, who may not gain
Thy vast horizon of the stars.

Yet though I breathe a fainter tone,
 And bring to Beauty's deathless shrine
 A lesser offering than thine,
Whose blooms in loftier soil are grown,

Mayhap the note that I have sung,
 Obedient to the Muse's call,
 Is not in vain; the coronal
Of fragile flowers not voidly flung.

And this the recompense I find:
 To pass, a cadence of her lyre—
 A flame to feed her altar-fire—
And breath on some supernal wind.

The Voice of Silence

Hath Sound alone a voice? Nay, 'tis not so:
 Silence can speak unto the inner ear,
 If it be finely tuned and keyed to hear—
A meaning-laden message, soft and low.

Silence hath secrets of the farther spheres,
 And echoes caught from the Eternal Sounds
 That, past all earthly and diurnal bounds,
Are symphonies unto Eternal Ears.

Alas! our baser senses but discern,
 At moments rare, some faint and broken note—
 Some few words from the Perfect Poem float
To us. Ah, would that we the whole might learn!

Weavings

Cast to the world, and lost forever,
 And over the heavens drawn again—
Lightly woven and broken ever—
 Endless gossamers of rain
Shimmer and vanish, seeking ever
 To veil the world and the skies in vain.

Out from the twilight valleys risen,
Over the heavens' windless gleam,
Slowly a woven calm is risen,
Bordered with the sunset-beam;
And, lo! my unquiet soul has risen
From world and sky to the heart of a dream.

The West Wind

O keen west wind with the sea's salt tang
And the breath of a distant strand
Say, what are the things whereof you speak
As you fly o'er the hills inland?

Methinks in your murmuring voice I hear
The thunderous roar of the sea,
The crashing waves on the rocky beach
That boom everlastingly.

Methinks you speak of the white-sailed ships
That cleave thro' the main apace,
With the canvas taut and a line of foam
At the stern to mark their race.

Methinks as you speak of the isles afar,
With a faint, sweet breath of balm—
The isles of the deep-blue sunset seas—
Of the bamboo and the palm.

Methinks I hear in your sighing voice
The tale of a storm at sea—
The maddened waves and the splintered wrecks—
Such are the things you tell to me.

Before Sunrise

I rose in that hushed hour before the dawn
Unveils its wonder old yet ever-new,
When still the night lies languidly upon
The earth, though stars are growing faint and few.

Up the long path I went, nor paused to rest
Along the cool, dark way, till on the hill
I stood, where dawn's first breeze my brow caressed
With mingled odorous breath and mountain chill.

To-west hung heavily the drowsy night,
    Weighted with fog, low-clinging, grey and dim,
Adown each valley and about each height,
    Thro' which the sinking stars appeared to swim.

I turned, and lo! how pale the eastland's face,
    As if it mourned the starlit night's decline,
Ere youthful day, coming with eager pace,
    With kisses should that cheek incarnadine.

At Nadir

I mark yon ruddy star go down
    O'er hills mysterious with night,
And far-off peaks that darkly frown
    In towering and impassive might.

At last it trembles on the crest
    Of some vague, mist-enshrouded height,
A moment seeming to arrest
    Its downward and unswerving flight.

The Besieging Billows

When the high, rock-battlemented shore
    Unyielding, grim and pitiless
The foaming, raging seawaves evermore
    Like fortress-storming legions press.

Though ever flung defeated, shattered, back
    Impotent, futile all their might
New billows form and rush to the attack
    Renewing the disastrous fight.

The ancient war continues night and day.
    Ne'er doth the sea its siege abate
And slow it wears the haughty shore away
    Relentlessly and sure as fate.

The Butterfly

I

O wonderful and wingèd flower,
That hoverest in the garden-close,

Finding, in mazes of the rose,
The rapture of a summer hour!

O symbol of Impermanence,
Thou art a word of Beauty's tongue,
A word that in her song is sung,
Appealing to the inner sense.

Of that high mystic harmony
All lovely things are notes and words—
The growth of flowers, the flight of birds,
The figured Signs, the foam-wrought sea,

The whitening gold of sudden dawn,
The sunset's garnet afterglow,
The cumulus, the noonlit snow,
The moon in irised clouds withdrawn.

Lacking (who knows?) a cloud, a tree,
A streamlet's purl, the ocean's roar
From Nature's multitudinous store—
Imperfect were the melody!

II

O Beauty, why so sad my heart?
Why stirs in me a nameless pain
Which seems like some remembered strain,
As on this product of thine art

Enraptured, marvelling I gaze,
And note how airily 'tis wrought—
A wingèd dream, a bodied thought,
The spirit of the summer days?

Thy Beauty opes, O butterfly,
The doors of being, with subtle sense
Of Beauty's frail impermanence,
And grief of knowing it must die.

Again I seem to know the tears
Of other lives, the woe and pain
Of days that died; resurgent wane
The moons of countless bygone years.

III

On other worlds, on other stars,
To us but tiny motes of light,
Or lost in distances of night
Beyond our system's farthest bars,

A priest to Beauty's service sworn,
I sought and served her all my days
With music and with hymns of praise.
In star-fall and the suns of morn

With thrilling heart her gaze I knew,
In other moons her bosom gleamed
And all the golden planet seemed
To shadow forth her shape and hue.

I grieved to watch the summers pass
With sun-led pageantries of bloom,
And sad aphelions assume
Their realm with crisping leaves and grass.

Mine was the grief of change and death,
Of fair things gone beyond recall,
The paling light of dawns, and all
The flowers' vanished hues and breath.

IV

From out the web of former lives,
The ancient, never-broken chain
Of love and sorrow, loss and gain,
One certain truth my heart derives—

Though Beauty passes, this I know,
From change and death, this verity:
Her spirit lives eternally—
'Tis but her forms that come and go.

V

Lo! I am Beauty's constant thrall,
Must ever on her voice await,
And follow through the maze of Fate
Her luring, strange and mystical.

Obedient to her summonings,
Forever must my heart aspire,
And seek, on wings of lyric fire,
To penetrate the heart of things.

Wherein she sits, augustly throned,
In loveliness that renders dumb—
The essence and the final Sum—
With peril and with wonder zoned.

What though I fail, my duller sense
Baffled as by a wall of stone?
The high desire, the search alone
Are their own prize and recompense.

The Meaning

Alas, that we are deaf and blind
To meanings all about us hid!
What secrets lurk the woods amid?
What prophecies are on the wind?

What tidings do the billows bring
And cry in vain upon the strand?
If we might only understand
The brooklet's cryptic murmuring!

The tongues of earth and air are strange.
And yet (who knows?) one little word
Learned from the language of the bird
Might make us lords of Fate and Change.

To the Nightshade

Sullen and sinister, darkly dull of leaf,
Thou rearest amid the brighter flowers,
Like a presage of evil in dreams of joyance—
Evil of beauty thy blossoms,
And purple like the agony of Death,
And their fruit as its livid consummation.
Such a flower art thou
As might spring from the rotting of ancient sin,
Its unavoidable latter confession,

Or from the corroded altar-stone,
Now merged with the blood of its victims—
A hideous and fruitful wedlock—
In some place of sacrifice to monstrous gods.

The Garden of Dreams

One day, when summer suns were kind,
I walked within my soul's domain,
Where inner summer held its reign,
And heard a voice, like some small wind
That wakes a breath, then sleeps again.

It said: "I come as messenger
From garths of dream whose flowers blow
Where clouds go by, and waters flow
Secret from thee; and breezes stir
Whose birth or death thou dost not know.

If thou wouldst have their faery blooms,
Send forth a thought to pluck them there
Most speedily: for, being more fair
Than earthly flow'rs, and with perfumes
No sun-conceived blossoms hear,

Fleeter than these, their hues are lost,
Their fragrance as a spirit fled."
Then, like a wind, the voice was dead.
In other flow'rs of dream engrossed,
I left those dreams unharvested;

Until, bethinking me of them,
I sent a thought in bloomless hours;
Returning soon, it said, "The flow'rs
Are vanished from each withered stem—
A harvest of the winds and show'rs."

Ode to Matter

O tissued fabric of the frame of things,
Thou art an alternating tide,
And Life a moment's foam
Thy shifting wave upflings.

Billowed with suns and worlds that roam
Where winds of Force direct with driving wings,
Thy depths immingle and divide—
A sea whereto the gulfs as shores abide.
In peaceless rounds of change,
Thy forms irreparably flee:
Inevitable laws estrange
All shapes of stars and worlds that be,
And like a mist's inconstant fantasy,
Ensphered anew, as other forms they range.
Lo! here a sun is smitten into night—
One with the cosmic mire;
And yonder startles into fire
The dust of stars destroyed,
Whose quickened worlds resume their ancient flight,
Till arms of darkness, rising from the void,
Drag down the pillared suns again;
And other systems rise and wane,
Rebuilt from star and asteroid.

Lo! is there end
Or rest unto thy toil—
Thou, who createst many forms,
Yet none that stay, of all thy fruitful soil.
Shall all the terms of living suns extend
And find thy labour incomplete?
All storms
Where stars irrevocably meet
Prepare not thy potential field
Unto some larger yield—
Than aught the systems show—some fruit more great,
Some flower ultimate?
Thine atoms pour
Through moulds of many worlds and suns,
As they have passed
In years beyond all memory and lore;
As they shall flee while Time his orbit runs,
Along abysmal aeons cast.
What strivest thou to build
With dust of systems reared and rent
And flame of suns blown out and lit again?
Dost toil with hands as yet unskilled
To some obscurely, known intent,

Far-sought through mists of weariness and pain?
Ah! dare we dream
That thou shalt dream no fairer thing than man,
No higher world than this?
That from thine unexplorable abyss
No stronger Life shall rise supreme,
Wrought from rejected dust whereof began
All former Life—
The dust remoulded through abyssal strife
Within the suns' uncompassable scheme?

Ode to Poetry

Handmaid of Beauty, yet a queen
In thine own sacred right,
Thou playest subtler chords unseen
The strains of an elusive quick delight
That Music's touch may not command
Albeit she possess
Eyes that behold the lightless land
Of ages yet unsped, and lend our sense
Some fleetingness
And magic of her vision's permanence.

Lo! in thy speech
The power and majesty that swing the sun
E'en as the worlds, and each
Dim atom of the system manifest,
Become articulate, although unguessed
The fulness of thy meaning, and unwon
The door of those dimensions enterless
That yet thou holdest, e'en as hues
That light hath wrapped in folds of clarity.
O star we may not lose
Though others pale and flee,
Thou art a Key unto the gate of Awe;
A herald of the runes I saw
In their unworded utterness;
A peak whose summit is invisible,
A plummet in the abrupt red heart of Hell.

The Pageant of Music

Last night I roamed within the walls of dream,
That, as a word of magic, strange, unsaid,
Are barrier to the thoughts of day. My tread
Was toward the morn, from whose unclouded gleam
Came music, seen and heard in pageantry—
Loud as the ocean's thunder tempest-bred,
Yet fair and delicate as flowers that shed
Their scent on meadows colored like the sea.

I heard and saw the music of all things—
Their sound-soul visible, that as a dawn,
For one age-moment bared the spirits's night.
Then, with prismatic notes, and voice of light,
And sounds and hues inseparable for wings,
The music-vision faded and was gone.

Autumn Dew

Amid the autumn grasses sere and dead
The lucent dewdrops glow and shine.
Are they the tears by elves and fairies shed
In sorrow for the year's decline?

The Eclipse

A thousand stars in the heavens blaze,
While sun and moon must hide their rays;
The glowing planets twinkle and gleam
While hidden is the sun's bright beam.
Unquenched they shine with a strange wild light.
But paler, paler than the sun.
What a weird, unearthly sight
Is each land they shine upon!
Let them gleam, 'tis but for a time,
Soon shall come the sun sublime,
And shine out in all his light.

The Falling Leaves

The leaves are falling, gold and red,
    About the old and dying year,
Making a couch for feet and head.
    Ah, who could wish a richer bier!

The Freedom of the Hills

Mine is the larger freedom of the hills
    That look afar on vale, and plain, and sea—
A living map extended wide below—
    In windswept, azure-domed supremacy.

No freedom equals mine, who gaze on all—
    Neither the freedom of the rolling main,
Of lashing, salty breeze and freshening spray,
    Nor of the equal stretches of the plain.

So I am nearer to the sky than they:
    The friendly sun bestows a stronger light,
And closer seems the myriad blossoming stars,
    That sow the illimitable fields of night.

Mine are the horizons that in distance fade,
    The longer vistas and the larger view.
Unto mine eyes are holden all the vales
    The city-studded plains that melt in blue.

I share them with the eagle and the hawk.
    So I am free as are the [ ] rills,
The drifting summer clouds and careless winds.
    Mine is the wider freedom of the hills.

The Hosts of Heaven

O suns and stars, to what strange, far-off end
What final fate tremendous and supreme,
Is ordered thy stupendous, awful scheme?
Whereto do all the ceaseless orbits tend,
Aphelions wherein the planets wend
To distances remote? What is His dream,
In which thy hosts to some far purpose gleam,
The use whereto He doth the systems bend?

* * *

How vast and all embracing is this plan
That wondrous, far-flung scheme we may not see—
Too bright, perhaps, its glory for our eyes!
Conceived ere Time and Space for us began.
May e'er men hope to pierce the mystery
And learn at last the secret of the skies?

Ode on the Future of Song

As yet yon stars are silver-faint,
Yea, wan as the beginning dreams
That fill the increasing gloom of sleep;
But soon their gleams
Shall utterly possess and paint
Our night with lusters of the further deep,
Yea, even as slumber's outer-space
Gives dreams unto the mind's far-inward place.

To me, who stand
Upon the threshold of the future's song,
The brightening of its dreams,
As now within a morn of stars, it seems
That these shall be
Not less effulgent, beautiful, nor strong
Than those which in the Past's illumined land
Shone the fulfillment and the prophecy
Of song that was and song to come.
For, simple and as complex as the day,
Shall song, that stands coeval with the stars,
Fade from the skies of Time?
Not till the stars are dumb,
The springs of morn run dry, and snow and rime
A strength to stay
And bind the sun with bars!
Hath light grown dull
Since yesteryear?

The Suns and the Void

Upon the stark, blue blankness of the sky,
The assailing armies of the stars have swept,
And all the night is splendid with their spears.

The azure emptiness hath grown a page,
Inscribed with countless characters of flame—
Gigantic hieroglyphs inscrutable,
Enblazonry eternal of the dark,
And ciphers bright whose key is yet unfound,
That burn as riddles to unnumbered eyes
On worlds uncountable.

The earth rolls on
Within its shadow—darkness that lays bare
The sister worlds, and legions of the suns
That flame remote, as day to unseen spheres,
And gleaming atoms on the night to us.
Enormous revelation of the dark!
The finite looks upon Infinity,
The endless star-processions that unfold
On midnight roads of the unceasing void.
O suns, thy light doth blind and stun the soul!
The imponderable abyss is as a weight
To crush the spirit utterly! I feel,
More strong than thunder on the astounded ear,
The vast, stupendous silence of the gulf.
Its darkness wraps me round, and I am lost,
All sense of self o'erwhelmed, and my soul steeped
In night, till it becomes a darkness, too.
What suns beyond the suns, what further voids
The night doth hide! What skies unseen are bright
To dwellers in Polaris' worlds! What depths
Of black, abysmal silence fall unsunned
Past Fomalhaut!

To George Sterling

His song shall waken the dull-sleeping throng,
    That dreams of sullen and of earth-bound things;
    He soars with Beauty where the Eternal sings,
And the Deep's insuperable chants prolong
The everlasting sovereignties of Song—
    Where caverned thunder from the mountains flings
    Its dirge o'er the dust of crumbled thrones and kings,
He stands defiant of Oblivion's wrong.

* * *

But ampler Liberty, divine and strange
    Hums in the song of his Promethean lyre,
        An echo of lost Time's immortal ones;
The tangled webs of mortal Death and Change
    Perish before his chanting lyric fire,
        That gleams in the paling light of sinking suns.

Moods of the Sea

How sad and melancholy is the sea
With that low murm'ring threnody it sings
Upon its strands, as if in memory
Of dead forgot, and disenabled kings.

How restless is the sea, when billows rise
And race its bosom o'er unceasingly;
No peace within the ocean lies
From shore to shore, no quiet in the sea—

How angry is the sea when tempests last
And loud the rearing billows [ ] and roar
And sullenly the foam-tipped breakers crash
Upon the yellow sands and rock-strewn shore.

Sonnets of the Seasons

Spring

O Spring, not only in the awakened earth,
    The leafing forests and the greening hills
    The gladsome impulse generously thrills.
The joy of buds unfolding and the birth
Of grasses, and the happiness and mirth
    Of all the newly freed and singing rills
    Whose rhythmic voices gyving Winter stills
Rouse in my breast where lately brumal dearth
Held sway. O wakened forces of the Spring,
    Thy strength and aspiration toward the sun
    Thine exultation and the joy are mine.
Oh! would that, as the streamlets, I might sing,
Would that my praising with the lark's were one!
    Then might I voice the joyance that is thine!

Summer

Now comes the Seasons' high and ardent noon
Fulfillment of Spring's youthful prophecy,
Full-flow'red and fruited. Hesitatingly
She follows on the last late showers of June.
Bringing the roses and a waxing moon
Enamoured of her beauty, fervently
The Sun-God leans, with oaths of constancy
To kiss her face. Ah! days of warmth and boon,
Wrapped in a haze of sunlit, drowsy peace
Oh! purple nights, slumbrously passionate
And bright with starry zones and coronals,
When birds weave webs of silver harmonies
Till air grows heavy with the aural weight,
And silence like a sweeter music falls.

The Wizardry of Winter

Behold the Winter's potent wizardry,
That hides in vestal white the barren ground,
And all the leaves that lie in banks around
Each stripped, bereft, and naked Autumn tree.
Behold his magic on the hill and lea,
His wonder-working hand, whereby are bound
The singing rivulets, so that no sound
Now strikes the pallid silence merrily.

How strange and white, beneath the cheerless skies,
The Winter-duranced land, far-visioned, lies.
Now break the clouds, and from a wind-borne seat
Of dismal gray, the Sun looks goldenly.
Lo! each tree stands a jewelled fantasy
And countless gems are 'neath our trampling feet!

The Cohorts of the Storm

To west the black titanic clouds reared high
In battle-form enormous and afar;
But soon on wind steeds fleet their ranks drew nigh,
Hasting to reach the elemental war.

Their skirmishers the sky's blue field o'erran
The massive, serried legions followed fast;

Then suddenly the awful battle 'gan
    With lightning flash and thunder's crashing blast.

The drenching rain in driving sheets poured down
    And overhead the storm in combat rolled;
Long hours its mighty cohorts strove, wind-blown,
    For some strange meed, as strove the kings of old.

Black night came on at last, and instantly,
    As if retreat had blown, the tempest ceased.
At once was stilled its loud artillery,
    And with the rain the clouds passed off to east.

I watched their rear-guard flee in ordered rout
    To some new battle-ground adown the sky,
And in its wake the gleaming stars leaped out
    And rode the crescent moon serene and high.

To the Morning Star

Thou art the star of hope that 'fore the dawn
Doth gild and gorgeously incarnadine
The eastern peaks [   ] doth shine
Above the faintly whitening horizon.

O star of hope and faith shine gently on
O Gleam [*sic*] thou bright within the orient sky
For by thy sign we know that dawn is nigh
That darkness and the night will soon be gone.

The Flower of the Night

The splendid aureate rose of Day
With evening fades and pines away,
And through the shadow-shrouded hours
The vast vague bloom of Darkness flow'rs.

A Sunset

As blood from some enormous hurt
The sanguine sunset leapt;
Across it, like a dabbled skirt,
The hurrying tempest swept.

War

He sits encrowned upon his awful throne
Of skulls; within the vast and ambient gloom
Which strive the red-flamed torches to illume
In vain, and leave full half its reach unknown.
A sword across his knees, he reigns alone
With merciless proud eyes, and mien of stone,
While 'fore him go like spectres from the tomb
In long review the victims of his doom,
In silence broken only for a groan
From bloodless lips. Here mighty kings o'erthrown
Look toward him with accusing eyes as go
They past, and once-great captains moan
And soldiers pass, with helms and swords made low
In ghastly file of shapes the dead assume.

Wings of Perfume

Unnamed, incognizable,
Save of inarticulate memory,
A quiver of scent from Earth's familiar night,
And, lo! the night and the earth
Are dropped like a cloak outworn,
And half-remembered twilight,
Somewhere beyond the intervening
Of time and dimension,
Arches above me, dark with columns,
Enormous, fantastic, not to be imagined on Earth,
Of a half-seen temple.
Through it, upon wings
Of an indescribable wind
That blows from the face of an alienated world—
A wind overpowering, vast
With its hints of unbelievable things
Struggling confusedly to be remembered—
Through it such fragrance is carried swiftly
From sacred gardens of scarce conceivable flowers
Rapt in the fluctuant ecstatic gloom
Between a blue sun lately set
And a green sun not yet risen.

The Island of a Dream

Oh! alien isle, sea-lost and isolate,
    What loud horizons of the irremediable sea
    Ensure thy strange, remote serenity,—
Beyond what last horizon isolate!

Lo! for thy sake, the world's allured young winds
    Shall roam passageless, desolate, forlorn,
    Seeking thee ever; shoreless and outworn,
To the sea's purple sink the world's old winds.

Like Heaven's one large inverted flower,
    The enchanted lotus of the purple light
    Sufficient; till the manifold, vast, white,
And deep moon-nenuphar supremely blows.

Autumn's Pall

But yesterday 'twas autumn and the leaves—
    All aureate and vermeil, strewed the ground
    And lay in drifted banks the trees around—
A fair and gorgeous sight. Night's hour, like thieves,
Have stol'n them all, and now the winter weaves,
    Where erst they lay, an ermine pall of snow.
    Yon woods where some lone bird for autumn grieves,
The hills and fields that pallid covering know.

The Music of the Gods

I walked one silent eve when loud and strong
    A music fell as from the empty sky—
    A sudden harmony, divine and high
That seemed of some unseen supernal throng,
Sweeping the heavens on mighty wings of song:
    Above, about, at once afar and nigh
    Surged waves of sound, that swelled in ecstasy
As music of the deep, sustained and long.
Invested by that sea as by the air
    My soul was swept to whirlwind heights of sound
And there depressed to maelstroms fathomless—
In antiphons of joy and vast despair,
Till from the music's culminating stress,
    I sank to earth with sight and hearing drowned.

The Night of Despair

About me closed the darkness of Despair
Whose dusky mists were chill upon my face.
Darkled and grew that heavy night apace;
Breathless and silent hung the ominous air
With dread and terror pregnant everywhere
And on the darkness I could dimly trace
Amorphous shapes in endless constant race
They passed. Beneath their fixed and pitiless stare
Who seemed accusing ghosts of futile days
My spirit flinched and desperate I turned
To where Death's gulfs made offer of their peace.
But did not try those deeps for staying fears.
The night wore on till lo, afar there burned
Hope's star that heralded the dawn's release.

Somnus

(A Fragment)

The bottom-lands of Lethe and of Night:
Beyond the fiery troubling of the stars,
The peaceful heavens hold in plenitude
A gloom that lies like drift of purple down
On lids oblivious—having but for light
The glimmer as of some lost afterglow.
Which, irretrievable of any sun,
Seems evermore to falter and to grope
'Mid forms and shades elusive. Like a scene
To one entranced with dark mandragora,
And dimmer than mirages of the moon,
Lies all the drowsy land, lapsing away
With Lethe to the sleep of nadir plains. . . .

At Midnight

Sleepless I stand at night's mysterious noon
Upon the hill, to watch the heavens unroll
Their star-emblazoned hieroglyphic scroll
And listen to the song the waters croon
To which the winds of night their harps entune—
The melodies which gathering to a whole

Do strangely, deeply stir and thrill the soul
Recalling music of some long-waned moon
Who love her beauty and her mystery.
Speak, too, of all her brooding loveliness
Wherewith my thrilling spirit holds commune
And, rapt in understanding sympathy,
Doth feel her [ ] mood upon me press.

The Fanes of Dawn

In opal mist involved, and silver snows,
    The mountains front the slow-unfolding morn,
    While half the west lies darkling, and forlorn
The last star flees unheeded as it rose;
Now what ethereal molten colour flows
    Along the stones of summits dim and worn?
    This amethystine-winged fire upborne
Of gems consumed from what cloud-furnace glows?

Above the mountains twice-sublime with fire,
    In lands of light, of colour, and of air,
        What walls and tow'rs whose wonder shall not last
Are builded—where the cloudy fanes aspire
    That house the visioned morning's purple flare,
        And with it melt upon the crystal vast.

The Summer Hills

How brown the rolling hills outspread—
The grass of spring is sere and dun;
From cloudless skies the flaying sun
Has bronzed its green. The Spring is dead,
As plain the sombre hills declare;
The flow'rs are gone that yesterday,
It seems, with mass of bloom, held sway;
No more the hills their liv'ry hear
This brown doth Summer's rule proclaim—
Fierce Summer, with his touch that seres
His sign on ev'ry hill appears,
His fervid heat, his breath of flame.

To George Sterling

O Beauty, goddess known and sung of old
They say that thou our later world hast fled
Her altars cold, her worship past and dead;
Now to the high, insatiate god of Gold
Alone man's knees are bent, their prayers said.
Yet haply still there be a few that hold
Her faith, and to her secret temple led,
Enwreath with long white amaranths her head.

High priest of these by right divine thou art
    Who singest here beside the western shore
        Immortal threnodies in Beauty's praise
Nor can her faith and ritual depart.
    Though men at false and rival shrines implore,
While such as thou to service give thy days.

The Wind-Threnody

As from the western mountains fade
    The glories of the afterglow,
    A zephyr cometh, soft and low
Like gentle, plaintive music played
    On tuneful lyres of long ago.

It steals amid the choric pines
    That at its thrilling touch resound,
    Vibrating with a mournful sound—
A plaint for Day, that slow declines
    Beyond the distant western bound.

The music grows and swells amain,
    A grand, full-volumed melody,
    Sad, sorrowful inexpressibly,
And laden with secret, world-old pain—
    Nature's eternal threnody.

The Voice in the Pines

Beauty, what mournest thou within the pines?
Surely thy voice is theirs,
Reverberent through the caverns of the soul
Like present grief which shares

The fainter sorrows of the past, that roll
In undertones nor ear nor thought defines.

Dost sorrow for thy deaths in other years—
Aeons that too are dead—
On vanished worlds remembered but of thee?
Or for the flowers, that, shed
But yesternoon, find now their threnody,
After the dews which were thy silent tears?

Black Enchantment

In forest-deeps wherefrom the twilight rose,
A silent ghost with thinnest cerement pale,
Disquieted, to walk the winds' repose
Above the tranced irremeable dale
O'er woods pervaded of one nightingale,
Where late the dreaming sunset was, I found
The dell of lilies, each one whitest grail
Of peace and pallid vision, that the ground
Uplifted for the quest of air, and light, and sound.

On all except the nightingale's swift song,
Each cup the charmèd silence holier,
Had poured, it seemed, the wavering light was long.
Till lo! what change grotesquely sinister,
With darkness poured as from a sepulchre!
An owl that hooted at the nightingale;
Lean mists that walkt the glades where no winds were,
And mid the lilies, flowers of swarthy dwale—
These things I saw ere yet the fluttering light could fail.

A night within the night was opened out—
Some iron bubble of enormous dread
From Death's abysm: Dwindled to a doubt,
The visible live world for me was fled;
Alone with all the immemorial dead,—
Sharing that burden with the breathless gloom—
I sensed the unheard intolerable tread
Of those unnumbered legions of the tomb.

The Burden of the Suns

Wherefore thy burden and thy toil, O Sun?
    Borne up the steep and hollow heavens afar
    Thy worlds retard thee, who were else a star,
Swift with white speed of many a lonelier one;
And heaving mightily, thy pulses run,
    Swollen with fires of effort. Shall Mizar
    Not pass thee, or the suns of Algebar?
And hopest thou to close with Procyon?

Howbeit, thou, and these, thy starrier kin,
    Transcending thee, strain ever, tho apart
        And with unequal speed, within the same
Black maze of night and Time, where all shall win,
    Tho with no path, nor clue, the hollow heart,
        Uncompassed and oblivious, whence they came.

The Castle of Dreams

It lies beyond the farthest sea,
This castle whereunto I flee
When life and time hang wearily.
Yet though so far, 'tis strangely nigh:
Within the breathing of a sigh
One gains the walls secure and high
    Of the Castle of Dreams.

Divinely beautiful and great,
Of pearl each dome and tower, and gate,
It stands, a hold of kingly state.
There gyving Time and Space are not,
And cares of Life are all forgot.
No breath of restless change is brought
    To the Castle of Dreams.

I walk each wondrous court and hall,
Their varied treasures mine at call,
For there I am the lord of all.
If gold and gems of land and sea,
And broad estates were offered me,
I would not take them for the key
    Of the Castle of Dreams.

A Dream of Oblivion

The day of Time was darkening to its end:
The sun hung chill within the blackened noon,
Its splendours one with night. From planets doomed
The wail of death to empty silence rose.
The stars were faint against the glooming vast,
Like wavering lights upon a windy plain
That one by one go out; and even as these,
The eternal suns expired, and left a void—
A huge and black Nirvana of the skies—
A visible Oblivion. Then came down
The darkness and the silence on all things,
The worlds that eddy like wind-driven leaves
Within the airless deep, and souls of men,
And on all Life. The universe was night,
And this strange, troubled dream of Time and Place
A still vacuity. These things I knew,
When, lo! beneath my feet the steadfast earth
Grew nothingness, and down the gulf I fell,
And with the darkness and the silence merged.

A Dream of Darkness

From dreams of light and sound one felt his soul
Borne out to some extremity of night
In voidness where the universe is thin.
Aghast and pale above the gulfs, the stars
Watched as he felt tremendous glooms
Until they shrank and drew [ ] back
From gulfs past any star's Titanic sight.

The Revelation

A voice decreed: "Let there be no more light;
    Reveal the gulfs and systems utterly."
    The veils and limits that infinity
Hath for its shields, were smitten of the light;
Horizonless, unsealed of depth or height,
    One after one, unto my scrutiny
    The deeps and their invested suns leapt free,
And billow-like, rolled on the shores of sight.

* * *

Nor interstice nor film of gloom remained
    To dull the stars' intolerable host
        Or stay the firmament's immeasured press,
That smote with revelation unrestrained,
    Till 'neath the weight of vastness uttermost
        My spirit's walls fell into nothingness.

The Dream-God's Realm

I wandered down Sleep's vast and sunless vale,
    Where silence and Cimmerian darkness lay
    That never moon nor stars disturb, nor Day
With sword or golden light. Beside the trail
I groping followed, through that secret dale,
    A deep and voiceless river stole its way—
    Dark Lethe's stream, owning whose opiate sway
I onward went without a doubt or fail.

Till, lo! the atramental veil of night
        That, stifling, hung about, behind, before,
    Was sudden parted by some unseen hand,
And on my vision leapt a marvelous sight—
        A green and joyous plain, with fair skies o'er,
    The Dream-God's sunlight-drenched, enchanted land.

Ephemera

We are but tiny insects of a day
That on a whirling planet toil and play—
To what end no one seems to know—till creep
We one by one aside, and fall asleep.

The Eternal Gleam

The tides of sunlight outward swim
    Where night, a dusky moon beguiles.
    The star of evening wanly smiles
O'er seas of twilight vast and dim.

With brightening vestal lucency
    Thou crownest, lonely vesper star,
    Yon line inexorable and far
That e'er withholds the day from me.

Thou hast the gleam that flamed divine
In billows of the sunset light
That leapt athwart the strands of night
And with its pure and lucent sign

Unto my soul thou beckonest:
My spirit yearns to burst its chains
And follow where the daylight wanes,
On wings of strong, divine unrest.

If I might gain the sunset's beam
O'ertake it in the distant flight
And bathe within its waves of light
A moment might I hold the gleam!

Evening

The tumult and the glare of day
With setting sun have died away;
All lands, all scenes, in silence lie
'Neath twinkling stars that gem the sky.
A holy calm o'er land and sea
Enshrouding all in mystery
Has dropped as though a Genii king
With magic word had bade each thing
To cease, and with the veil of night
All earth had hidden from our sight.

The Harbour of the Past

Watched over by insuperable peaks,
Beneath a leaden sky and copper sun,
Surrounded by a desert treeless, dun,
Where never comes a cloud, nor tempest shrieks
In that still haven lie, with idle beaks
And lifeless sails, the Years, their voyage run,
The harbour of the Past forever won
That each dead epoch with its cargo seeks.

The shore by lurid beacon-fires is gemmed
Whose light stains as with blood the billows spent,
And sepulchres are strewn the whole extent
Betwixt the mountains and the water hemmed—
White tombs of kings once augustly enthroned,
And now by listless, dusty winds bemoaned.

In Extremis

Within Life's arc of light I stand
    That lyeth white and clear
To calmly watch upon each hand
    The Shadow creeping near.

Slowly the arc grows narrower
    The encroaching night draws on;
Black, pitiless its bastions rear,
    The light will soon be gone.

The Inscription

Science hath found the secret key
    That opes to modern sight the door
    Unto the hieroglyphic lore
Of Egypt, Ur, and Nineveh.

In buried cities long forgot
    Her eyes the inscription strange divine
    And read the emblematic sign
In time-defying granite wrought.

But who shall read the hieroglyphs
    The sea inscribes upon its shore?
    Who penetrate the hidden lore
Engraved upon the eternal cliffs?

Could we but know the meaning held
    Within those runes the billows write
    What learning strange were ours, what light
Surpassing all the lore of Eld!

Lost Beauty

Whither doth Beauty pass? What is the law
    Whereby her forms and colours bright and rare
    Merge in the vapid, achromatic air?
Doth she herself into herself withdraw?
Mayhap the gleam of dawn, the sunset's glow
    The fragile hues that paint the flowers of Spring
    And all the songs the birds and brooklets sing,
Like streams refluent, whence they issued flow.

* * *

Yet, ah, shall ever sunrise render back
The gold of dawns that that [*sic*] ravished us of eld?
The splendours of the later sunsets lack
Some magic gleam of those we once beheld.
Nor may we gain from yonder songster's tone
The dulcet notes of birds forever flown.

Nature's Orchestra

In yon sunlit meadow, hark
To the singing of the lark
And the quail in coverts near
To each other calling clear
Voice of some lone robin floats
From an oak, and hoarser note
Of the blackbirds settling nigh.
Bluejays call, as past they fly
And their strident voices fall
In a blending musical
With the sweet tones of the thrush
And the bluebird in yon bush
In the woods a brooklet sings,
And the wistful whisperings
Of the wind amid the trees,
Blend with songs of birds and bees
And the streamlet's melody,
In a perfect harmony.

The Past

Naught of the Past is left but memories—
A wreath of withered roses on its tomb
That, keeping yet a ghost of their perfume
[no more written]

The Present

We stand within the Present's sun and bloom—
The garden of the living hours, yet glance
We backward to the Past's romance,
Or onward to the Future's unlit gloom.

The Future

Albeit we plant the Future's seed each day
Potent with fate each thought, and word, and deed
We know not what shall spring from that hidden seed.
Rank thistles or red roses—who can say?

Time the Wonder

Time holds the keys of all eternity
Its warder grim is he;
The Past he shuts and locks forevermore,
Then opes the Future's door.

The Palace of Jewels

It rears beside the cliff-confronted sea,
Where, spurred by winds, the waves aspire in foam—
A palace towering large and massively,
To flower in minaret and dome.

Naught but the ocean's music echoes there;
No lutes pervade its halls with mirth and sigh;
And wanders love, through close and pleasance fair,
The velvet, figured butterfly.

Within, in silence tapestried and old,
And dusk that lingers through the widest day,
Are heapéd treasure-chests, that, spilling hold
Jewels of varied hue and ray.

Here caskets weirdly wrought and prodigal
Of opals color-clouded, and the fire,
Thrilling in crystal through the sombre hall,
Wherewith the diamonds aspire.

And sapphires lighten, all astorm with blue,
Beside the deeper emerald's mimic sea;
And slumberous rubies, with a burst of hue,
Awaken intermittently.

The Past

Drawn hither by the tides of change and chance
Betwixt the dead past and the future's gloom

We stand within the present's sun and bloom—
The garden of the living hours. Yet glance
We ever backward to the past's romance
Regretting that no wizard may relume
Its glamour—and the flash of sword and plume—
The Greek and Turk serve only to enhance.
Ay, of the Past is left but memories—
A wraith of withered roses on its tomb
That only breathe a ghost of sweet perfume
And yet are eloquent of brilliancies
Long turned to dust, which one at moments sees
Some memory of their former state resume.

The Potion of Dreams

What occult Circe of the hours of sleep
Mixeth the Cup of Dreams with potent art?
How doth the sorceress cunningly impart
To it such wondrous virtues, and where steep
That powerful potion? Opium poppies' grew
Nor hasheesh from far India's mystic land
Have not such properties, nor can command
Visions of more fantastic form and hue.

Pleasure and pain in mingling mystical
Are in that cup. There past and present meet,
With pageantry of earthly sights and sounds.
Abysses bottomless, heights that appall
With plainlands infinite about their feet,
And seas horizonless, lie in its bounds.

The Power of Eld

Beneath my dome of sleep, secure-immersed
And filled of peace, such blinded power of scath
As Samson once employed, was loosed in wrath,
And tumult with tempestuous arm dispersed
The pillared silence: came a wind accurst,
That, shuddering, as from hidden peril fled—
A sign; and then the past's uncharneled dread
In swarming visions on the darkness burst.

* * *

Betrayed by Sleep unto the might of Eld,
I knew the terror of its kings, the fear
Of thrones abased by some resistless flood;
Howlings of prophets mingled in mine ear
With death-lament of cities, far-beheld
'Neath drenching flame that made the night as blood.

Romance

In vain, Romance, we seek thy mystic land
Though e'er our holden eyes shall see afar
As beacon-light, thy fatal siren star
That gleams above a strange, elusive strand.
Shall yet, where all the barring Years are dead,
The earth we know to secret darkness hurled,
Our questing feet upon some farther world
Unto thy strange and radiant realm be led.
Shall yet we gain once more from mist and night
And barren years, thy large and younger light?
Thy golden sands our feet may never gain,
Though oh how beautiful we see them shine!
Forever like the dim horizon line
We watch them fade across the fruitless main.

The Song of the Worlds

Along our sun-appointed ways
Gulf into gulf expires;
We know the length of peaceless gyres,
The urge that never stays.

Flung in the bonds of solar force,
We measure sky on sky,
Where marginless immensity
Protracts our labored course.

Across the hyaline profound
Our bridging circles run;
Within far-sunk abysses spun
We consummate their round.

We mark our gleaming sisters whirl,
Gulf-alienated far,

Where puny world and giant star
Seem but as atom-swirl.

Fonts of incalculable fire,
The further suns outblaze;
Rushing adown torrential ways,
Their gleams advance, retire.

Planet and star, in one unrest,
The ceaseless systems flame.
O universe, unto what aim
Thine orbit-streaming quest?

Oh! culminate fore'er withheld!
Oh! purpose dark alway!
Through desert night and futile day
Our cosmic search impelled

Finds no conclusive boundaries,
Nor comprehending mark;
No limitations of the dark,
Nor shore of spacial seas.

Along the sequent vasts of Time
Whose chasmal aeons fall,
Age upon age eventual,
Our gyres unswerving climb.

Borne by the years' unebbing tide,
We find immensitude,
Where dreamt horizon-lines elude,
And no confines abide.

Prisoned in Time's infinity,
Twin with eternal space,
How shall our gulf-engirdling race
Avail to set us free?

In vain through gyral years we think
To reach beyond the abyss
Some void-ulterior precipice,
Some space-restraining brink.

Cursed with immutable unrest,
The sun-impulse that goads
Along reiterated roads,
Upon a circled quest,

Whereto is found no binding bourne,
    We shall not still to rest,
    Until, to lasting night addressed,
The master suns, outworn,

From shadowed, darkling sovereignty—
    Their time-rescinded reigns—
    Relax and loose our olden chains,
And cast us gulfward, free.

Sonnet on Music

Strange melodies unplayed my spirit hears
    Through lyric flute and soft guitar, or in
    The harmonious sobbing of the violin.
Music of laughter greets my subtler ears,
Or of the pain and anguish of the years.
    From stirring harp, or lute's melodious din,
    Or some cathedral organ's tone, I win
The larger music of the circling spheres.

* * *

Forever through the outer melodies
Come subtle hints of vaster harmonies:
    In rhythm of torrents and of brooks I dream
    Faint echoes of Life's everlasting Stream,
    And in the ocean's sound, of earth supreme,
The resonance of mightier, wider Seas.

Sonnet on Oblivion

Not as a sea of flame whose waves and deeps
    Shall gulf the suns and worlds—but as a night,
    A darkness and a silence past all light,
Beyond all sound, Oblivion waits and sleeps.
Within its absolute encircling sweeps
    The universe—a stream of stars that sight
    Deems countless, but upon whose gleaming flight
Like some eternal tide, Oblivion creeps

A darkness and a silence! There shall draw
    To one eclipse the systems and disperse
    This strange and troubled dream of Time and Place.

Then, sun nor world shall be nor light nor law—
    But endless night and emptiness of space—
A vast Nirvana of the universe.

Sonnet to the Sphinx

O riddle of the years, that in this desert place
O'er Egypt's desolation guard doth keep—
Here where her shattered glories buried sleep,—
Upon thy sealèd lips and mocking face
Which hold the secrets grim of Time and Space,
We look, and question thee. Before thee creep
How many, and from out their darkness deep
Crave light and knowledge! Ne'er in any case
Dost thou an answer make, for on thine eyes
And lips hath Silence laid her awful seal,—
    Her order and her spell inviolate.
But oh! if thou should speak, who art all wise
    Heeding at last our myriad-voiced appeal,
What might we learn, of life, and death, and fate!

Sphinx and Medusa

The old constraint of an essential bond
    Hath linkt them in my mind: opposed they stare,
    Twin silences, that through Time's Otherwhere,
The ruinous past, thus each to each respond,
One with mysterious gaze that sees beyond
    The straining suns, calm as the voidness there;
    And one with eyes like deserts of despair,
Flameless as granite, clear as diamond.

They gaze across the past . . . Yet thought must see
        That eve of time when man no longer yearns,
    Grown deaf before Life's Sphinx, whose lips are barred;
When from the spaces of Eternity,
        Silence, a rigorous Medusa, turns
    On the lost world the stress of her regard.

The Sphinx of the Infinite

The mystery beyond all mysteries,
Of which involves the lesser in itself,

At night the shadows: Many a flaming sun,
Before the Sphinx whose eyes are firmaments,
With all the constellations, hath availed
As might the lonely fen-light to illume
The abyss whereon it hovers. All the worlds
(Where Life, a dreamer in the night of Time,
Sees an eternal dawn upon the dark
Which is the curtain of impending sleep)
Have not resolved the riddle of its silence,
And falter at the last. The very gods,
From out their alien gloom, or light unknown,
Lift eyes of mighty question, and are mute,
While all the reflex of the empty gulf
Makes live the flaming mirror of their gaze.

The Tartarus of the Suns

Beyond the orbit of the farthest sun,
A desert darkness lies—immeasured night
That knows nor eve nor dawn, where only drift
Dethroned and aimless suns, and world unlit.
Thereto are cast the disenabled stars,
Like those great Titans that high Zeus hurled,
By will supreme, from the Olympian peak
To Tartarus, the nadir of all space.

Discarded dust and cinders of the Plan,
Darkened and chill, they haunt the silent gloom,
And wait their brothers, suns that reign afar;
Till these shall come, with all their subject worlds,
Whose dust hath dreamed of Immortality,
And Night succeed unto their flaming thrones.

The Temple of Night

Fear-compassing, night's temple arches high,
    Indefinitely doming hill and plain,
    With massive walls that comprehend the main
And clasp the distances of sand that lie
Forgot and desolate. Against the sky
    It rises bold and vast, with towers that gain
    The ether's desert and immense domain
And in the wastes of outer sunlight die.

* * *

Lo! this is Beauty's fellest, perfect shrine
Her consecrated temple, pure, divine,
With wind-swung flower-censers rendered sweet.
The moon and star, her steadfast symbols gleam,
And wistful-sighing wind and cadenced stream,
With lyric symphonies the goddess greet.

The Throne of Winter

Yon heaven-aspiring peaks, imperial, lone,
That seem the West's stupendous coronet,
With many a titanic jewel set,
Are Winter's high and everlasting throne
From which he holds an undisturbed sway,
Silence and Solitude his ministers
With Ice and Snow, before whom e'er disperse
Summer's invading armies in dismay.

He reigns in awe-inspiring majesty
And dazzling, chilly royal pomp and show,
Splendours august no kings or emperors know
Upon him, where he sits eternally
Within his icy court, his jewelled hand
Clasping a sceptre glittering and grand.

Time

O Time, great satrap of Eternity,
Gigantic sifter of our destinies,
To whose stern, inexorable decrees
Both king and mendicant must bow the knee,
Thine is an all-embracing sovereignty;
All men must go their life and striving cease
At thy strong bidding; nothing may appease
Or stay thy doom; none may evade or flee.

Thou sitt'st apart, thy glass within thy hand,
The glass wherein the grains of death and fate
Drop silently, as flees each wingéd hour.
And irrevocably doth fall that gleaming sand
A never-ceasing stream, on which do wait
The tides of life and death, and wealth and power.

To a Cloud

O cloud in the sky,
You will and you can
Be a mountain or camel—
Why not a man?

O cloud in the sky,
Be a castle alight for the woman I love,
With the splendour of sunset inviting the night.
Be a terrace of palms lifting crowns in the air,
Tossing kisses to stars in the ether so rare—
But holding the earth with a thousand of thongs,
And singing through centuries love-burdened songs
Because of your grip in the soil!
Be strong down below to the gentle above.

Be a chariot of fire!
Let your steed be the flame
Of the sun in his ire—
Of the sun in his sweep
From deep unto deep
In the measureless march of the limitless arch
That is lost for a name.
And there is in the heat of your fervency beat—
Beat out the crown she should wear.
Oh, crown her, and carry her far
From the hush of the noon to the still of the star.

O cloud, be a boat;
And with sails a-spread, float—
Don't drive—only drift with the tide
Of a pulsating world
That rises and falls as the primal need calls
With the sensuous sweep of soft breezes at play
With her odorous hair,
With her lips and her eyes—
Where mystery lies—
With the dark skin a-hint of the Tubal Cain tint—
With the lips which are copper-hued coffers of kisses,
Each pledge of bewildering blessing of blisses,
Oh, play with her gently, swift winds of the west,
Make her couch on that quarter-deck royal with rest.

O cloud, if you can be a mouse or a mountain,
Be wise. Be a man!
Touch tenderly
Ivory arms fashioned slenderly,
Caress with a palm a-promuse [*sic*] with passion
The rare curve of the cheek,
And bury within that adorable chin
The kisses a painter could dream but not paint.
And strip from the shoulder the drapery's ban.
Let the matchless bust dawn on the eyes of a man!
Then sweep from the sight the last vestige of light,
And wrap that warm form in the clasp of delight,
And bathe her with kisses while blessing the night.

To a Mariposa Lily

Thou art the chalice of the sun;
    Filled from the fountains of his light,
Thy rimming petals overrun
    With nectar morning-pure and bright.

Fit cup art thou, O flow'r, to hold
    Such drink surpassing and divine—
Wrought of the finest vestal gold,
    And brimmed with sunlight's crystal wine.

To a Snowdrop

Dainty flower, snowy-white,
Shrinking modestly from sight,
Here within the woodland's heart,
As a lantern shaped thou art—
Such a lamp as elf or fay
Bear to light them on their way
To some dell where in a ring
At midnight, they dance and sing.

To Ambition

Achievement's spur, a spirit thou of fire
That in the bosoms of the high and great
Hath ever fiercely burned, without abate;
Whose flame hath made the lowly day aspire

To royal thrones, and lifted myriads higher;
Thou mak'st and unmak'st dynasty and state,
And oft on thee hath hung an empire's fate.
For all advance is to thy urging due
And mighty evils in thy path ensue.
The pages of all history to stain
Thy spirit doth both good and bad imbue
<And drives them on> to seek their ends amain.

To the Crescent Moon

I am half-wearied by the moon's wide flight,
Yet too complete were evening's offered rest:
Come thou upon the still and sleeping west
And wash the shadows with a dream of light.

Make thou for me such twilight as of Sleep,
And fill with visions borne on filmy wings
That borderland—with dreamy flutterings
That vaguely venture as from Slumber's deep.

To the Morning Star

Triumphant rise, O star, on pinions fleet,
Before the east with budding dawn grows white,
And shine with dark-dispelling, steady light.
Through hours that passed with leaden, laggard feet,
Devoid of rest, lo! I have watched to greet
Thine aureate eye as from the bonds of night
Thou break'st, and soar'st above the eastern height,
Where soon the hosts of dark and day shall meet.

* * *

Vanquish, O star of hope, with conquering ray
Black Doubt and Fear that have companioned me,
While all the weary hours, forsaken of sleep,
Tormented, I have tossed. Drive them away,
As sudden dawn drives night, and bring with thee
Assurance blest of morn—and slumber deep.

To Thomas Paine

O thou who dared the sacred truth proclaim
Who took the stand alone but unafraid

By calumny and danger undismayed
How have they soiled and trampled on thy fame!
How ignorance doth execrate thy name,
Superstition taught, whose minions laid
Gainst thee the charge of infidel and made
Thy name its synonym. But all the blame
By hierophant and layman on thee placed
Shall yet be theirs, as men who helped delay
The righteous cause of Truth and Liberty,
And when the rule of Superstition is abased
No name of kings (than thou) upon that day
Shall higher stand, as one who made men free.

To Thomas Paine

O priest of Truth and herald of the light,
Thou didst proclaim as might the morning star,
That shining trumpet at the lips of dawn,
The fading of the priests and powers of gloom.
Yet have they striven to cast upon thy ray
The mist exhaled from Superstition's mire—
A breath of scum still foul upon the earth,
Still making blind the gaze that else might see.
It shall not hide thy light forever thus;
And though it hang between thee and men's eyes,
Stainless art thou: no marsh can harm a star.

Twilight

Of his great realm, the mighty sovereign Day
Doth for a space his pinioned flight delay
Ere he his scepter to the night resign.
Now all is silent, save that in the pine
The wind laments the passing daylight's sway
In low, sad notes. Now all is turning gray
As slowly doth the fading reign decline
And dim, uncertain, in the world. How far
And faint one little solitary star
Doth on the azure robe of evening shine
To herald with its lonely gleam of light
As deep'ning dusk doth with the dark combine
The stately coming of the queenly Night.
As doth the morning star foreshadow Day.

The Twilight Woods

As eve to purple turns the afterglow
That lately with a rich and fervent red
Illumed the sunset skies, my feet are led
By whispering spirits of the winds that blow
At this grey hour, and many secrets know,
To where the oaks and pines meet overhead
In plots to keep away the light. I tread
Beneath their archways pensively and slow.

Here darkening twilight is a sorcery
Whereby all things are rendered weird and strange:
Bushes and trees fantastic shapes assume,
And shadows lurk within the forest's range
Felt but unseen, for when I turn they flee
To darker depths of consecrated gloom.

The Vampire Night

Sunset as of the world's concluding day:
Vain struggles of the sun to climb once more
The irremeable sky with reddening light;
And then, abrupt and unavoidable,
The drop of his exhausted, flameless orb
Into the cold ultimity of space.
Bereft, bewildered, lost, the planet lies,
Wrapt with the tightening grave-cloth of the gloom;
And silence comes, deliberate, assured,
Like Lethe at the feet of gods that stand,
Unkingdomed, disenabled, on its brink.

What change is this that quickens awe confirmed
To live, pulsating fear? Upon the chords
Of the tense trees, what eldritch hand is laid
That startles into sound such latent dread
As of the damned, within Hell's spacious murk
Eddying invisibly? Or is the wind
Fraught with a resurrection of the dead—
Ghosts lately born, that knowing not themselves
As phantoms, cry a common fear, and shriek
Each from the other? Lo, I seem to hark
The gabblings of the grave, where speak anights

The neighbouring dead; strange outcry of the corpse
Unhallowed by the ghoul's disturbing hand,
And mumblings out of brainless skulls.

The darkness speaks, her echoing word the wind
That shudders through the stillness like a fear.
All dreams of terror inexpressible
Crowd on the gloom at that invoking voice—
Phantasmal terrors, imageless, to sight
That incommunicably limn themselves
Upon the mind; and maleficent powers
Whose eddyings intensify the dusk,
Albeit bodiless. About the soul
They surge with unseen hands that grope and claw,
Felt as the clutch of metal by the mind,
Though light as silence to the shrinking clay.

With fingers of eternal dread the dark
Reaches, and claims its prey; who ventures forth,
The vampire night shall drink his very soul
And leave a living fear within its place!

The Waning Moon

As pale and wan as vapours that at eve
    Steal ghostly-like across the darkling plain,
    Low in the twilight West the Moon doth wane.
Night after night I marked her glories leave,
The dark Earth of some brilliancy bereave,
    Till now, a haggard shade, the Moon is fain
    To fly the rule she may no more maintain,
The argent pomp and state her pale beams weave.

O Queen, forsake thine empire of the Night,
    And swiftly seek the regions dim to-west,
        Whence may'st thou soon return, and robed anew
In gleaming splendours of thy fuller light,
    As earthly queens in jeweled robes are dressed,
        Hold court supreme within the starry blue.

The Abyss Triumphant

1911–1912

Antony to Cleopatra

Lie still: the sultry, large, Egyptian moon,
An amber face with hair of trailing flame,
Hath found the breasted hills beyond the Nile,
And rests a little. Let thy royal head
Upon my bosom find a kindred peace,
This interim of languor-laden dreams,
Which is the truce of passion: Turn thy lips,
Flower-like, and lay them on thy weary flesh,
And veins o'erworn of pleasure; let thy hair,
Enwound about our mingled arms, run on,
Nor disentwine the happy knees and thighs
Our long delight hath wedded . . . We shall lie
And deep within subsiding pulses feel
A drowsy joy that is not ecstasy
And wakeful peace, more dear than Lethe's draught,
Like welling from out the central fount of Love,
A wine with poppies laden, while we dream
Of blissful nights that were, and things to be.
Star by star
The splendid night of our desire goes down
To join the nights of Babylon and Ur,
And stately worlds forgotten; Dawn shall rise,
A hueless nenuphar in heavenly pools,
With Tyrian shores of cloud land circled round.
And flames ardent and crimson, opening
Its wide and magic petals, measureless,
Whose perfume is the balmy wind that blows
From Syria, and the Persian incense-bearing shores
Of all the royal East.

Poetry

O poetry, not on the written page
Alone mayst those be found, for ocean tides
Have pulsing rhythm and the tempests rage
And gentle breeze thy rhyming flow abides;
One hears thee in the seaward pilgrimage
Of streams, and where adown the mountain sides
Water rills in cataracts, and out in space
The planets ceaseless swing with rhythmic pace.

The Last Night

I dreamed a dream: I stood upon a height,
A mountain's utmost eminence of snow.
Beholding ashen plains outflung below
To a far sea-horizon, dim and white.
Beneath the spectral sun's expiring light
The world lay shrouded in a deathly glow;
Its last fear-laden voice, a wind, came low;
The distant sea lay hushed, as with affright.

I watched, until the pale and flickering sun,
In agony and fierce despair, flamed high,
And shadow-slain, went out upon the gloom.
Then Night, that war of gulf-born Titans won,
Impended for a breath on wings of doom.
And through the air fell like a falling sky.

The Eternal Snows

Above the rugged realm of fir and pine,
Aggressive pinnacles, supreme and high,
In snow eternal keenly pierce the sky,
Inviolately white save when the shine
Of morning hues them, or the sunset's wine
Doth drench their slopes in crimson. Pure they lie,
Beyond all earthly dreams of purity,
And hieroglyphed with Beauty's mystic sign.

O snows remote, untrod, that gleam secure
From all the desecrating years of Time,
That, vestal still, shall front Eternity,
Thou art to me as some Ideal sublime,
That from its eminence, unwon and pure,
Speaks with the voice of what my soul might be.

The Moonlight Desert

Above the desert's dark-obscured expanse
The rounded moon uplooms; at once laid clear
The waste leaps on the sight, the far and near
Known equally. As in a silver trance,
Its sand agleam, the desert lies outrolled.
How bright, seen through the burnt-out atmosphere,

The moon and the augmented stars appear,
Yet how aloof, incurious and cold!

Silent as they the waste outspreads, in white
Unbroken, save where lonely boulders cast
Their dusky-purple shadows on the sand—
Holding Death's terror and its wisdom fast
Within that silence—sinister and bright,
A dead, unutterably ancient land.

Nocturne

Intensified and re-enforced with clouds,
In searchless secrecy descends the night;
Against the shrinking lakes of western light,
The hills ambiguous stand, disguised with shrouds
Of mist-inwoven and unfeatured gloom;
A little and engulfed from sight, they sink
In rising tides of dark upon whose brink,
Of chartless waves no beacon-stars illume.

Lost utterly are earth and firmament,
As in some final night of doubts and fears,
Wherein the abysses of Oblivion lie.
Till, lo! the heaven-eclipsing clouds are rent,
And through the rift a lone, bright star brightly peers,
Like some great watchful and unsleeping Eye.

Ode to Music

O woven fabric and bright web of sound,
Whose threads are magical,
And with swift weaving thrall
And hold the spirit bound!
We may not know whence thy strange sorceries fall—
Whether they be Earth's voices wild and strong,
Her high and perfect song,
Or broken dreams of higher worlds unfound.
For, lo, thou art as dreams,
And to thy realm all hidden things belong—
All fugitive and evanescent gleams
The soul hath vainly sought;
All mystic immanence;

All visions of ungrasped magnificence,
And great ideals pinnacled in thought;
All paths with marvel fraught
That lead to lands obscure:
For, lo, upon thy road of sound we pass,
Seeking thy magic lure,
To vales mist-implicated and unsure,
Where all seems strange as visions in a glass;
And wonder-haunted hills,
Where Beauty is an echo and a dream
In sighing pines, and rills
Clouded and deep with imaged tree and sky;
And where bright rivers gleam
Past cities towering high,
Each wonderful as some cloud-fantasy.

Thou loosenest the bondage of the years,
Making the spirit free
Of all sublunar joys and fears.
Who mounts on thine imperious wings shall see
The ways of life as threads of day and night;
Serene above their change,
His eyes shall know but far transcendent things,
His ears shall hark but voices free and strange;
Vast seas of outer light
Shall beat upon his sight,
Eternal winds shall touch him with their wings;
His heart shall thrill
To larger, purer joy, and grief more deep
Than earth may know;
And e'en as dews of morning fill
The opened flower, into his soul shall flow
High melodies, like tears that angels weep.
Then shall he penetrate
The veils and outer barriers of sound,
And near the soul of melody,
Where, rapt in aural splendors ultimate,
His soul shall see
The marvel and the glory that surround
Eternal Beauty's shrine;
And catch afar the glint divine
Of her moon-colored robe, or haply hear,

With world-oblivious ear,
Some echo of her voice's mystery.

Thou hast Love's power to find
The soul's most secret chords, that else were still,
And stir'st them till they thrill
Disclosed to least, faint movements of thy wind.
Thine aural sorcery
O'erwhelms the heart as sunset storms the sight,
For thou art Beauty bodied forth in sound—
Her colors bright
And diverse forms expressed in harmony:
Within thy bound,
The flare of morning is become a song,
And tree and flower a music sweet and long.
And in thy speech
The power and majesty that swing
Planet and sun, and each
Dim atom of the system manifest,
Become articulate, expressed
Like ocean in the brooklet's whispering.
Beyond the woof of finite things,
Thy threads of wonder deep-entangled lie—
Time's intertexturings
Within Eternity—
With Song, mayhap, to be his memories;
For Beauty borders nigh
The ultimate, eternal Verities.

The Dream-Weaver

Who weaveth the web of dreams?
    He hath wrought a fabric strange
Whose threads are the moon's white beams
    And the hues that pass and change
In the sunset's coloured gleams;

Whose woof is in the joy of flowers,
    That wake in the dawn of spring
And the music of passing showers,
    And the song the thrushes sing
Through the sunshine-colored hours.

He hath wrought a fabric dread—
A web that is hued with night,
With fear as its awful thread;
Whose warp is the ghostly might
Of the unremembered dead.

I have sought the weaver of dreams,
In the soul's unfathomed deep;
I have followed a clue that gleams
Through the labyrinth of sleep,
Of a wind that sweeps the spheres.

And lost in the Titan surge
Of a wind that sweeps the stars
I have neared the farthest verge,
Where the ends of night are bars,
And the day and darkness merge.

But in vain is the endless quest:
For, thin as a thread of wind,
The weaver eludes the test;
And hideth where thought is blind
In depths 'neath the soul's unrest.

Ode to the Abyss

O many-gulfed, unalterable one,
Whose deep sustains
Far-drifting world and sun,
Thou wast ere ever star put out on thee;
And thou shalt be
When never world remains;
When all the suns' triumphant strength and pride
Is sunk in voidness absolute,
And their majestic music wide
In vaster silence rendered mute.
And though God's will were night to dusk the blue,
And law to cancel and disperse
The tangled tissues of the universe,
His might were impotent to conquer thee,
O indivisible infinity!
Thy darks subdue
All light that treads thee down a space,
Exulting over thine archetypal deeps.

The cycles die, and lo! thy darkness reaps
The flame of mightiest stars;
In aeon-implicating wars
Thou tearest planets from their place;
Worlds granite-spined
To thine erodents yield
Their treasures centrally confined
In crypts by continental pillars sealed.
What suns and worlds have been thy prey
Through unhorizoned reaches of the past!
What spheres that now essay
Time's undimensioned vast,
Shall plunge forgotten to thy gloom at length
With life that cried its query of the Night
To ears with silence filled!
What worlds unborn shall dare thy strength,
Girt by a sun's unwearied might,
And dip to darkness when the sun is stilled!

O incontestable Abyss,
What light in thine embrace of darkness sleeps—
What blaze of a sidereal multitude
No peopled world is left to miss!
What motion is at rest within thy deeps—
What gyres of planets long become thy food—
Worlds unconstrainable
That plunged therein to peace
Like tempest-worn and crew-forsaken ships;
And suns that fell
To huge and ultimate eclipse,
And from the eternal stances found release!
What sound thy gulfs of silence hold!
Stupendous thunder of the meeting stars
And crash of orbits that diverged,
With Life's thin song are merged;
Thy quietudes enfold
Paean and threnody as one,
And battle-blare of unremembered wars
With festal songs
Sung in the Romes of ruined spheres;
And music that belongs
To undiscoverable younger years
With words of yesterday.

Ah! who may stay
Thy soundless world-devouring tide?
O thou whose hands pluck out the light of stars,
Are worlds but as a destined fruit for thee?
May no sufficient bars
Nor marks inveterate abide
As shores to baffle thine unbillowing sea?
Still and unstriving now,
What plottest thou,
Within thy universe-ulterior deeps,
Dark as the final lull of suns?
What new advancement of the night
On citadels of stars around whose might
Thy slow encroachment runs,
And crouching silence, thunder-potent, sleeps?

Medusa

As drear and barren as the glooms of Death,
It lies, a windless land of livid dawns,
Nude to a desolate firmament, with hills
That seem the gibbous bones of the mummied Earth,
And plains whose hollow face is rivelled deep
With gullies twisting like a serpent's track.
The leprous touch of Death is on its stones,
Where for his token visible, the Head
Is throned upon a heap of monstrous rocks
Rough-mounded like some shattered pyramid
In a thwartly cloven hill-ravine, that seems
The unhealing scar of huge Tellurian wars.
Her lethal beauty crowned with twining snakes
That mingle with her hair, the Gorgon reigns.
Her eyes are clouds wherein black lightnings lurk,
Yet, even as men that seek the glance of Life,
The gazers come, where, coiled and serpent-swift,
Those levins wait. As round an altar-base
Her victims lie, distorted, blackened forms
Of postured horror smitten into stone—
Time caught in meshes of Eternity—
Drawn back from dust and ruin of the years,
And given to all the future of the world.
The land is claimed of Death: the daylight comes

Half-strangled in the changing webs of cloud
That unseen spiders of bewildered winds
Weave and unweave across the lurid sun
In upper air. Below, no zephyr comes
To break with life the circling spell of doom.
Long vapor-serpents twist about the moon,
And in the windy murkness of the sky
The guttering stars are wild as candle-flames
That near the socket.

Thus the land shall be,
And Death shall wait, throned in Medusa's eyes,
Till in the irremeable webs of night
The sun is snared, and the corroded moon
A dust upon the gulfs, and all the stars
Rotted and fallen like rivets from the sky,
Letting the darkness down upon all things.

The Messengers

Catching a little wind's unrest,
The dandelion-crests dissolve,
Where swooping wings of air involve
And lift them to a scattered quest.

Snared in the tangled zephyr-coil,
They try the day to hidden ends—
The messengers that Beauty sends
With words of waking to the soil.

Chant to Sirius

What nights retard thee, O Sirius!
Thy light is as a spear,
And thou penetratest them
As a warrior that stabbeth his foe
Even to the center of his life.
Thy rays reach farther than the gulfs;
They form a bridge thereover
That shall endure till the links of the universe
Are unfastened, and drop apart,
And all the gulfs are one,
Dissevered by suns no longer.

How strong art thou in thy place!
Thou stridest thine orbit,
And the darkness shakes beneath thee,
As a road that is trodden by an army.
Thou art a god
In thy temple that is hollowed with light
In the night of infinitude,
And whose floor is the lower void;
Thy worlds are as priests and ministers therein.
Thou furrowest space,
Even as an husbandman,
And sowest it with alien seed;
It beareth alien fruits,
And these are thy testimony,
Even as the crops of his fields
Are the testimony of an husbandman.

The Horizon

Thou art the place our eager, hastening feet
May never reach, though far the quest is sped,
Though over land and sea our search is led,
Forever doth thy mystic line retreat.

Far-veiled in blue, when we arise at dawn
Thou beckonest, O one elusive, fair,
And we must follow through the morning air
With hoping hearts, forever, ever on.

In purple and in gold we see, at eve
Thy distant barrier drawn across the west;
Yet still we shall pursue the weary quest,
And thou, O luring one, will e'er deceive.

A Dream of Beauty

I dreamed that each most lovely, perfect thing
That Nature hath, of sound and form and hue—
The winds, the grass, the light-concentering dew,
The gleam and swiftness of the sea-bird's wing;
Blueness of sea and sky, and gold of storm
Transmuted by the sunset, and the flame
Of autumn-colored leaves, before me came,
And, meeting, merged to one diviner form.

Incarnate Beauty 'twas, whose spirit thrills
Through glaucous ocean and the greener hills,
And in the cloud-bewildered peaks is pent.
Her face the light of fallen planets wore,
But as I gazed, in doubt and wonderment,
Mine eyes were dazzled, and I saw no more.

A Live-Oak Leaf

How marvellous this bit of green
    I hold, and soon shall throw away!
Its subtile veins, its vivid sheen
    Seem fragment of a god's array.

In all the hidden toil of earth,
    Which is the more laborious part—
To rear the oak's enormous girth,
    Or shape its leaves with poignant art?

Wind-Ripples

Did Beauty's unseen spirit pass
    With tread unstayable and fleet?
Surely I saw the crested grass
    Bow 'neath supernal feet!

A Song from Hell

This song I got me from the nether pits,
Where, as a witches' cauldron-brew, that blends
Envenomed roots and herbs malignly foul,
With poison-essence drawn from charnel things,
And carrion found by night, the various damned
Bubble and seethe with their own agony,
And cry to upward firmamental gulfs
(Reddened with blotching flame as though with stars)
A chant that rears like some distillment weird,
Atwist with urge of pain from writhing lips:—

We are the damned—the stain and moil
    That Death has washed from earthly time;
    Drawn down by tides of Hell, we boil
Like toads within a torrid slime.

Our sins were great—a deadly charge—
And yet less heavy than our fate:
We pour through Hell's alembic large,
Each soul transformed to vital hate;

The good that in our hearts remained
By sin untainted, now is one
With vileness cankeringly ingrained;
By earth and Hell we stand undone—

For that which earth unfinished left,
The consummation of the pit.
From out the insuperable cleft,
To where its lords presiding sit,

And watch with calm contestless sight,
We burn, by double test refined
To clearest evil—purgèd quite
Of good or mercy from the mind.

Our souls are lined to vast despair,
As to some nadir-founded rock,
Where never hope descends to mock
Beyond the dip of terrene air.

We heighten to a hate that beats
In rage all impotently strong
Against the worlds that league with wrong,
Whose pain each other's pain completes.

Ah, would our hate were hands to draw
The lords of earth and hell beneath!
Ah, would our hate were venomed teeth
To rend them through their mail of law!

Ah, would that we might cleave with hate
The roof, and base, and walls of Hell—
Wrench at its pillars till they fell
With ruin indiscriminate!

Immovably it stands, with springs
Of fire to tear its inward glooms,
Wherefrom, ascending high, our fumes
Are breath of incense to its kings.

The Palace of Jewels

Fronting the sea's blue chambers fluctuant—
Those floors of azure, marble veined with foam—
It rears, a golden palace culminant
In cusp of tower and round of dome.

Naught but the ocean's music echoes there;
No lutes pervade its halls with mirth and sigh;
And glances lone, through close and pleasance fair,
The velvet, figured butterfly.

Within, in silence tapestried and old,
And dusk that lingers through the widest day,
Are heapéd treasure-chests that, spilling, hold
Jewels of iris-changéd ray.

Here caskets weirdly wrought are prodigal
Of hue-tempestuous opals, and the fire,
A pulse of crystal in the sombre hall,
Wherewith the diamonds aspire;

Deep sapphires, clouded to the core with blue;
Beryls that blend the fire of sky and sea;
And slumberous rubies, with a burst of hue,
Arousing intermittently.

They wage a truceless war within the gloom,
Each with its swift and varying beam for lance—
A kindling strife that runs from room to room,
With hues that waver or advance.

The diamonds' front of shifting onset leaps
Where lambent rubies lurk athwart, with spears
In sunset dipt—each line a flame that creeps,
Alternate glows and disappears.

A flare that stabs, like some keen battle-call
Upstartles 'mid the hesitating strife;
With rush of beams that clash, triumph, or fall,
The jewels leap to myriad life.

Against the gloom their irised swords unite,
With shadow-sundering blades and points that fret.
From flickering looms they scatter wefts of light,
To catch the dusk as in a net.

Uneasily the twilight-edges start
    Before the balas ruby's orange ire,
Or mimic lightning from the diamond's heart,
    Whose blood is everlasting fire.

Poured through the vessels of their alchemy,
    The daylight is become a gorgeous thing—
A flame that soars and falls unquietly,
    A spirit of a colored wing.

What dawns and sunsets march from room to room
    Beneath the noon or twilight of the sky!
What jewels fed with many suns illume,
    Make each a mimic day, and die!

Like blood within a vein, the sunlight swirls,
    Racing from gem to gem, with fires that wed
Mysterious, ocean-sad, dream-hearted pearls,
    And heliotropes stabbed through with red;

Or run where vistaed amethysts enfold
    Their flame with purple of some vague confine,
And overbrimming ruby-flagons hold
    The light like some deep-glowing wine.

Through evening halls the scattered jewels burn
    Like broken chains of fire within the night,
Till comes the moon, and from her heavenly urn,
    Bestows a stream of subtler light

On gems that seem some clear and stellar dew,
    Orbed in the regions past the springs of morn;
And gems like magic flowers that fold anew
    In lands beyond the sunset-bourn.

The Star-Treader

I

A voice cried to me in a dawn of dreams,
Saying, "Make haste: the webs of death and birth
Are brushed away, and all the threads of earth
Wear to the breaking; spaceward gleams
Thine ancient pathway of the suns,
Whose flame is part of thee;
And the deep gulfs abide coevally

Whose darkness runs
Through all thy spirit's mystery.
Go forth, and tread unharmed the blaze
Of stars wherethrough thou camest in old days;
Pierce without fear each vast
Whose hugeness crushed thee not within the past.
A hand strikes off the chains of Time,
A hand swings back the door of years;
Now fall earth's bonds of gladness and of tears,
And opens the strait dream to space sublime."

II

Who rides a dream, what hand shall stay!
What eye shall note or measure mete
His passage on a purpose fleet,
The thread and weaving of his way!
It caught me from the clasping world,
And swept beyond the brink of Sense,
My soul was flung, and poised, and whirled
Like to a planet chained and hurled
With solar lightning strong and tense.
Swift as communicated rays
That leap from severed suns a gloom
Within whose waste no suns illume,
The wingèd dream fulfilled its ways.
Through years reversed and lit again
I followed that unending chain
Wherein the suns are links of light;
Retraced through lineal, ordered spheres
The twisting of the threads of years
In weavings wrought of noon and night;
Through stars and deeps I watched the dream unroll,
Those folds that form the raiment of the soul.

III

Enkindling dawns of memory,
Each sun had radiance to relume
A sealed, disused, and darkened room
Within the soul's immensity.
Their alien ciphers shown and lit,
I understood what each had writ

Upon my spirit's scroll;
Again I wore mine ancient lives,
And knew the freedom and the gyves
That formed and marked my soul.

IV

I delved in each forgotten mind,
The units that had builded me,
Whose deepnesses before were blind
And formless as infinity—
Knowing again each former world—
From planet unto planet whirled
Through gulfs that mightily divide
Like to an intervital sleep.
One world I found, where souls abide
Like winds that rest upon a rose;
Thereto they creep
To loose all burden of old woes.
And one there was, a garden-close
Whose blooms are grown of ancient sin
And death the sap that wells and flows:
The spirits weep that dwell therein.
And one I knew, where chords of pain
With stridors fill the Senses' lyre;
And one, where Beauty's olden chain
Is forged anew with stranger loveliness,
In flame-soft links of never-quenched desire
And ineluctable duress.

V

Where no terrestrial dreams had trod
My vision entered undismayed,
And Life her hidden realms displayed
To me as to a curious god.
Where colored suns of systems triplicate
Bestow on planets weird, ineffable,
Green light that orbs them like an outer sea,
And large auroral noons that alternate
With skies like sunset held without abate,
Life's touch renewed incomprehensibly
The strains of mirth and grief's harmonious spell.

Dead passions like to stars relit
Shone in the gloom of ways forgot;
Where crownless gods in darkness sit
The day was full on altars hot.
I heard—enisled in those melodic seas—
The central music of the Pleiades,
And to Alcyone my soul
Swayed with the stars that own her song's control.
Unchallenged, glad, I trod, a revenant
In worlds Edenic longly lost;
Or dwelt in spheres that sing to those,
Through space no light has crossed,
Diverse as Hell's mad antiphone uptossed
To Heaven's angelic chant.

VI

What vasts the dream went out to find!
I seemed beyond the world's recall
In gulfs where darkness is a wall
To render strong Antares blind!
In unimagined spheres I found
The sequence of my being's round—
Some life where firstling meed of Song,
The strange imperishable leaf,
Was placed on brows that starry Grief
Had crowned, and Pain anointed long;
Some avatar where Love
Sang like the last great star at morn
Ere the pale orb of Death filled all its sky;
Some life in fresher years unworn
Upon a world whereof
Peace was a robe like to the calms that lie
On pools aglow with latter spring:
There Time's pellucid surface took
Clear image of all things, nor shook
Till the black cleaving of Oblivion's wing;
Some earlier awakening
In pristine years, when giant strife
Of forces darkly whirled
First forged the thing called Life—
Hot from the furnace of the suns—
Upon the anvil of a world.

VII

Thus knew I those anterior ones
Whose lives in mine were blent;
Till, lo! my dream, that held a night
Where Rigel sends no message of his might,
Was emptied of the trodden stars,
And dwindled to the sun's extent—
The brain's familiar prison-bars,
And raiment of the sorrow and the mirth
Wrought by the shuttles intricate of earth.

The Invisible Host

Invisible, the armies of the Wind
    Through all the clouded daylight hours went past,
Toward some far-distant and unguessed-of bourn,
    In columns long, invincible, and vast.

Unpausingly their winged squadrons poured
    To wild and warlike songs and martial strains,
By unseen fingers played upon the pines,
    Over the tree-crowned hills and dusty plains.

They rose on pinions terrible and swift,
    Driving the massed and somber clouds before,
Then sank to earth and roused the sleeping dust,
    That swept in vague and formless column's o'er.

They stripped the plundered trees of what few leaves
    Were missed, in haste, by Autumn's robber hands;
And on their wings they bore the Autumn off
    And brought the winter to the waiting lands.

To George Sterling

What questioners have met the gaze of Time,
    Whose searchless eyes unyielding theirs denied,
    Till sank the casual monarch's baseless pride,
And transitory fames of sword or rhyme!
What fames from gulfs monotonous shall climb,
    Whose eyes ephemeral, unverified,
    Shall that enduring scrutiny abide
As men that face the noontide sun sublime!

* * *

One after one the searches stare and fall,
    Abased before its unabated scorn,
But this thy fame, in days eventual,
    'Mid ruins desolate shall stand unworn,
Confronting Time in vastness musical,
    Like Memnon's statue staring at the morn.

The Dream-Bridge

All drear and barren seemed the hours,
    That passed rain-swept and tempest-blown.
The dead leaves fell like brownish notes
    Within the rain's grey monotone.

There came a lapse between the showers;
    The clouds grew rich with sunset gleams;
Then o'er the sky a rainbow sprang—
    A bridge unto the Land of Dreams.

The Nemesis of Suns

Lo, what are these, the gyres of sun and world,
    Fulfilled with daylight by each toiling sun—
    Lo, what are these but webs of radiance spun
Beneath the roof of Night, and torn or furled
By Night at will? All opposite powers upwhirled
    Are less than chaff to this imperious one—
    As wind-tossed chaff, until its sport be done,
Scattered, and lifted up, and downward hurled.

All gyres are held within the path unspanned
    Of Night's aeonian compass—loosely pent
        As with the embrace of lethal-tightening weight;
All suns are grasped within the hollow hand
    Of Night, the godhead sole, omnipotent,
        Whose other names are Nemesis and Fate.

Retrospect and Forecast

Turn round, O Life, and know with eyes aghast
The breast that fed thee—Death, disguiseless, stern:
Even now, within my mouth, from tomb and urn,
The dust is sweet. All nurture that thou hast

Was once as thou, and fed with lips made fast
On Death, whose sateless mouth it fed in turn.
Kingdoms abased, and Thrones that starward yearn,
All are but ghouls that batten on the past.

Monstrous and dread, must it forever abide,
This inescapable alternity?
Must beauty blossom, rooted in decay,
And night devour its flaming hues alway?
Sickening, will Life not turn eventually,
Or ravenous Death at last be satisfied?

The Song of a Comet

Pale plummet of the stark immensities,
From perished heavens cast, I fall and flare
Through gulfs by stellar orbits girdled round;
And spaces bare
Of sparkless night between the galaxies—
By path of sun nor circling planet bound.
No star allots my lone and cyclic gyre;
I mark the systems vanish one by one;
Among the swarming worlds I lunge,
And sudden plunge
Close to the zones of solar fire;
Or 'mid the mighty wrack of stars undone,
Flash, and with momentary rays
Compel the dark to yield
Their aimless forms, whose once far-potent blaze
In ashes chill is now inurned.
Upon the shadowy heavens half-revealed,
I show their planets turned,
Whose strange ephemerae,
On adamantine tablets deeply written,
In cities long unlitten,
Have left their history
And lore beyond redemption or surmise.
Adown contiguous skies,
I pass the thickening brume
Of systems yet unshaped, that hang immense
Along mysterious shores of gloom;
Or see—unimplicated in their doom—
The final and disastrous gyre

Of blinded suns that meet,
And from their mingled heat
And battle-clouds intense,
Overspread the deep with fire.

Upon the Lion's track,
Or far beyond the abysms of the Lyre,
I thread, through mazes of the zodiac,
Mine orbit placed amid
The multiple and irised stars, or hid,
Unsolved and intricate,
In many a planet-swinging sun's estate.
At times I steal in solitary flight
Along the rim of the exterior night
That rounds the universe;
And then return,
Past outer footholds of sidereal light,
To see the systems gather and disperse;
And learn
What vast and multifarious marvels wait
In the dim void that has no ultimate;
What wraiths of suns extinguished long ago
On alien welkins burn;
What flaming blossoms grow
From the black battlefields of cosmic wars;
What stellar hells, or ampler spheres sublime,
Enisled in diverse time,
Are wrought from sharded moons and meteors;
And haply I discern
What paler fires, to mine own self akin,
Still haunt the night's eternal corridors,
Or in the toils of great Arcturus spin.
Then, restless still, I rise
Through vaults of mightier gloom, to watch the dark
Snatch at the flame of failing suns;
Or mark
That midden of the stagnant nadir skies
Where many a fated orbit runs.
An arrow sped from some forgotten bow,
Through change of firmaments and systems sent,
And finding bourn nor bars,
I fly, nor know
For what remoter mark my flight is meant.

The Canyon

A Titan furrow in the hills,
    Ploughed there a million years ago,
The steep and high-walled canyon winds
    From yonder peaks to plains below.

Said the Dreamer

My dreams were nests of horror, whimsey-wrought
With orts and shreds from old abysses brought;
Were eyries built by condor-wingèd awe,
Enskied on sombre pinnacles of thought.

Fantastical, I saw the visions shift
Like bubbles that a Titan's breath might lift,
Drowning in seas more deep than his despair—
Iron-colored, soon to shatter or to drift;

Or like illumined crystals fallen from hands
Of gods, that cloud interiorly with lands
Of wider spheres exalted past the sun,
Or burst while thought in idle question stands.

Conscious of gulfs in which I dared not gaze,
I passed on faltering and imperiled ways,
Through lands where hoary mountains danced and roared
To baleful pygmies piping hellish lays.

The flames that wait against the end of things
Were light and limit to my wanderings.
Through deserts bleaching like the bones of death
Aback I fled, and faltered on spent wings

In night Cimmerian, thronged with sorceries,
Where lightnings flamed on empty sands and seas;
Or feared the leopard-crouch of pallid shapes
In Saracenic arches of black trees.

Then in the dream I dreamt that Time was done:
Light still endured, whose touch I might not shun,
Though at my back I heard the lips of Night
Puff out the flaring flambeau of the sun.

I leaned from some black precipice, to see
The pits beneath. One came, not far from me,

Who hurled therein the sockets of the stars
And shell of worlds that rattled emptily.

Saturn

Now were the Titans gathered round their king
In a waste region slipping toward the verge
Of drear extremities that clasp the world—
A land half-moulded by the hasty gods,
Grotesque, misfeatured, blackly gnarled with stone,
And left beneath the bright scorn of the stars;
Or worn and marred from conflict with the deep,
Conterminate, of Chaos. Here they stood,
Old Saturn midmost, like a central peak
Among the lesser mounts that guard its base.
Defeat, that gloamed within each countenance
Like the first tinge of death, upon a sun
Gathering like some dusk vapor, found them cold,
Heavy of limb, and halting as with weight
Of threatened worlds and trembling firmaments.
A wind cried round them like a trumpet-voice
Of phantom hosts—hurried, importunate,
And intermittent with a tightening fear.
Far off the sunset sprang, and the hard clouds,
Molten among the peaks, seemed furnaces
In which to make the fetters of the world.

Seared by the lightning of the younger gods,
They saw, beyond the grim and crouching hills,
Those levins thrust like spears into the heart
Of swollen clouds, or cleaving the dark sky
Like swords colossal. Then, as the Titans watched,
The night rose like a black, enormous mist
Around them wherein naught was visible
Save the sharp levin leaping in the north;
And no sound came except of seas remote
That seemed like Chaos ravening past the verge
Of all the world, fed with the crumbling coasts
Of Matter.

Till the moon, discovering
That harsh swart wilderness of sand and stone
Tissued and twisted in chaotic weld,

Lit with illusory fire each Titan's form,
They sate in silence, mute as stranded orbs—
The wrack of Time, upcast on ruinous coasts,
And in the slow withdrawal of the tide
Unvexed awhile. Small solace could they take
From that wan radiance glistering frostily
Upon the desert seized in iron silence,
Like a false triumph over contestless Fates,
Or a mirage of life in wastes of death.
Yet were they moved to speak, and Saturn's voice,
Seeming the soul of that tremendous land
Set free in sound, startled the haughty stars:

"O Titans, gods, sustainers of the world,
Is this the end? Must Earth go down to Chaos,
Lacking our strength, beneath the unpractised sway
Of godlings vain, precipitate with youth,
Who think, unrecking of disastrous chance,
To bind their will as reins upon the sun,
Or stand as columns to the ponderous heavens?
Must we behold with eyes of impotence
That universal wrack, even though it whelm
These our usurpers in impartial doom
Beneath the shards and fragments of the world?
Were it not preferable to return,
And, meeting them in fight unswervable,
Drag down the earth, ourselves, and these our foes,
One sacrifice unto the gods of Chaos?
Why should we stay, and live the tragedy
Of power that survives its use?"

Now spake
Enceladus, when that the echoings
Of Saturn's voice had fled remote, and seemed
Dead thunders caught and flung from star to star:
"Wouldst hurl thy kingdom down the nightward gulf
Like to a stone a curious child might cast
To test the fall of some dark precipice?
Patience and caution should we take as mail,
Not rashness for a weapon—too keen sword
That cuts the strainèd knot of destiny,
Never to be tied again. Were it not best
To watch the slow procedure of the days,

That we may grasp a time more opportune
When desperation is not all our strength
Nor the foe newly filled with victory?
Then may we hope to conquer back thy realm
For thee, not for the gods of nothingness?"

He ceased, and after him no lesser god
Gave voice upon the shaken silences,
None venturing to risk comparison,
Inevitable then, of eloquence
With his; but, like the ambiguity
Of signal stars and lesser overcast
And merged in one confusion by the moon,
Silence possessed that throng, till Saturn rose.
Around his form the light intensified,
And strengthened with addition wild and strange,
Investing him as with a ghostly robe
And gathering like a crown about his brow.
His sword, whereon the shadows lay like rust,
He took, and dipping it within the moon
Made clean its length of blade and from it cast
Swift flickerings at the stars. And then his voice
Came like a torrent, and from out his eyes
Streamed wilder power that mingled with the sound.

And his resurgent power, in glance and word,
Poured through the Titans' souls and was become
The fountains of their own, and at his flame
Their fires relumined twice-rebellious rose,
Leaping against the stronghold of the stars.
And now they turned, majestic with resolve,
Where, red upon the forefront of the north,
Arcturus was a beacon to the winds.
And with the flickering winds, that lightly struck
The desert dust, then spring again in air,
They passed athwart the foreland of the north,
Against their march they saw the shrunken waste,
A rivelled region like a world grown old
Whose sterile breast knew not the lips of life
In all its epoch; or a world that was
The nurse of infant Death, ere he became
Too large, too strong for its restraining arms,
And towered athwart the suns.

And there they crossed
Metallic slopes that rang like monstrous shields
Under their tread, and dully clanging plains
Like body-mail of greater, vaster gods.
Where hills made gibbous shadows in the moon,
They heard the eldritch laughters of the wind,
Seeming the mirth of doom; and 'neath their gaze
Gaunt valleys deepened like an old despair.
Yet strode they on through the moon's fantasies,
Bold with resolve, across a land like doubt.

And now they passed among huge mountain-bulks,
Themselves like ambulant mountains, moving slow
'Mid fettered brethren, adding weight and gloom
To that mute conclave great against the stars.
Emerging thence the Titans marched where still
Their own portentous shadows went before
Like night that fled but shrunk not, dusking all
That desert way.

And now they came where sleep,
The sleep of weary victory, had seized
The younger gods as captives, borne beyond
All flight of mounting battle-ecstasies
In that deep triumph of forgetfulness.
Upon that sleep the striding Titans broke,
Vague and immense at first like forming dreams
To those disturbèd gods, in mist of drowse
Purblind and doubtful yet, though soon they knew
Their erst-defeated foes, and rising stood
In silent ranks expectant, that appeared
To move, with shaking of astonished fires
That bristled forth deployed like awful plumes
Between the brightening desert and the sky.
Then, sudden as the waking from a dream,
The battle sprang, where striving deities
Moved brightly through the whirled and stricken air,
Sweeping it to a froth of fire; and all
That ancient, deep-established desert rocked,
Shaken as by an onset of the gulfs
Of gathered and impatient Chaos, while,
Above the place where central battle burned,
The moon and stars drew back in dazzlement,

Paling to more secluded distances.
Lo, where the moon's uncertain light had wrought
Disordered shadows and chimeras dim,
Hiding the hideous desert with mirage,
Or deepening it with gulfs and glooms of hell,
Mightier confusion, chaos absolute,
Was grown the one thing sure in sky or world.
Typhonian maelstroms caught in fiery storms,
Torn by the sweep of Olympian weaponries—
Crescented blades that met with rounds of shields;
Grappling of shapes, seen through the riven blaze
An instant, then once more obscure and known
Only by giant heavings of that war
Of furious gods and rousèd elements—
These, round one swollen center, hung ensphered
Upon the blasted sand and molten rocks.

So huge that chaos, complicate within
With movements of gigantic legionry,
Where Jove and Saturn, thunder-crested, led
In onset never stayed—so strong the strife
Of differing impulse, that decision found
No foothold, till that first confusion should
In ordered conflict re-arrange and stand
With its true forces known. This seemed remote
With that wide struggle pending terribly,
As if the spectrumed wings of Time had made
A truce with white Eternity, and both
Stood watching from afar.

Through drifts of haze
The broadening moon, made ominous with red,
Glared from the westering night. And now that war
Built for itself, far up, a cope of cloud
And drew it down, far off, upon all sides,
Impervious to the moon and sworded stars.
And by their own wild light the gods fought on
'Neath that stupendous concave like a sky
Filled and illumined with glare of shattered suns.
And cast by their own light, upon that sky
The gods' own shadows moved like shapen gloom,
Phantasmagoric, changed and amplified,
A shifting frieze that flickered dreadfully

In spectral battle indecisive. Then,
Swift as it had begun, the contest turned
And on the heaving Titans' massive front
It seemed that all the motion and the strength
Self-thwarting and confounded, of that strife,
Was flung in centered impact terrible,
With rush of all that fire, tempestuous-blown
As if before some wind of further space
Striking the earth. Lo, all the Titans' flame
Bent back upon themselves and they were hurled
In vaster disarray, with vanguard piled
On rear and center. Saturn could not stem
The loosened torrents of long-pent defeat;
He, with his hosts, was but as drift thereon,
Borne wildly down the whelmed and reeling world.

Hurling like slanted rain, the violet levin
Fell over the flight of Titans, and behind,
In striding menace, all-victorious Jove
Loomed like some craggy cloud with thunders crowned
And footed with the winds. In that defeat,
With Jove's pursuit deepened and manifold,
Few found escape unscathed, and some went down
Like senile suns that grapple with the dark,
And reel in flame tremendous, and are still.

Ebbing, the battle left those elder gods
Thrown back on iron shores of their despair,
A darker and a vaster Tartarus.
The victor gods, their storms and thunders spent,
Went dwindling northward like embattled clouds,
And, where the lingering haze of fight dissolved,
The pallor of the dawn began to spread
On darkness purple like the pain of death.
Ringed with that desolation Saturn stood
Mute, and the Titans answered unto him
With brother silence. Motionless, they appeared
Some peristyle of topless columns great,
Alone enduring of a fallen fane
In wastes of an immenser world whence Life
And Faith have vanished, whose enshadowed orb
Verges oblivionward. And Twilight slow
Crept round those lofty shapes august and seemed

Such as might be the ghostly, muffled noon
Of mightier suns that totter down to death.

Then turned they, passing from that dismal place
Blasted anew with battle, ere the dawn,
Striding in flame athwart stupendous chasms
And wasteful plains, should overtake them there,
Bowed with too heavy a burden of defeat.
Slowly they turned, and passed upon the west
Where, like a weariness immovable
In menace huge, the plain its monstrous bulk,
The peaks its hydra heads, the whole world crouched
Against their march with the diminished stars.

So fell the Titans—a gigantic rain
From out the battle's midmost vestiture
Of blackly-closing densities of cloud,
That darkened more intensely when their flame
Out-ruining, left hollow half the clefts
And fast recess of concaves innermost
Which, e'en as lightning-sheets continuous,
The fight had brimmed with glut of raging fire.
They poised by Jove's all potent hand unseen
In middle space where Tartarus was dim,
Impended till his slackening hold allowed
Such downfall as of earthquake-loosened peaks
That plunge enormously from topmost walls
Of cragged Earth, to cloud-withholden seas.

So fell they that the vast endured not less
Disrupture of the universal law
Than if the clear ethereal skies should see
The wrenching of the planets from their course,
With wide confusion felt among the stars
O'er breadth of voidness hitherto uncrossed.
Through unimpeding air with nadir-aimed
Resistless speed, they dropped apace, and saw
The gulf of Tartarus opening under them
Like visible Oblivion, for the time
Ere they were one with it. Like midnight stars
That near the sea's long margin of eclipse,
The clearness of their light grew dim with red,
Ere one by one the Titans sat, and gloom

Met over them, and silence smoothed its plumes
Above the roar and ruin of their fall.

So plunged they to that dark receptacle
Whose bottom is the nadir of all things.
The brood of night, at last they were returned
To shelter of her wings original
To burn with unabated fire of rage
And heat of aspiration in the dusk
Where claritude of flame and rust of night
Are ranked alike in one futility.
Knowing the pain of useless, baffled strength,
That turns and eats upon itself, they sat,
Deep-gloomed by overtopping walls of Hell
And shadowed by Cyclopean world.

The Shadow of the Unattained

O mists that move upon the breeze,
    On borrowed wings that have the power
    To shape and shift ye for an hour
Along the hills, among the trees!

O mists that hang upon the pines,
    And from the many-pointed green,
    Confused with grey for all its sheen,
Drip slowly down in shaken lines!

What phantom voice has come to me
    With hush of magic on the heart—
    Fainter than winds that breathe apart
The folds of twilight's drapery?

Ah, why the swift imperious sense
    As of horizons far, forlorn,
    Of griefs wherewith the stars might mourn,
And bonds of alien exigence?

Is it that ye are less of Time
    Than flower and wind, than hill and tree,
    That with the voice of dreams to me,
Of visions from a hidden clime,

Ye call, and all the griefs of earth
    Are overcast with starrier woe—

Sorrow that I may never know
Attainment, and the vision's worth;

And grief that sighs in Beauty's breath—
Beauty, whose lyric laughters hold
A sadder music learned of old,
An echo from the halls of Death?

Akin to thine, a sadness lies
In dawn-anterior moons that set
Through night's receding violet,
That thickens down the western skies,

Or in last summer's whitened grass,
Ghostly above the green of spring,
And lonely birds that lowlier sing
When colored autumns sadly pass,

In all of strangely beautiful,
A wistful or impassioned pain—
In cobwebs laden with the rain
Through fullest morn's white, listening lull;

Or the wild rose's single rim
Of simplest petals exquisite,
And irised dragon-flies that flit
Through mesh of shadows, fine and dim.

Lo, past all present beauties fall
The shadows of the unattained;
From purest song that ear hath gained,
Uncompassable echoes call.

In quest of visions half-forbid,
My soul must put aside the screen,
And walk in regions vaguely seen,
Round Mind's half-conscious borders hid,

As one who seeks a mystic bloom
On ways beset with nightly chance—
Circled with alien vigilance,
And rustling of the ghostly gloom.

II

Desirous dreams imperative,
What wings are thine of baffled flight!

What spheres mysterious to the light—
Skies where empyreal colors live

Past zeniths of the violet's wing,
And ethers of seraphic sound,
Prolonged swift music, free of bound,—
Await thy search and entering!

Still shall I strive, nor hope to find
Their entrance's fantasmal clue:
The road that one must walk thereto
Is thinner than a thread of wind.

Their fires of cloudy mystery
Sing all unheard, except when fall
Into my soul antiphonal,
Like starlight on the sleeping sea,

Their least low spectral echoings.
And thought's arising wave must break
Each glimmering image that they make—
Vague vision of exotic things

All alienate and unretained.
Like faintest iris on the sky,
What ghostly dreams appear and die
That sleep nor day has wholly gained!

Cliff-shadows edged with opal foam,
Sloping to meet the shadowy sea;
Pale streams that fall forgetfully
Into the morning's mirrored dome;

III

White flowers with colored shadows crossed;
Translucent-winged butterflies,
And hueless birds of haunted skies,
In iridescent twilight lost—

Such things my soul soliciteth,
And far delight of lyric spheres,
With unintelligible tears
In clearest realms of tear-white Death—

A land of strange forgotten dooms,
And fair as ancient death is fair,

For stranger beauty broodeth there,
Like moonlight on the sand of tombs:

Dull permanence of foam that clings
On moveless wave and soundless sand,
And stirless amaranths that stand
In garths forgot of winds and wings;

Time in those gardens by the shore,
Moves softlier than the feet of Sin;
It seems a god hath wept therein,
And saddened them forevermore.

....

I turn; the mists have taken flight;
Above the fallen sunset-gleam,
Lost, as the fabric of a dream,
The silence thickens into night.

The Pursuer

Ascendant from what dead profundity,
Of lives that Death, methought, had compassed round—
Sealed with the night of suns, forever bound
With dust of systems,—comest thou to me,
Despair, whose other name in memory
Is tongueless now—whence comest, thus enwound
With Night's forgotten purples, to astound
All present days with old inveteracy?

O shape of subtler horrors, here unguessed,
Have I not climbed secure from their abyss,
Those lower spheres by trampling Death deprest?
Those tearest me beyond the hells of this,
Down chasms dreadful for the light of tears,
And ampler glooms alive with crawling fears!

Echo of Memnon

I wandered ere the dream was done
Where over Nilus' nenuphars,
With all its ears of quivering stars,
The darkness listened for the sun.

Ere shadows were, ere night was gone,
I found the one whom suns had sought,
And waiting at his feet, methought
Had speech with Memnon in the dawn. . . .

Sad as the last, lamenting star
He sang, and clear as morning's gold:
Unto his voice I saw unfold
The hesitant, pale nenuphar.

But dolorous like the peal of dooms,
And proclamation of the night,
The waste returned that voice of light
With echo from its hollow tombs!

Nero

This Rome, that was the toil of many men,
The consummation of laborious years—
Fulfillment's crown to visions of the dead
And image of the wide desire of kings—
Is made my darkling dream's effulgency,
Fuel of vision, brief embodiment
Of wandering will and wastage of the strong
Fierce ecstasy of one tremendous hour,
When ages piled on ages like a pyre
Flamed to the years behind and years to be.

Yet any sunset were as much as this,
Save for the music forced from tongueless things,
The rape of Matter's huge, unchorded harp
By the many-fingered fire—a music pierced
With the tense voice of Life, more quick to cry
Its agony—and save that I believed
The radiance redder for the blood of men.
Destruction hastens and intensifies
The process that is beauty, manifests
Ranges of form unknown before, and gives
Motion, and voice, and hue, where otherwise
Bleak inexpressiveness had levelled all.

If one create, there is the lengthy toil;
The labored years and days league toward an end
Less than the measure of desire, mayhap,

After the sure consuming of all strength
And strain of faculties that otherwhere
Were loosed upon enjoyment; and at last
Remains to one capacity nor power
For pleasure in the thing that he hath made.
But on destruction hangs but little use
Of time or faculty, but all is turned
To the one purpose, unobstructed, pure,
Of sensuous rapture and observant joy;
And from the intensities of death and ruin
One draws a heightened and completer life,
And both extends and vindicates himself.

I would I were a god, with all the scope
Of attributes that are the essential core
Of godhead, and its visibility.
I am but emperor, and hold awhile
The power to hasten death upon its way,
And cry a halt to worn and lagging Life
For others, but for mine own self may not
Delay the one nor bid the other speed.
There have been many kings, and they are dead,
And have no power in death save what the wind
Confers upon their blown and brainless dust
To vex the eyeballs of posterity.
But were I God, I would be overlord
Of many kings, and were as breath to guide
Their dust of destiny. And were I God,
Exempt from this mortality which clogs
Perception and clear exercise of will,
What rapture it would be, if but to watch
Destruction crouching at the back of Time,
The tongueless dooms which dog the travelling suns;
The vampire, Silence, at the breast of worlds,
Fire without light that gnaws the base of things,
And Lethe's mounting tide that rots the stone
Of fundamental spheres. This were enough
Till such time as the dazzled wings of will
Came up with power's accession, scarcely felt
For very suddenness. Then I would urge
The strong contention and conflicting might
Of Chaos and Creation—matching them,
Those immemorial powers inimical,

And all their stars and gulfs subservient,
Dynasts of time, and anarchs of the dark—
In closer war reverseless, and would set
New discord at the universal core—
A Samson-principle to bring it down
In one magnificence of ruin. Yea,
The monster, Chaos, were mine unleashed hound,
And all my power Destruction's own right arm!

I would exult to mark the smouldering stars
Renew beneath my breath their elder fire
And feed upon themselves to nothingness.
The might of suns—slow-paced with swinging weight
Of myriad worlds—were made at my desire
One orb of roaring and torrential light,
Through which the voice of Life were audible,
And singing of the immemorial dead,
Whose dust is loosened into vaporous wings
With soaring wrack of systems ruinous.
And were I weary of the glare of these,
I would tear out the eyes of light, and stand
Above a chaos of extinguished suns,
That crowd and grind and shiver thunderously,
Lending vast voice and motion by no ray
To the stretched silence of the blinded gulfs.
Thus would I give my godhead space and speech
For its assertion, and thus pleasure it,
Hastening the feet of Time with cast of worlds
Like careless pebbles, or, with shattered suns,
Brightening the aspect of Eternity.

The Mad Wind

What hast thou seen, O wind,
Of beauty or of terror,
Surpassing, denied to us,
That with precipitate wings,
Mad and ecstatical,
Thou spurnest the hollows and trees
That offer thee refuge of peace,
And findest within the sky
No safety nor respite
From the memory of thy vision?

Finis

It seemed that from the west
The live red flame of sunset,
Eating the dead blue sky
And cold insensate peaks,
Was loosened slowly, and fell.
Above it a few red stars
Burned down like low candle-flames
Into the gaunt black sockets
Of the chill insensible mountains.
But in the ascendant skies
(Cloudless, like some vast corpse
Unfeatured, cerementless)
Succeeded nor star nor planet.
It may have been that black,
Pulseless, dead stars arose
And crossed as of old the heavens.
But came no living orb,
Nor comet seeming the ghost,
Homeless, of an outcast world
Seeking its former place
That is no more nor shall be
In all the cosmos again.
Null, blank and meaningless
As a burnt scroll that blackens
With the passing of the fire,
Lay the dead infinite skies.
Lo! in the halls of Time,
I thought, the torches are out—
The triumph of the gods
Or funereal pomp of demons
For which their flames were lit
Over and quiet at last
With the closing peace of night,
Whose dumb impassible skies
Enfold the living world
As the sea a sinking pebble.

Ode to Light

What sky beheld thy primal birth,
When ageless night's dimensionless extent
First knew division, and the girth
Of formless heaven's constraint and measurement;
And when thy touch was laid
On chaos, till its atom-surge
Subsided as the breast
Of ocean, when above the night's unrest
The morning leaps, arrayed
In vesture of unshadowed skies?
Was it in any deep our sight descries,
Or past the verge
Of vision in a firmament withheld,
That, like a flower from the primordial dust,
Thy sun original upsprang—
Lone, ere the constellations sang
Their youthful paean unexcelled,
Bright in the first completion of their choir—
Their fulness ere the hand of Death outthrust
Broke that continuity of younger fire?
Burns yet thine earliest star?
Or sank its flame
Ere came
Aldebaran and Algebar:
Or stout Orion rose fulfilled
With all his starry frame?
Ere any world that now
Treads to a sun unchilled,
Might look upon its flaming brow?
How flared the seed,
Sown by the years' innumerous hands,
Through firmamental lands?
What stellar blooms myriad-hued
Restrainlessly ensued,
And died to bring
Thy present burgeoning!
What seed was spent
Ere, all unpent,
It reared perfected and magnificent!

In the Desert

I met the night in unfamiliar lands,
In realmless desolations, drear and far,
Where no life was, nor any shard remained
Of tomb or cenotaph: all salient things
Long since had fed the prone monotony
Of the null forgetful sands. Here darkness came
Directly as a king who mounts the throne
Of some Cimmerian primogeniture.
A waif of day, I wandered beneath stars
That seemed the unnumbered steely eyes of Death
Seeking the lost necropoles.

A wind
Rose loudly on the middle night, and passed,
Laden with nameless, immemorial dust,
The shapeless ghost of empires. In that dark
Alien and secret as the heart of death,
I knew not if the wind, remembering
Walls that were great upon its ancient way,
Sang now their threnody, or if the dust,
Tongueless itself, found in the shrilling wind
A tongue for its regret. I, wandering there,
Felt but the dust's unseen, mysterious kiss,
Heard but the grievous wind. . . . So have I known
Lost visions vaguely grasp at memory
And fall back unrecalled. . . . Then, laden still
With sorrow and with dustiness of Eld,
Stirring the desert dark, the wind went on
To leave its dwindling burden at the feet
Of splendid morning unendurable.

The Return of Hyperion

The dungeon-clefts of Tartarus
Are close beyond the mountains
That are bound like a giant's girdle
About the unstirred, unbreathing east.
Alike on mountain and plain
The night is as some iron dream
That closes the soul in a crypt of dread,

Apart from touch or sense of earth,
As in the space of eternity.

What unseen light perturbs the darkness?
Behold! it stirs and fluctuates
Between the mountains and the stars
That are set as guards above the prison
Of the captive Titan-god. I know
That in the depths beneath, Hyperion
Divides the pillared vault of dark
And briefly stands upon its ruin.
Then light is laid upon the peaks,
As the hand of one who climbs beyond;
And now, the sun! The sentinel stars
Are dead with overpotent flame,
And in their place Hyperion stands.
The night is loosened from the land
As a dream from the mind of the dreamer;
A great wind blows across the dawn,
Like the wind of the movement of the world.

To the Daemon Sublimity

I wane and weary: come, thou swifter One,
With vans of ether-sundering instancy,
Zoned with essential night and sovereignty
Of flame septuple, strong to blind or stun
Beyond the bolted levin. Though Earth, undone,
Fail to thy meteor-fraught epiphany,
Though Time be as a chasm-riven sea,
Come thou, and bear me to thy chosen sun.

Yea, in the fiery fastness of the star
That thine empyreal wings most often find,
Thy lordliest eyrie, lone in gulf and gloom,
Leave me and lose me, safe from wasting war
Of finite things unworthy, and resigned
To some apotheosis of bright doom.

Atlantis

Above its domes the gulfs accumulate.
Far up, the sea-gales blare their bitter screed:
But here the buried waters take no heed—

Deaf, and with welded lips pressed down by weight
Of the upper ocean. Dim, interminate,
In cities over-webbed with sombre weed,
Where galleons crumble and the krakens breed,
The slow tide coils through sunken court and gate.

From out the ocean's phosphor-starry dome,
A ghostly light is dubitably shed
On altars of a goddess garlanded
With blossoms of some weird and hueless vine;
And, wingèd, fleet, through skies beneath the foam,
Like silent birds the sea-things dart and shine.

Averted Malefice

Where mandrakes, crying from the moonless fen,
Told how a witch, with eyes of owl or bat,
Found, and each root maleficently fat
Pulled for her waiting cauldron, on my ken
Upstole, escaping to the world of men,
A vapor as of some infernal vat;
Across the stars it clomb, and caught thereat
As if their bright regard to veil again.

Despite the web, methought they knew, appalled,
The stealthier weft in which all sound was still. . . .
Then sprang, as if the night found breath anew,
A wind whereby the stars were disenthralled. . . .
Far off, I heard the cry of frustrate ill,
A witch that wailed above her curdled brew.

The Balance

The world upheld their pillars for awhile:
Now, where imperial On and Carthage stood,
The hot wind sifts across the solitude
The sand that once was wall and peristyle;
Or furrows like the main each tawny mile
Where, ocean-deep above its ancient food
Of cities fame-forgot, the waste is nude,
Traceless as billows of each sunken pile.

Lo! for that wrong shall vengeance come at last,
When the devouring earth, in ruin one

With royal walls and palaces undone,
In dust far-blown from orbit of the past,
Shall drift, and winds that wrangle through the vast
Immingle it with ashes of the sun.

The Cherry-Snows

The cherry-snows are falling now;
Down from the blossom-clouded sky
Of zephyr-troubled twig and bough,
In widely settling whirls they fly.

The orchard earth, unclothed and brown,
Is wintry-hued with petals white:
Even as the snow they glimmer down:
Brief as the snow's their stainless white.

Copan

Around its walls the forests of the west
    Gloom, as about some mystery's final pale
    Might lie its multifold exterior veil.
Sculptured with signs and meanings unconfessed,
Its lordly fanes and palaces attest
    A past before whose wall of darkness fail
    Reason and fancy, finding not the tale
Erased by time from history's palimpsest.

Within this place, that from the gloom of Eld
    Still meets the light, a people came and went
        Like whirls of dust between its columns blown—
An alien race, whose record, shadow-held,
    Is sealed with those of others long forespent
        That died in sunless planets lost and lone.

A Dead City

Twilight ascends the abandoned ramps of noon
Within an ancient land, whose after-time
Unfathomably shadows its ruined prime.
Like rising mist the night increases soon
Round shattered palaces, ere yet the moon
On mute, unsentried walls and turrets climb,

And touch with pallor of sepulchral rime
The desert where a city's bones are strewn.

She comes at last: unsepultured, they show
In all the hoary starkness of old stone.
From out a shadow like the lips of Death
Issues a wind, that through the ruins blown,
Cries like a prophet's ghost, with wailing breath,
The weirds of finished and forgotten woe.

The Eldritch Dark

Now as the twilight's doubtful interval
Closes with night's accomplished certainty,
A wizard wind goes crying eerily,
And on the wold misshapen shadows crawl,
Miming the trees, whose voices climb and fall,
Imploring, in Sabbatic ecstasy,
The sky where vapor-mounted phantoms flee
From the scythed moon impendent over all.

Twin veils of covering cloud and silence, thrown
Across the movement and the sound of things,
Make blank the night, till in the broken west
The moon's ensanguined blade awhile is shown. . . .
The night grows whole again. . . . The shadows rest,
Gathered beneath a greater shadow's wings.

Epitaph for the Earth

Somewhere in Space the disunited dust
That formed a visible comparted world,
Floats in unnoticed formlessness, nor mars
With stain of fleck the ethereal claritude
Of vacancy; nor with its monads driven,
Separate, irrelevant, athwart the suns,
Impedes the tangled multitudinous passage
Of rays that cross each other like the thrust
Of unrelenting swords.
    The tombs that tooth
With granite mouths successive glut of Life
At last are not distinguished from the lips
Of earlier-crumbled earth. And man himself—

An evanescent peak of foam that pointed
One wave, subsided now, of matter's tide
Leaves but bequest of stories that he took
From forms long antecedent, that were not
As he; that shall not thus combine again
In all the future sequences of Change.

With hope of some far-off, supernal goal,
Changeless, and independent of the years
He strove on low and shifting ways, and sent
Commissioned dreams ethereal-wing'd before,
On summits that achievement's laggard feet
Scarcely approached, till on one lesser peak
He knew his own futility at last—
Himself an immaterial trick of Chance.

Fairy Lanterns

'Tis said these blossom-lanterns light
 The elves upon their midnight way;
 That fairy toil and elfin play
Receive their beams of magic white.

I marvel not if it be true;
 I know this flower has lighted me
 Nearer to Beauty's mystery,
And past the veils of secrets new.

The Fugitives

O fugitive fragrances
That tremble heavenward
Unceasing, or if ye linger,
Halt but as memories
On the verge of forgetfulness,
Why must ye pass so fleetly
On wings that are less than wind,
To a death unknowable?
Soon ye are gone, and the air
Forgets your faint unrest
In the garden's breathlessness,
Where fall the snows of silence.

Lament of the Stars

One tone is mute within the starry singing,
The unison fulfilled, complete before;
One chord within the music sounds no more,
And from the stir of flames forever winging
The pinions of our sister, motionless
In pits of indefinable duress,
Are fallen beyond all recovery
By exultation of the flying dance,
Or rhythms holding as with sleep or trance
The maze of stars that only death may free—
Flung through the void's expanse.

In gulfs depressed nor in the gulfs exalted
Shall shade nor lightening of her flame be found;
In space that litten orbits gird around,
Nor in the bottomless abyss unvaulted
Of unenvironed, all out-lying night.
Allotted gyre nor lawless comet-flight
Shall find, and with its venturous ray return
From gloom of undiscoverable scope,
One ray of her to gladden into hope
The doubtful eyes denied that truthward yearn,
The faltering feet that grope.

Beyond restrainless boundary-nights surpassing
All luminous horizons limited,
The substance and the light of her have fed
Ruin and silence of the night's amassing:
Abandoned worlds forever morningless;
Suns without worlds, in frory beamlessness
Girt for the longer gyre funereal;
Inviolate silence, earless, unawaking
That once was sound, and level calm unbreaking
Where motion's many ways in oneness fall
Of sleep beyond forsaking.

Circled with limitation unexceeded
Our eyes behold exterior mysteries
And gods unascertainable as these—
Shadows and shapes irresolubly heeded;
Phantoms that tower, and substance scarcely known.
Our sister knows all mysteries one alone,

One shape, one shadow, crowding out the skies;
Whose eyeless head and lipless face debar
All others nameless or familiar,
Filling with night all former lips and eyes
Of god, and ghost, and star:

For her all shapes have fed the shape of night;
All darker forms, and dubious forms, or pallid,
Are met and reconciled where none is valid.
But unto us solution nor respite
Of mystery's multiform incessancy
From unexplored or system-trodden sky
Shall come; but as a load importunate,
Enigma past and mystery foreseen
Weigh mightily upon us, and between
Our sorrow deepens, and our songs abate
In cadences of threne.

A gloom that gathers silence looms more closely,
And quiet centering darkness at its heart;
But from the certitude of night depart
Uncertain god nor eidolon less ghostly;
But stronger grown with strength obtained from light
That failed, and power lent by the stronger night,
Perplex us with new mystery, and doubt
If these our flames, that deathward toss and fall
Be festal lights or lights funereal
For mightier gods within the gulfs without,
Phantoms more cryptical.

New shadows from the wings of Time unfolding
Across the depth and eminence of years,
Fall deeplier with the broadening gloom of fears.
Prophetic-eyed, with planet-hosts beholding
The night take form upon the face of suns,
We see (thus grief's vaticination runs—
Presageful sorrow for our sister slain)
A night wherein all sorrow shall be past,
One with night's single mystery at last;
Nor vocal sun nor singing world remain
As Time's elegiast.

Lethe

I flow beneath the columns that upbear
The world, and all of heaven and limbo and hell;
Foamless I glide, where sounds nor glimmers tell
My motion nadirward: no moment's flare
Gives each to each the shapes that, unaware,
Convening upon my verge, essay the spell
Of essential night-thick waters that compel
One face from pain and rapture and despair.

The fruitless earth's denied and cheated sons
Meet here, where fruitful and unfruitful cease.
And when their lords, the mightier, hidden Ones,
Have drained all worlds, till being's wine is low,
Shall they not come, and from the oblivious flow
Drink at one draft a universe of peace?

The Masque of Forsaken Gods

Scene: A moonlit glade on a summer midnight.

THE POET

How pale the sapphire of the central night,
Wherein the stars turn grey! The summer's green,
Edgèd and strong by day, is dull and faint
Beneath the moon's all-monorating mood,
That in this absence of the impassioned sun
Sways to a sleep of sound and calm of color
The live and vivid aspect of the world.
Even thought itself is strangely overcome,
And like the pale beginning of a dream.
Here were the theater of a miracle,
If such, within a world long alienate
From its first dreams, and shut with skeptic years,
Might now befall.

THE PHILOSOPHER

The Huntress rides no more
Across the upturned faces of the stars:
'Tis but the dead shell of a frozen world,
Glittering with desolation. Earth's old gods—
The gods that haunt like dreams each planet's youth—

Are fled from years incredulous, and tired
With penetrating of manifolded masks
That give but emptiness they served to hide.
Remains not faith enough to bring them back—
Pan to his wood, Diana to her moon,
And all the powers that once made populous
A haggard world where Time grows weary now.
Yet Youth, that lives, might for a little claim
That vanished pantheon, on such a night,
When, under the flowering marvel of the moon,
The films of time wear perilously thin,
And thought looks backward to the simpler years,
Till all the vision seems but just beyond.
If one have faith, it may be that he shall
Behold them once—once only, and no more,
Because of Time's inhospitality,
For which they may not stay.

THE POET

The quiet light
Surges and fumes like to a spectral sea
Whereof relimning foundered shapes are born!
Is it a throng of luminous white clouds—
Phantoms of some old storm's death-driven Titans,
That float beneath the moon, and speak with voices
Like the last echoes of a thunder spent?
'Tis the forsaken gods, that wind a foothold
About the magic circle which the moon
Draws like some old enchantress round the glade.

THE PHILOSOPHER

I see them not; the vision is addressed
Only to thine acute and eager youth.

JOVE

All heaven and earth were once my throne;
Now I have but the wind alone
For shifting judgment-seat.
The pillared world supported me:
Yet man's old incredulity
Left nothing for my feet.

PAN

Man hath forgotten me:
Yet seems it that my memory
Saddens the wistful voices of the wood;
Within each erst-frequented spot
Echo forgets my music not,
Nor earth my tread where trampling years have stood.

ARTEMIS

Time hath grown cold
Toward beauty loved of old.
The gods must quake
When dreams and hopes forsake
The heart of man,
And disillusion's ban,
More chill than stone,
Rears till the former throne
Of loveliness
Is dark and tenantless.
Now must I weep—
Homeless within the deep
Where once of old
Mine orbèd chariot rolled—
And mourn in vain
Man's immemorial pain
Uncomforted
Of light and beauty fled.

APOLLO

Time wearied of my song—
A satiate and capricious king
Who for his pleasure bade me sing,
First of his minstrel throng;
Till, cloyed with melody,
His ear grew faint to voice and lyre;
Forgotten then of Time's desire,
His thought was void of me.

APHRODITE

I, born of sound and foam,
Child of the sea and wind,

Was fire upon mankind—
Fuelled with Syria, and with Greece and Rome.
Time fanned me with his breath,
Love found new warmth in me,
And Life its ecstasy,
Till I grew deadly with the wind of death.

A NYMPH

How can the world be still so beautiful
When beauty's self is fled? 'Tis like the mute
And marble loveliness of some dead girl;
And we that hover here are as the spirit
Of former voice and motion and live color
In that which shall not stir nor speak again.

ANOTHER NYMPH

Nay, rather say this lovely, lifeless world
Is but a rigid semblance, counterfeiting
The world which was: nor have the gods retained
Such power as once informed and rendered vital
The cryptic irresponsiveness of stone—
That statue which Pygmalion made and loved.

ATÈ

I, who was discord among men,
Alone of all Time's hierarchy
Find that Time hath no need of me,
No lack that I might fill again.

THE POET

Tell me, O gods, are ye forever doomed
To fall and flutter among spatial winds,
Finding release nor foothold anywhere—
Debarred from doors of all the suns, like spirits
Whose names are blotted from the lists of time,
Though they themselves yet wander undestroyed?

THE GODS TOGETHER

Throneless, discrowned, and impotent,
In man's sad disillusionment,
We passed with Earth's returnless youth,
Who were the semblances of truth,

The veils that hid the vacantness
Infinite, naked, meaningless,
The blank and universal Sphinx
Each world confronts at last—and sinks.
New gods forefend awhile the gaze
Of man—each one a veil that stays—
Till the new gods, discredited,
Like mist that melts with noon, are fled—
That power oppressive, limitless,
The tyranny of nothingness.
Our power is dead upon the earth
With the first dews and dawns of time,
But in the far and younger clime
Of other worlds, it hath rebirth.
Yea, though we find not entrance here—
Astray like feathers on the wind,
To neither earth nor heaven consigned—
Fresh altars in a distant sphere
Are keen with fragrance, bright with fire,
New hearths to warm us from the night,
Till, banished thence, we pass in flight
While all the flames of dream expire.

The Maze of Sleep

Sleep is a pathless labyrinth,
Dark to the gaze of moons and suns,
Through which the exile clue of dreams,
A gossamer thread, obscurely runs.

The Medusa of the Skies

Like a worm-fretted visage from the tomb,
The moon unswathes her hollow, shrunken head,
Launching such light as foulders on the dead
From pallid skies more death-like than the gloom.
Under her beams the breasted lands assume
Dead hues, and charnel shapes unceremented;
And shadows that towering sepulchers might shed
More livid as the shadows on dials of doom.

On hills like tumuli, and waters mute,
A whiteness steals as of a world made still

When reptant Death at last rears absolute—
An earth now frozen by malefice of eyes
Aeonian dooms and realm-deep rigors fill—
The gaze of that Medusa of the skies.

The Night Forest

Incumbent seemingly
On the serrate points of peaks
That end the visible west,
The rounded moon yet floods
The valleys hitherward
With fall of torrential light,
Ere from the overmost
Dividing mountain-cusp
She slip to the lower dark.
But here, on an eastward slope
Pointed and thick with its pine,
The forest scarcely remembers
Her light that is gone as a vision
Or ecstasy too poignant
And perilous for duration.
Withdrawn in what darker web
Or dimension of dream I know not,
In silence pre-occupied
And solemnest rectitude,
The pines uprear, and no sigh
For the rapture of moonlight past
Comes from their bosom of boughs.
Far in their secrecy
I stand, and the burdenous dusk,
Dull, but at times made keen
With tingle of fragrances,
Falls on me as a veil
Between my soul and the world.
What veil of trance, O pines,
Divides you from my soul,
That I feel but enter not
Your distances of dream?
Ah! strange, imperative sense
Of world-deep mystery
That shakes from out your boughs—

A fragrance keener still,
Piercing the inner mind.

The wind shall question you
Of the dream I may not gain,
And all its sombreness
And depth immeasurable,
Shall tremble away in sound
Of speech not understood
That my heart must break to hear.

Nirvana

Poised as a god whose lone, detachèd post,
An eyrie, pends between the boundary-marks
Of finite years and those unvaried darks
That veil Eternity, I saw the host
Of suns and worlds, swept from the furthermost
Of night—confusion as of dust with sparks—
Whirl toward the opposing brink; as one who harks
Some warning trumpet. Time, a withered ghost,
Fled with them: disunited orbs that late
Were atoms of the universal frame,
They passed to some eternal fragment-heap.
And, lo! the gods, from space discorporate,
Who were its life and vital spirit, came,
Drawn voidward by the vampire-lips of Sleep!

Ode on Imagination

Imagination's eyes
Outreach and distance far
The vision of the greatest star
That measures instantaneously—
Enisled therein as in a sea—
Its cincture of the system-laden skies.
Abysses closed about with night
A tribute yield
To her retardless sight;
And Matter's walls reveal the candent ores
Rock-held in furnaces of planet-cores.
She penetrates the sun's transplendent shield,
And through that inner vastness, sphered and dire,

Pierces his dreadful heart, whose gurge of fire
Heaves outward, riven by Titanic throes,
And fills his frame with tide and cataract
Of thunder-pulsing, incandescent streams.
Her eyes exact
From the Moon-Sphinx that wanes and grows
In wastes celestial, alien dreams
Brought down on wings of spectral beams.
Adown the clefts of under-space,
She rides, her steed a falling star,
To seek, where void and vagueness are,
Some mark or certainty of place.
Upon their heavenly precipice,
The gathered suns shrink back aghast
From that interminate abyss,
And threat of sightless anarchs vast.

She stands endued
With supermundane crown, and vestitures
Of emperies that include
All underworlds and overworlds of dream—
Domains with shadow bound,
Cimmerian and profound,
And heights of some Himalaya supreme
Where moon-transcending light endures.
She roams in grey, fantasmal lands, where grow
In scarce-discernèd fields and closes blind,
Faint blossoms stirred by wings of eidolons;
Or wanders all bemused and slow
In woods where only nameless echoes go
And wraiths of ancient wind:
In twilight there she shuns
The strident day, while ecstasy and grief
Speak only in vague whispers like the leaf.

Upon some supersensual eminence
She hears the fragments of a thunder loud,
Where lightnings of ulterior Truth intense
Flame through the walls of hollow cloud.
But these she may not wholly grasp
With unsupernal clasp.
Her eyes inevitably see,
'Neath rounds and changes of exterior things,

The movements of Essentiality—
Of ageless principles—that alter not
To temporal alterings—
Unswerved by shattered worlds upbuilt once more,
And stars no longer hot;
Or broken constellations strewn
Like coals about the heavenly floor,
And rush of night upon the noon
Of their lost worlds, unsphered retrievelessly
In icy deserts of the sky.
From the beginning of the spheres,
When systems nebulous out-thrown
Drove back the brinks
Of nullity with limitary marks,
Till end of suns and sunless death of years,
To her are known
The unevident inseparable links
That bind all deeps, all suns, all days and darks.

Pine Needles

O little lances, dipt in grey,
And set in order straight and clean,
How exquisitely clear and keen
Your points against the cobalt day!

Attesting what consummate art
Ye fringe the limpid firmament,
O little lances, keenly sent
To pierce with beauty to the heart.

The Price

Behind each thing a shadow lies;
Beauty hath ever its cost:
Within the moonlight-flooded skies
How many stars are lost!

The Retribution

Old Egypt's gods, Osiris, Ammon, Thoth,
Came on my dream in thunder, and their feet
Revealed were as the levin's fire and heat.

The hosts of Rome, the Arab and the Goth
Have left their altars dark, yet stern and wroth
In olden power they stood, whose wings were fleet,
And mighty as with strength of storms that meet
In mingled foam of clouds and ocean-froth.

Above my dream, with arch of dreaded wings,
In judgment and in sentence of what crime
I knew not, sate the gods outcast of time.
They passed, and lo! a plague of darkness fell,
Unsleeping, and accurst with nameless things,
And dreams that stood the ministers of Hell.

Shadow of Nightmare

What gulf-ascended hand is this, that grips
My spirit as with chains, and from the sound
And light of dreamland, draws me to the bound
Where darkness waits with wide, expectant lips?
Albeit thereat my footing holds, nor slips,
The night-born menace and the fear confound
All days and hours of gladness, girt around
With sense of near, unswervable eclipse.

So lies a land whose noon is plagued with whirr
Of bats, than their own shadows swarthier,
That trace their passing upon white abodes,
Wherein from court to court, from room to room,
In hieroglyphics of abhorrent doom,
Is trailed the slime of slowly crawling toads.

The Snow-Blossoms

But yestereve the winter trees
    Reared leafless, blackly bare,
Their twigs and branches poignant-marked
    Upon the sunset-flare.

White-petaled, opens now the dawn,
    And in its pallid glow,
Revealed, each leaf-lorn, barren tree
    Stands white with flowers of snow.

A Song of Dreams

A voice came to me from the night, and said,
What profit hast thou in thy dreaming
Of the years that are set
And the years yet unrisen?
Hast thou found them tillable lands?
Is there fruit that thou canst pluck therein,
Or any harvest to be mown?
Shalt thou dig for gold in the mines of the past,
Or trade for merchandise
In the years where all is desolate?
Are they a sea that will bring thee to any shore,
Or a desert that vergeth upon aught but the waste?
Shalt thou drink from the springs that are emptied,
Or find sustenance in shadows?
What value hath the future given thee?
Is there aught in the days yet dark
That thou canst hold with thy hands?
Are they a fortress
That will afford thee protection
Against the swords of the world?
Is there justice in them
To balance the world's inequity,
Or benefit to outweigh its loss?

Then spake I in answer, saying,
Of my dreams I have made a road,
And my soul goeth out thereon
To that unto which no eye has opened,
Nor ear become keen to hearken:
To the glories that are shut past all access
Of the keys of sense;
Whose walls are hidden by the air,
And whose doors are concealed with clarity.
And the road is travelled of secret things,
Coming to me from afar;
Of bodiless powers,
And beauties without color or form
Holden by any loveliness seen of earth.
And of my dreams I have builded an inn
Wherein these are as guests.
And unto it come the dead

For a little rest and refuge
From the hollowness of the unharvestable wind,
And the burden of too great space.

The fields of the past are not void to me,
Who harvest with the scythe of thought;
Nor the orchards of future years unfruitful
To the hands of visionings.
I have retrieved from the darkness
The years and the things that were lost,
And they are held in the light of my dreams
With the spirits of years unborn
And of things yet bodiless.
As in an hospitable house,
They shall live while the dreams abide.

The Song of the Stars

From the final reach of the upper night
To the nether darks where the comets die,
From the outmost bourn of the reigns of light
To the central gloom of the midmost sky,
In our mazeful gyres we fly.
And our flight is a choral chant of flame,
That ceaseless fares to the outer void,
With the undersong of the peopled spheres,
The voices of comet and asteroid,
And the wail of the spheres destroyed.
Forever we sing to a god unseen—
In the dark shall our voices fail?
The void is his robe inviolate,
The night is his awful veil—
How our fires grow dim and pale!

From the ordered gyres goes ever afar
Our song of flame o'er the void unknown,
Where circles nor world, nor comet, nor star.
Shall it die ere it reach His throne?

On the shoreless deeps of the seas of gloom
Sailing, we venture afar and wide,
Where ever await the tempests of doom,
Where the silent maelstroms lurk and hide,
And the darkling reefs abide.

And the change and ruin of stars is a song
That rises and ebbs in a tide of fire—
A music whose notes are of dreadful flame,
Whose harmonies ever leap high'r
Where the suns and the worlds expire.
Is such music not fit for a god?
Yet ever the deep is a dark,
And ever the night is a void,
Nor brightens a word nor a mark
To show if our God may hark.

From the gyres of change goes ever afar
Our flaming chant o'er the deep unknown,
The song of the death of planet and star.
Shall it die ere it reach His throne?

In our shadows of light the planets sweep,
And endure for the span of our prime—
Globed atoms that hazard the termless deep
With races that bow to the law of Time,
And yet cherish a dream sublime.
And they cry to the god behind the veil.
Yet how should their voices pass the night,
The silence that waits in the rayless void,
If he hear not our music of light,
And the thundrous song of our might?
And they strive in the gloom for truth—
Yet how should they pierce the veil,
When we, with our splendors of flame,
In the darkness faint and fail,
Our fires how feeble and pale!

From the ordered gyres goes ever afar
Our song of flame o'er the void unknown,
Where circles nor world, nor comet, nor star,
Shall it die ere it reach His throne?

Song to Oblivion

Art thou more fair
For all the beauty gathered up in thee,
As gold and gems within some lightless sea?
For light of flowers, and bloom of tinted air,
Art thou more fair?

Art thou more strong
For powers that turn to thee as unto sleep?
For world and star that find thy ways more deep
Than light may tread, too wearisome for song.
Art thou more strong?

Nay! thou art bare
For power and beauty on thine impotence
Bestowed by fruitful Time's magnificence;
For fruit of all things strong, and bloom of fair,
Thou still art bare.

The Soul of the Sea

A wind comes in from the sea,
And rolls through the hollow dark
Like loud, tempestuous waters.
As the swift recurrent tide,
It pours adown the sky,
And rears at the cliffs of night
Uppiled against the vast.

Like the soul of the sea—
Hungry, unsatisfied
With ravin of shores and of ships—
Come forth on the land to seek
New prey of tideless coasts,
It raves, made hoarse with desire,
And the sounds of the night are dumb
With the sound of its passing.

The Summer Moon

How is it, O moon, that melting
Unstintedly, prodigally,
On the peaks' hard majesty,
Till they seem diaphanous
And fluctuant as a veil,
And pouring thy rapturous light
Through pine and oak and laurel,
Till the summer-sharpened green,
Softening and tremulous,
Is a luster of liquid silver—

How is it that I find,
When I turn again to thee,
That thy lost and wasted light
Is regained in one magic breath?

To the Darkness

Thou hast taken the light of many suns,
And they are sealed in the prison-house of gloom.
Even as candle-flames
Hast thou taken the souls of men
With winds from out a hollow place;
They are hid in the abyss as in a sea,
And the gulfs are over them,
As the weight of many mountains,
As the depth of many seas;
Thy shields are between them and the light;
They are past its burden and bitterness;
The spears of the day shall not touch them,
The chains of the sun shall not hale them forth.

Many men there were,
In the days that are now of thy realm,
That thou hast sealed with the seal of many deeps;
Their feet were as eagles' wings in the quest of Truth—
Aye, mightily they desired her face,
Hunting her through the lands of life
As men in the blankness of the waste
That seek for a buried treasure-house of kings.
But against them were the veils
That hands may not rend nor sabers pierce;
And Truth was withheld from them
As a water that is seen afar at dawn,
And at noon is lost in the sand
Before the feet of the traveller.
The world was a barrenness,
And the gardens were as the waste.
And they turned them to the adventure of the dark,
To the travelling of the land without roads,
To the sailing of the sea that hath no beacons.
Why have they not returned?
Their quest hath found end in thee,
Or surely they had fared

Once more to the place whence they came,
As men that have journeyed to a fruitless land.
They have looked on thy face,
And to them it is the countenance of Truth.
Thy silence is sweeter to them than the voice of love,
Thine embrace more dear than the clasp of the beloved.
They are fed with the emptiness past the veil,
And their hunger is filled;
They have found the waters of peace,
And are athirst no more.
They know a rest that is deeper than the gulfs,
And whose seal is unbreakable as the seal of the void;
They sleep the sleep of the suns,
And the vast is a garment unto them.

To the Sun

Thy light is as an eminence unto thee,
And thou art upheld by the pillars of thy strength.
Thy power is a foundation for the worlds:
They are builded thereon as upon a lofty rock
Whereto no enemy hath access.
Thou puttest forth thy rays, and they hold the sky
As in the hollow of an immense hand.
Thou erectest thy light as four walls
And a roof with many beams and pillars.
Thy flame is a stronghold based as a mountain:
Its bastions are tall, and firm like stone.

The worlds are bound with the ropes of thy will,
Like steeds are they stayed and constrained
By the reins of invisible lightnings.
With bands that are stouter than iron manifold,
And stronger than the cords of the gulfs,
Thou withholdest them from the brink
Of outward and perilous deeps,
Lest they perish in the desolations of the night,
Or be stricken of strange suns;
Lest they be caught in the pitfalls of the abyss,
Or fall into the furnace of Arcturus.
Thy law is as a shore unto them,
And they are restrained thereby as the sea.
Thou art food and drink to the worlds:

Yea, by the sustenance are they sustained,
That they falter not upon the road of space
Whose goal is Hercules.
When thy pillars of force are withdrawn,
And the walls of thy light fall inward,
And thy head is covered with the Shadow,
The worlds shall wander as men bewildered
In the wasteness void of life and barren.
Athirst and unfed shall they be
When the springs of thy strength are dust
And thy fields of light are black with dearth.
They shall perish from the ways
That thou showest no longer,
And emptiness shall close above them.

The Unremembered

What stern prenatal palls occlude from us
Once-dominant Signs, once-rampant arms! How strait
The sunless road, suspended, separate,
That leads from death to birth! Not luminous
With lodestar, or with star calamitous,
The Past is closed as by the night-black spate
Of planet-gulfing seas—its keyless gate
Lost in Avernian shadows cavernous.

In his bleak mercy, Death forever strips
The soul of light and memory, rendering blind
Our vision, lest surmounted deeps appal,
As when on mountain-heights a glance behind
Betrays with knowledge, and the climber slips
Down gulfs of fear to some enormous fall.

White Death

Methought the world was bound with final frost:
The sun, made hueless as with fear and awe,
Illumined still the lands it could not thaw.
Then on my road, with instant evening crost,
Death stood, and in its dusky veils enwound,
Mine eyes forgot the light, until I came
Where poured the inseparate, unshadowed flame
Of phantom suns in self-irradiance drowned.

Death lay revealed in all its haggardness:
Immitigable wastes horizonless;
Profundities that held nor bar nor veil;
All hues wherewith the suns and world were dyed
In light invariable nullified;
All darkness rendered shelterless and pale.

The Winds

To me the winds that die and start,
And strive in wars that never cease,
Are dearer than the level peace
That lies unstirred at summer's heart.

More dear to me the shadowed wold,
Where, with report of tempest rife,
The air intensifies with life,
Than quiet fields of summer's gold.

I am the winds' admitted friend:
I share those ancient mysteries
They whisper to the trembling trees
Or roar along the heavens' end.

And when my spirit listless stands
With folded wings that do not live,
Their own assuageless wings they give
To lift her from the stirless lands.

Within the place unmanifest
Where central Truth is immanent,
Lies there a vast, entire content
Of sound and movement one in rest?

I know not this: yet in my heart
I feel that where all truths concur,
The shrine is peaceless with the stir
Of winds that enter and depart.

The Morning Pool

All night the pool held mysteries,
    Vague depths of night that lay in dream,
Where phantoms of the pale-white stars
    Wandered, with darkness-tangled gleam.

And now it holds the limpid light
  And shadeless azure of the skies,
Wherein, like some enclaspèd gem,
  The morning's golden glamour lies.

The Abyss Triumphant

The force of suns had waned beyond recall.
Chaos was re-established over all,
Where lifeless atoms through forgetful deeps
Fled unrelated, cold, immusical.

Above the tumult heaven alone endured;
Long since the bursting walls of hell had poured
Demon and damned to peace erstwhile denied,
Within the Abyss God's might had not immured.

(He could but thwart it with creative mace. . . .)
And now it rose about the heavenly base,
Mordant at pillars rotten through and through
Of Matter's last, most firm abiding-place.

Bastion and minaret began to nod,
Till all the pile, unmindful of His rod,
Dissolved in thunder, and the void Abyss
Caught like a quicksand at the feet of God!

The Last Goddess

(A Fragment)

To laud the loves of old,
I sought for splendors fabulous and far:
The curls of one were black Circean petals
Of poppies blown by night
In the sad gardens of a sinful star;
Her eyes were mystic metals,
Wrought with a secret told
By lost archangels in their flight
To women of the worlds that stray
On the red verges of the nether day;
Her voice was like a lulling music blown
At sunset from an isle of spells
Across a lake of rosy nenuphar;
And yet therein

Betimes I caught the chill and crystal bells
That grieved, and grieved alone,
Above the fallen din
Of cities drowsed with revelry and sin.

Satan Unrepentant

Lost from those archangelic thrones that star,
Fadeless and fixed, heaven's light of azure bliss;
Forbanned of all His splendor and depressed
Beyond the birth of the first sun, and lower
Than the last star's decline, I still endure,
Abased, majestic, fallen, beautiful,
And unregretful in the doubted dark,
Throneless, that greatens chaos-ward, albeit
From chanting stars that throng the nave of night
Lost echoes wander here, and of His praise
With ringing moons for cymbals dinned afar,
And shouted from the flaming mouths of suns.

The shadows of impalpable blank deeps—
Deep upon deep accumulate—close down,
Around my head concentered, while above,
In the lit, loftier blue, star after star
Spins endless orbits betwixt me and heaven;
And at my feet mysterious Chaos breaks,
Abrupt, immeasurable. Round His throne
Throbs now the rhythmic resonance of suns,
Incessant, perfect, music infinite:
I, throneless, hear the discords of the dark,
And roar of ruin uncreate, than which
Some vast cacophony of dragons, heard
In wasted worlds, were purer melody.

The universe His tyranny constrains
Turns on: in old and consummated gulfs
The stars that wield His judgement wait at hand,
And in new deeps Apocalyptic suns
Prepare His coming: lo, His mighty whim
To rear and mar, goes forth enormously
In nights and constellations! Darkness hears
Enragèd suns that bellow down the deep
God's ravenous and insatiable will;

And He is strong with change, and rideth forth
In whirlwind clothed, with thunders and with doom
To the red stars: God's throne is reared of change;
Its myriad and successive hands support
Like music His omnipotence, that fails
If mercy or if justice interrupt
The sequence of that tyranny, begun
Upon injustice, and doomed evermore
To stand thereby.

I, who with will not less
Than His, but lesser strength, opposed to Him
This unsubmissive brow and lifted mind,
He holds remote in nullity and night
Doubtful between old Chaos and the deeps
Betrayed by Time to vassalage. Methinks
All tyrants fear whom they may not destroy,
And I, that am of essence one with His,
Though less in measure, He may not destroy,
And but withstands in gulfs of dark suspense,
A secret dread for ever: for God knows
This quiet will irrevocably set
Against His own, and this my prime revolt
Yet stubborn, and confirmed eternally.
And with the hatred born of fear, and fed
Ever thereby, God hates me, and His gaze
Sees the bright menace of mine eyes afar
Through midnight, and the innumerable blaze
Of servile suns: lo, strong in tyranny,
The despot trembles that I stand opposed!
For fain am I to hush the anguished cries
Of Substance, broken on the racks of change,
Of Matter tortured into life; and God,
Knowing this, dreads evermore some huge mishap—
That in the vigils of Omnipotence,
Once careless, I shall enter heaven, or He,
Himself, with weight of some unwonted act,
Thoughtless perturb His balanced tyranny,
To mine advance of watchful aspiration.

With rumored thunder and enormous groan
(Burden of sound that heavens overborne
Let slip from deep to deep, even to this

Where climb the huge cacophonies of Chaos)
God's universe moves on. Confirmed in pride,
In patient majesty serene and strong,
I wait the dreamt, inevitable hour
Fulfilled of orbits ultimate, when God,
Whether through His mischance or mine own deed,
Or rise of other and extremer Strength,
Shall vanish, and the lightened universe
No more remember Him than Silence does
An ancient thunder. I know not if these,
Mine all-indomitable eyes, shall see
A maimed and dwindled Godhead cast among
The stars of His creating, and beneath
The unnumbered rush of swift and shining feet
Trodden into night; or mark the fiery breath
Of His infuriate suns blaze forth upon
And scorch that coarsened Essence; or His flame,
A mightier comet, roar and redden down,
Portentous unto Chaos. I but wait,
In strong majestic patience equable,
That hour of consummation and of doom,
Of justice, and rebellion justified.

The Titans in Tartarus

Low in the far-flung shadow of the world,
Under the moveless stretch of glooms great wing'd
That brood the abyss, vague Tartarus lapsed remote
Through zones of spacial silence. Night and Time,
Agreeing once, had made thereof a place
Immediate unto Chaos, and removed
From temporal clamor and terrestrial hush,
In gulfs world-sundered from the sun. Far up
Light was, a gossamer of frailest blue,
Above the lift of Cyclopean walls,
And flight of crags incredible through heavens
Of darkness, and ethereal space of eve,
Sheer, everlasting. But within the abyss
The silence of the death of suns was come,
And the far light seemed as the ghost of days
Flown and forgotten; or as memory
Sent through the drifts of drear Oblivion

To the forgetful dead. But unto them,
The fall'n Titanic gods disconsolate,
It shone as might a throne supreme and lost—
Phantasmal, unattainable, athwart
The chasm of downfall and defeat. Apart
In the waste darkness round, the purblind air
Scarcely their presence each to each betrayed,
Who, to the gaze of those but newly fallen,
Had seemed as clouds upon a moonless midnight—
Black, formless, without substance, motionless.
The flaming tumult of disastrous fight,
Taking their outward fire, had left them bleak
As their own statues, who yet ached within.
And battle-splendours gloomed with rust were strewn
Around them, where the darkness heeded not
If rust or clearest splendours were: downcast
Were ineffectual blade and useless mail,
Left to the barren and devouring dust
That knew not nor should know the sun.

Abrupt
The change, from impact and surprise of strife—
From the embattled world, where searing war
Had lately flamed through indecisive lands
Open to sun and stars—to this drear deep,
This unity of night and misery,
Of desolation, silence, and defeat
Intolerable, sure. Speechless beneath
That gloom the Titans lay, where like the strong
Suspense of noiseless and enormous wings,
Immediate breathless menace infinite,
Came hideous, myriad-eyed Despair. With minds
Tortured, and anguished gaze, they saw the dark
Writhe to unnumbered forms of subtlest fear,
Such terrors as attend the night of suns
For the strange impotence of gods dethroned,
The face of Chaos with a thousand leers,
And phantoms pointing at eternal gulfs.

Dark with defeat, gigantically dumb,
Like Memnons morningless, that have survived
The dawn-voiced vibrant sun's last silencing,
The Titans waited. Time, that hath for hue

In the swift light and cloud-surprise of Change,
All iris that enchants the sunset foam,
Now, with grey silence clad, dismal and slow,
Through the grey darkness waned, as one that hath
No hope, foreworn upon an endless way.
All desolation and all hopelessness
Had hushed, it seemed, a deep that was the tomb—
So huge that dark—of all magnificence,
Aeons of splendour, whole antiquities
Of Time-forgotten glories. There the gods,
Sleepless in midst as of Oblivion,
Abiding, fronted anguish infinite,
And all the strong renewal of despair
Throughout Tartarean, dark eternity.

The Cloud-Islands

What islands marvellous are these,
    That gem the sunset's tides of light—
Opals aglow in saffron seas?
    How beautiful they lie, and bright,
Like some new-found Hesperides!

What varied, changing magic hues
    Tint gorgeously each shore and hill!
What blazing, vivid golds and blues
    Their seaward winding valleys fill!
What amethysts their peaks suffuse!

Close held by curving arms of land
    That out within the ocean reach,
I mark a faery city stand,
    Set high upon a sloping beach
That burns with fire of shimmering sand.

Of sunset-light is formed each wall;
    Each dome a rainbow-bubble seems;
And every spire that towers tall
    A ray of golden moonlight gleams;
Of opal-flame in every hall.

Alas! how quickly dims their glow!
    What veils their dreamy splendors mar!
Like broken dreams the islands go,

As down from strands of cloud and star,
The sinking tides of daylight flow.

Remembered Light

The years are a falling of snow,
Slow but without cessation,
On hills and mountains and flowers and worlds that were;
But snow, and the crawling night wherein it fell,
May be washed away in one swifter hour of flame:
Thus it was that some slant of sunset
In the chasms of pilèd cloud—
Transient mountains that made a new horizon,
Uplifting the west to fantastic pinnacles—
Smote warm in a buried realm of the spirit,
Till the snows of forgetfulness were gone.
Clear in the vistas of memory,
The peaks of a world long unremembered
Soared further than clouds but fell not,
Based on hills that shook not nor melted
With that burden enormous, hardly to be believed.
Rent with stupendous chasms,
Full of an umber twilight,
I beheld that larger world:
Bright was the twilight, clear like ethereal wine
Above, but low in the clefts it thickened,
Dull as with duskier tincture.
Like whimsical wings outspread but unstirring,
Flowers that seemed spirits of the twilight
That must pass with its passing—
Too fragile for day or for darkness—
Fed the dusk with more delicate hues than its own;
Stars that were nearer, more radiant than ours,
Quivered and pulsed in the clear thin gold of the sky.

These things I beheld
Till the gold was shaken with flight
Of fantastical wings like broken shadows
Forerunning the darkness;
Till the twilight shivered with outcry of eldritch voices
Like pain's last cry ere oblivion.

The Sorrow of the Winds

O winds that pass uncomforted
Through all the peaceful meads of spring,
And tell the trees your sorrowing,
That they must mourn till ye are fled!

Think ye the Tyrian distance holds
The crystal of unbroken sleep?
That those forgetful purples keep
No veiled, contentious greens and golds?

Half with communicated grief,
Half that they are not free to pass
With you across the flickering grass,
Mourns each inclinèd bough and leaf.

And I, with soul disquieted,
Shall find within the haunted spring
No peace, till your strange sorrowing
Is down the Tyrian distance fled.

Luna Aeternalis

By an alien dream despatched and driven
In a land to strange stars given,
Stars that summoned forth the moon,
Singing a strange red eldritch rune,
I heard the coming of the moon
With tremulous rim that clomb and rang,
Whose rondure on the horizon rang
A gong distinct with silvern clang,
Re-echoing distantly, until,
Arisen soon,
In silent silver stood the moon
Above the horizon ringing still.

Half-waned and hollow was her brow,
And caverned by the night; but now
Her twilight turned the stars' loud rune
To muted music in a swoon,
Her low light lulled the stars to drowse,
Flicker and fail, and vaguely rouse:
I felt the silence come and go

As the red stars muttered low . . .

Old with moonlight lay the night,
And on the desert lay
Ancient and unending light
That assured not of the day;
For the half-moon stood to stay
Fixèd at the heavens' height
And eternal ere the day.
Triumphant stood the moon
In a false and cold and constant noon:
Surely in conflict fell
The true, lost sun of noon;
The golden might of Uriel
Met some white demon of the moon.

By an alien dream despatched and driven,
I found a land to demons given,
To silvern, silent demons given
That flew and fluttered from out the moon,
Weaving about her tomb-white face
With mop and mow and mad grimace,
And circling down from the semilune
In a dim and Saturnalian dance,
To pirouette and pause and prance,
To withdraw and advance,
All in a wan eternal dance.

[In the Ultimate Valleys]

In ultimate lone valleys evermore,
    Immutable large purple blossoms bloom,
    Munificent, unfading suns illume,
And amplest moons are perfect evermore.

The sole blue silence of the dreaming day,
    In arch complete, stands open o'er the land;
    Flowers and horizons to the sun expand
In self-same silence through the sleeping day.

But in the night, pale dolors dwell, and dreams
    Impalpable take slow and spectral flight;
    That lucid land forgetful, in the night
Remembers flown and fugitive sad dreams.

And in an alien, immemorial vale,
Unworn, immutable wan marbles are:
At altars to an immemorial star,
The hushed winds worship in an alien vale.

The Nereid

Her face the sinking stars desire:
Unto her place the slow deeps bring
Shadow of errant winds that wing
O'er sterile gulfs of foam and fire.

Her beauty is the light of pearls.
All stars and dreams and sunsets die
To make the fluctuant glooms that lie
Around her; and low noonlight swirls

Down ocean's firmamental deep
To weave for her who glimmers there
Elusive visions, vague and fair;
And night is as a dreamless sleep:

She has not known the night's unrest
Nor the white curse of clearer day;
The tremors of the tempest play
Like slow delight about her breast.

The berylline pallors of her face
Illume the kingdom of the drowned.
In her the love that none has found,
The unflowering rapture, folded grace.

Await some lover strayed and lone,
Some god misled, who shall not come
Though the decrescent seas lie dumb
And sunken in their wells of stone.

But nevermore of him, perchance,
Her enigmatic musings are,
Whose purpling tresses float afar
In grottoes of the last romance.

Serene, an immanence of fire
She dwells for ever, ocean-thralled,
Soul of the sea's vast emerald.
Her face the sinking stars desire.

A Phantasy at Twilight

1913–1917

The Ghoul

He seemed, in implicit deeper night
    Of cypress, and the glade of cedarn gloom,
    A shadow come from catacomb or tomb,
The shade of midnight's subterranean might
Upthrown to strengthen darkness, and affright,
    Light's rear and remnant, and defer the doom
    Of phantoms—ere the haled dawn relume
The woodland fanes of Hecatean rite.

When half the conclave of the glooms was gone,
    Gigantical I saw his form define,
        And sombre on the sun's eternal ways;
And fantoms languid in the night's decline,
    Were, thinnest mist-ranks paling tow'rd the dawn,
        O'er the black tarns of his abhorrent gaze.

The Land of Evil Stars

'Neath blue days, and gold, and green,
Blooms the glorious land serene,
Flaming shields of dawns between;
And the rapt white flowers suffice
To illume
With their bright eyes
Fluctuant ecstatic gloom
'Twixt the fallen emerald sun
And the unrisen azure one.

But the season of the night
Comes in all the suns' despite;
And, ah, gorgeous then their sorrows
At departure into morrows
Of remoter lands forgot—
Until now remembered not
For the lovelier flowers of this
And each lake's pure lucency,
And recalled regretfully,
Regretfully, for leaving *this*.

In the star-possessèd night
The land knows another light—

All the small and evil rays
Of the sorcerous orbs ablaze
With ecstatical intense
Hate and still malevolence—
Dwelling on the fields below
From the ascendancy of even
Till the suns, re-entering heaven,
Glorify with triple glow
The dim flowers smitten low.

Ah, not cold, or kind, as ours,
The stars of those remotest hours!
Peace and pallor of the flowers
They have fevered, they have marred
With the poison of their light,
With distillèd bale and blight
Of a red, accurst regard:
All the toil of sunlight hours
They undo
With their wild eyes—
Eldritch and ecstatic eyes,
Stooping timeward from the skies,
Burning redly in the dew.

The Clouds

Their tow'rs are builded far;
They have strange sorcery
To draw from out the sea
Their palaces more swift than shadows are—

Their lucent halls and domes
That house the western sun,
And when his stay is done,
Are yet the stars' more dim and hallowed homes.

Their minarets uppiled
A rich enchantment be,
Their pillars, mystery,
Their walls, a magic unexplained and wild.

Their tow'rs are builded far;
Upon the world's extremes,
They stay fleet sunset dreams,
Ere those shall hasten to the twilight star.

Remote upon blue noon,
Their temples white and fair
Lure fainter wings, that there
Find sanctuary sure—ah, not too soon!

They have strange sorcery
To build upon the wind
Their tow'rs supreme-designed,
And less enduring than the shadows be.

The Doom of America

Thou hast striven after strange gods, O America: in the temples of latter time, thou hast lifted up Baal and Mammon and Moloch.
Thou hearkenest wholly unto these, thine ears seek after the flattery of subtle and false oracles:
They are filled therewith, they are grossly satisfied: neither shalt thou hear the Lord if His thunders bespeak thee, nor heed His prophets except with mockery.
O bride that wast given unto God of former time! O sharer in the covenant of the Most High:
Thou doest adultery with bestial deities:
Yea, thou deniest it not, in the marts thou confirmest the report of thy shame with mirth.
O breaker of faith, thou fearest not, thou art graceless: thou hast forgotten the promise of the jealousy of the Lord, and the prophecy of His vengeance:
O fornicatrix! thou art entirely naked; thou art bare even of shame.

Thou hast built innumerable furnaces for altars to the greed of thy gods: thou hast drawn forth the demons of the elements and enforced them to labour with groaning and shrieking in the service of Mammon.
But the smell of thine altars is not pleasant to the true God, neither do the stars approve it:
It is a stench to the nostrils of Alcyone; the cry of the sacrifice is a howl of abomination in the ears of Altair.
The stars have cursed thee with red conjunctions, with a most fatal configuration:
They are leagued with God in a conspiracy against thee.
Thou canst not hear the menace of His mirth, who fashioneth the levins of reckoning:

Neither dost thou observe how the planets of midnight shake with an evil and unheard laughter:
In her cold hollow heat, the pale moon hath a most black and secret mirth:
The years and the days of thine end have been assigned to the work thereof, and God hath already named their attendant angels:
Time and the sun have been notified as to thy doom; thou alone knowest it not.

O foolish, O indiscreet, thou hast taken to thee many alien peoples, the stranger is become thy possessor:
They shall be invoked against thee soon, they shall be given over to the task of thy confusion, even to the redoubling thereof:
The curse of Babel shall be upon thee.
Shall the Beasts of the Abyss that thou hast taken for deities, countervail the flaming might of the seraphim, the sunlike wrath of the Most Righteous?
Mammon shall be aghast in the light of thine end, Moloch shall reel amain before the thunder of thine undoing.

Art thou stronger than Rome, art thou greater than Babylon, that, sinning as these sinned, thou shalt abide where they abode not, nor be stricken as these were stricken?
Nay, thou art less than these were, the term of thy fornication shall be briefer than theirs;
Doom shall come upon thee ere thou art made ready, and the chariots thereof shall be swifter than comets.

O scorner of poets and prophets, of them that are soothsayers: O mocker of the trumpets of Truth: I know that thou wilt not heed me: thou wilt pause a little, thou wilt pass on with derision and forget:
For thine ears are withholden, the rumour of the preparation of doom may not reach so far; and seals are upon thine eyes like eyelids.
Perhaps thou wilt remember me, in the days like tempestuous night, when thine ears shall be thronged with the thousand noises of the labour of death, and around thee shall gather and multiply the rumours of manifold division:
When many confusions are increased upon thee.
But now thou sayest, Ha, ha, am I not armoured with cities, is not my metropolis a shield of adamant embossed with iron?
Am I not fortified? Have I not swift messengers that I have taken captive in the kingdom of the wind?

Am I not ringed about with demons of the deep, with strangers from the vast that I have enslaved and compelled to my service?
Yea! but the strength of iron and stone availeth and saveth not when the heart is corrupted;
Neither shall the weapons of genii protect against the rot and rust of the spirit.

O thou unseemly one, whose actions are not meet: who hast suffered thy merchants to wax as kings: who admittest the multitude to thy councils:
In the end they shall betray thee to the desert and the dust.
In that day thy captains and divers peoples shall divide thee from within: the strong shall be at strife with the strong:
Also, the heathen of his multitude shall sunder thee from round about: he whose heart is entire within him, who is not forsworn as thou:
Who hath not departed from his god as thou from thine.
O twice-confounded: in the end they shall render thee to the Abyss, to the blind and earless One who receiveth but rendereth not in turn:
Abaddon shall take charge of thee.

In the far time to come, ere the end of the black cycle, thy memory shall be but as the writing on a stone that hath crumbled, that the wind hath lifted grain by grain and diffused afar:
The wise and the patient shall hardly regather the characters of that writing, nor put together the import thereof.
Only some wind, that hath blown always within thy loneliest and most ancient waste, shall have remembrance of thee then.
Even thy magic shall be forgotten: the desert peoples latterly thy remnant, will hardly have the same names for thy devils in that day made free and ranging as aforetime.
Also, thy high and haughty cities shall in those years be such that they who builded would scarcely say if this were their handiwork:
Neither shall they endure as the stone of old time, as the pillars of Rome and Tyre that builded mightily, of Egypt whose toil shall be a testimony to the stars of the last and endless night.

Nightmare

As though a thousand vampires, from the day
Fleeing unseen, oppressed that nightly deep,
The straitening and darkened skies of sleep
Closed on the dreamland date in which I lay.

Eternal tensions numbed the wings of time
While through unending narrow ways I sought
Awakening; up precipitous gloom I thought
To reach the dawn, far-pinnacled sublime.

Rejected at the closen gates of light
I turned, and down new dreams and shadows fled,
Where beetling shapes of veiled, colossal dread
With Gothic wings enormous arched the night.

The City of the Titans

I saw a city in a lonely land:
Foursquare, it fronted upon gulfs of fire;
Behind, the night of Erebus hung entire;
And deserts gloomed or glimmered on each hand.

Sunken it seemed, past any star or sun,
Yet strong with bastion, proud with tower and dome:
An archetypal, Titan-builded Rome,
Dread, thunder-named, the seat of gods foredone.

Outreaching time, beyond destruction based,
Immensely piled upon the prostrate waste
And cinctured with insuperable deeps,

The city dreamed in darkness evermore,
Pregnant with crypts of terrible strange lore
And doom-fraught arsenals in lampless keeps.

Desire of Vastness

Supreme with night, what high mysteriarch—
The undreamt-of god beyond the trinal noon
Of elder suns empyreal—past the moon
Circling some wild world outmost in the dark—
Lays on me this unfathomed wish to hark
What central sea with plume-plucked midnight strewn,

Plangent to what enormous plenilune
That lifts in silence, hinderless and stark?

The brazen empire of the bournless waste,
The unstayed dominions of the brazen sky—
These I desire, and all things wide and deep;
And, lifted past the level years, would taste
The cup of an Olympian ecstasy,
Titanic dream, and Cyclopean sleep.

The Medusa of Despair

I may not mask for ever with the grace
Of woven flowers thine eyes of staring stone:
Ere the lithe adders and the garlands blown,
Parting their tangle, have disclosed thy face
Lethal as are the pale young suns in space—
Ere my life take the likeness of thine own—
Get hence! the dark gods languish on their throne,
And flameless grow the Furies they embrace.

Regressive, through what realms of elder doom
Where even the swart vans of Time are stunned,
Seek thou some tall Cimmerian citadel,
And proud demonian capitals unsunned
Whose ramparts, ominous with horrent gloom,
Heave worldward on the unwaning light of hell.

The Refuge of Beauty

From regions of the sun's half-dreamt decay,
All day the cruel rain strikes darkly down;
And from the night thy fatal stars shall frown—
Beauty, wilt thou abide this night and day?

Roofless, at portals dark and desperate,
Wilt thou a shelter unrefused implore,
And past the tomb's too-hospitable door
Evade thy lover in eluding Hate?

Alas, for what have I to offer thee?—
Chill halls of mind, dank rooms of memory
Where thou shalt dwell with woes and thoughts infirm;

This rumor-throngèd citadel of Sense,
Trembling before some nameless imminence;
And fellow-guestship with the glutless Worm.

The Years Restored

I said: Their thunders are forever dumb:
    Time and the sun find not that former might;
    Kings have not thrones and kingdoms in the Night—
Who sit with tarnished crowns and fingers numb,
Dropping the sceptre. Of the Past's great sum,
    Our hands reach but the symbols recondite,
    Tho broken crypts accord the prying light
The gold long dim in Herculaneum.

I spoke: Nor saw, in realms with memory zoned,
    The restoration of the mightier years—
        Free from the dust of dead reality,
The perfect Dream in light eternal throned;
        Now how, with thunders uttered silently,
    Death strikes loud echoes out of Life that hears.

The Witch in the Graveyard

Scene: A forsaken graveyard, by moonlight. Enter two witches.

FIRST WITCH

Sit, sister, now that haggish Hecate
Appropriate and ghastly favor sheds,
And with wild light forwards our enterprise;
And watch the weighted eyelids of each grave,
As never mother watched her babe, to mark,
At zenith of the necromantic moon,
The stir of that disquiet, when the dead,
From suckling nightmares of the charnel dark
Or long insomnia on a mouldy couch,
Impelled like wan somnambulists, arise—
Constrained to emerge and walk, or seated each
On his own tombstone, shrouded council hold,
Or commerce with the sooty wings of hell.
All omens of this influential hour
When all dark powers, thronging to the dark,

Promote enchantment with their wavèd wings,
And brim the wind with potency malign—
A dew of dread to aid our cauldron—these
Observe thou closely, while I seek afield
All requisite swart herbs of venefice
And evil roots unto our usance ripe.

(The first witch departs, leaving the other among the tombs, and returns after a time, in the course of her search.)

FIRST WITCH

Sister, what seest or what hearest thou?

SECOND WITCH

I see
The moonlight, and the slowly moving gleam
That westers hour by hour on tomb and stone;
And shrivelled lilies, tossed i' the winter's breath
With their attenuate shadows, as might dance
Phantom with flaffing phantom; at my side,
The white and shuddering grasses of the grave,
With nettles, and the parching fumitory,
Whose leaves, root-trellised on the bones of death,
Will rasp and bristle to the lightest wind.

(The first witch moves on, and approaches again, after an interval.)

FIRST WITCH

Sister, what seest or what hearest thou?

SECOND WITCH

I see
The mound-stretched gossamers, cradles to the dew;
Moon-wefted briers, and the cypress-trees
With shadow swathed, or cerements of the moon;
And corpse-lights borne from aisle to secret aisle
Within the footless forest. . . .
Now I hear
The lich-owl, shrieking lethal prophecy;
And whimpering winds, the children of the air,
Lost in the glades of mystery and gloom.

(The first witch disappears, and passes again shortly.)

FIRST WITCH

Sister, what seest or what hearest thou?

SECOND WITCH

I see
The ghost-white owl, with huge, sulphureous eyes,
That veers in prone, unwhispered flight, and hear
The small shriek of the moon-adventuring mole,
Griped in mid-graveyard. . . . And I see
Where some wild shadow shakes, though the pale wind
Of midnight stirs far off . . . and hear
Curst mandragores that gibber to the moon,
Though no man treads anigh. . . .
(After an interval)
Some predal hand doth hold the wandering air;
Now dies the throttled wind with rattling breath,
And round about a breathing Silence prowls.
(After another interval)
I hear the cheeping of the bat-lipped ghouls,
Aroused beneath the vaulted cypresses
Far off; and lipless muttering of tombs,
With clash of bones bestirred in ancient charnels
Beneath their shroud of unclean light that crawls. . . .
Earth shudders, and rank odours 'gin to rise
From tombs a-crack; and shaken out all at once
From mid-air, and directly 'neath the moon,
Meseems what hanging wing divides the light,
Like a black film of mist, or thickest shadow:
But on the tomb there is no shadow!

FIRST WITCH

Enough! 'twill be a prosperous night, methinks,
For commerce of the demons with the dead,
And for us too, when every omen's good,
And fraught with promise of a potent brew.

The Sea-Gods

Beneath the sunset and the sea
Their coral-builded cities be;
They keep an old forgotten reign,
A purple, far supremacy.

The azure-girdled suns that roam,
And moons that tred the silvering foam,
Are vague above their ocean-vales;
And shaken dawns their evenings dome.

Their eyes like changing emeralds gleam
Through twilights of the Tyrian stream;
And with blue weeds their tresses flow,
As in a dark, confusèd dream.

But often, when long afterglows
In cold and spectral evenings close,
On lonely seas they rise, and cry
From foam left grey by sunset's rose.

Or in the mystic waves and wan,
Hushed by the moon's marmoreal dawn,
They moan as moans the muted surf
On shores of windless isles withdrawn.

Known to their dim supremacy
The deep's forgotten secrets be;
Their old, eternal vestures are
The purples of the flowing sea.

The Ministers of Law

The glories and the perils of thy day
Are one, O Man! Thou goest to thine end
With Powers, and for a little thou dost wend
With marshalled Majesties upon their way:
But thee the dread Necessities betray
That nurse, and fearful Splendors that befriend;
And thee shall alien Dominations rend. . . .
Deemest the triumph of the worlds to stay,
Or step by step, through eons overpassed,
Stride with the suns upon their road of awe?
Thou travelest brief ways that end and sink—
Urged by the hurrying planets; and the vast,
Prone-rushing constellations of the Law
Thunder and press behind thee at the brink.

Decadence

By some strange antepast I have consumed
In a former star foregone the fruits of this;
And frost and dust commingle in the kiss
Of love, with my forsaken self entombed.

Quenched as of night and Lethe, the great fire
Wherewith to lordlier suns my spirit burned,
Bequeathes but ashes, long and long inurned,
To feed the darkling altars of desire.

O soul not all the further stars might fill,
Nor any god constrain your stubborn will
Nor silence this your mouth with heaven's wine.

How wearily, how humbly shall you crave
From the low Earth an everlasting grave,
And from the dust its ancient anodyne!

Somnus

The flowing silence of Lethe
Thro gulfs of more than Erebean gloom—
Beyond the fiery troubling of the stars
And moons made pale with travail
Or the loud seas exulting to the sun—
The lapse of oblivion—of night utterness.
The thunder-driven chariots of storm.
The sun, which is the golden lamp of noon,
Whose hours elude the groping light—
Lost in the hollow silence
Or dimmer than mirages of the moon—
In gloom declivous as to under-gloom—
Less than the foam of Lethe seem the worlds—
Softer than the fall of lotos-petals.

To Beauty

(A Fragment)

Beauty, whose all-potential hand
Forever holds the fertile stars in fee,
What aeons serve thine empery,
What deeps are vast to thy demand!

All which Immensity,
Furrowed by fire, and sown by laboring suns
Hath brought to fruit within the patient past,
In heritage thou hast;
And all the flaming promise of the spheres
Which in remoter years
Shall be fulfilled at last
After the toil of long aphelions.
The advancing heavens still advance
Thy sun-supported feet;
From out the gulfs of divagance
Stars on thine errands meet;
Who bruit thy briefest word
In cyclic thunders heard
By gods upon their echo-shaken throne;
Who fledge thy flight
With ever-travelling light
To constellate the eyeless night unknown.

The City of Destruction

(A Fragment)

I

The incognizable kings of Night, within their unrevealed abyss,
Have built them a metropolis against the kingdoms of the light.

Its mountain-passing ramparts climb exalted from the nadir flats
In black, Babelian ziggurats that tier the dusk of nether time.

Prodigious, dire and indistinct, with horns that lift the heavens' doom,
Its turrets crowd the skyless gloom huge as the night of hells extinct.

The hostile gulfs for armor wear its walls as of a thousand Romes;
The swollen menace of its domes enhelms the swart, inimic air.

The Powers to darkness ministrant have fortressed them supremely well,
Building their dreadful citadel with massed, eternal adamant

Quarried from out the core entire of suns that night and ice entomb;
Their secret furnaces relume the stone that once was stellar fire.

The monstrous lamps of Death and Mars like demon moons emblaze
their halls;
The watch-fires on the infernal walls flame like a crown of fallen stars.

II

From out the sunken courts resound colossal engineries of doom;
Some slow, malign, tremendous loom dismally rumbles underground;

Loud shuttles clack implacably; unknown machines, with clangorous ire,
Beat in their hearts of throbbing fire the instants of eternity;

The crooked arms of titan cranes, with grasp Briarean, momently
Lift to the dim, Tartarean sky a nameless freight in stretchèd chains;

And Acheronian waters roar, constrained, relentless, subterrene,
Where at their evil toil unseen the hellish wheels moan evermore.

The Orchid of Beauty

Beauty, thou orchid of immortal bloom,
Spring from the fire and dust of perished spheres,
How art thou tall in these autumnal years
With the red rain of immemorial doom,
And fragrant where the lesser suns illume,
For sustenance of Life's forgotten tears.
Ever thy splendor and thy light appears
Like dawn from out the midnight of the tomb.

Colors, and glints, and glamors unrecalled,
Richly thy petals intricate revive:
Blossom, whose roots are in eternity,
The faithful soul, the sentience darkly thralled,
In dream and wonder evermore shall strive
At Edens lost of time and memory.

A Phantasy of Twilight

Ere yet the soaring after-fire was flown,
I found a city in the twilight lone—
    Asleep in lapse of some forgotten land
And griping horizons of deserts prone.

Ah, strange with time and ruinous it was!
The seeping sand through idle gates did pass;
    The garths were barren, and each breasted grave
Was rock-reluctant to the nursling grass!

But in the dusking palaces I saw
Twilight rebuild the broken thrones of Law—
    Affording unto fanes long-desecrate,
What elder glooms of mystery and awe!

And walls and columns, in the ghostly gleam,
Lit as with memory of a past supreme,
    Held mightier form portentous for awhile,
Ere night should whelm them like a crumbling dream.

And, lo, from courts and arches, unconfined,
Rode forth, unto some desert bourn assigned,
    The evanescent pomps of ghostly dust,
On thin and momentary manes of wind!

Beauty Implacable

White Beauty, bending from a throne sublime,
Hath claimed my lips with kisses keen as snow:
Now through my harp the tremors come and go
Of things not stirred with urgencies of time;
Now from the lunar mountains, old and lone,
In dream I watch the neighboring world remote;
Or on the dim Uranian waters float
After a star-like sun from zone to zone.

Lo! in her praise, the stern, the fearful one,
Whose love is as the light of snows afar,
Whose ways are difficult, what word shall be?
I, desolate with Beauty, and undone,
Say Death is not so strong to change or mar,
And Love and Life not so desired as she.

The Nameless Wraith

As one who seeks the silver moth of night
Where moonless gardens lose the afterglow,
My soul went forth ineffably, to know
Some vaguer vision unrevealed of light.

From halcyon fells whereon the falcons range,
From Hesper, and the sunsets mountain-born,
And from the trembling freshness of the morn
I turned me to a dreamland still and strange.

It seemed the hueless ashes of the day
And darkened glories filled that glooming world:
The spectrum of hesternal suns was furled
In immemorial valleys vast and grey.

Ruins, and wrecks of many a foundered year,
Doubtfully known, bestrewed the unvisioned verge,
Where, from unsounding reaches of blind surge,
Some nameless wraith of beauty fluttered near.

Was it the dove from shrines of lost delight?
The nightingale from love's necropolis?
What dream-led messenger of time's abyss
Came from the dark, and vanished in the night?

The Ancient Quest

O giant stars, born of eternal night,
    O wingéd flames wherewith the void is sown,
As dreadful prophets of a God unknown,
        Ye speak the law in light!

Had we but sight to see and comprehend,
    Your countless fires were as a language plain
To tell us all that we have sought in vain;
        The quest were at an end.

O younger worlds, whose tireless-pinioned flight
    Climbs eagerly the sheer and topless deep!
O shrivelled planets that obscurely creep
        On orbits sunk in night!

Alike ye falter in unceasing gloom
    That shrouds the deathless Truth ye may not find;
Alike for ye the faming suns are blind,
        And light may not illume.

For Life whose God-ambitious eyes would see
    The stellar-manifested truth sublime,
Must gaze with sight immutable as Time,
        Large as Infinity.

Aspect of Iron

From iron mountains graven on the sky—
A sharp horizon past the burnished noon
And all the desert's grasp of bronze—were hewn
Amidst remote, mute giant Memnons high

The granite sentries of Eternity
That stand distinct above each brazen dune,
Or glittering lutes, metallic to the moon,
And on whose breast the shields of mornings lie.

All other lands I know are not as this:
Girt with strange rigors of definitude,
Exactnesses of iron permanence
As the last height that fronts the last abyss.

Beyond the Door

Alas! the evanescence of a dream,
That, like a rose, shall never blossom more!
A glimpse of unguessed things, and then the door
Of waking sense clangs to. Alas! the Gleam,
The visioned Secret and the Light supreme,
That one at moments nears, when, lo! the pall
Of veiling darkness drops and covers all—
The darkness of the daylight's aureate beam!

Leaving but an elusive memory—
A heavenly cadence, a supernal word,
Never but half-recalled. In dreams are heard
Who knows what tidings from Eternity,
Transcendent, strange! Alas! we may not bring
Aught past the gateway of Awakening!

The Harlot of the World

O Life, thou harlot who beguilest all!
Beautiful in thy house, the golden world.
Abidest thou, where Powers pinion-furled
And flying Splendors follow to thy call.

Innumerous like the stars or like the dust,
Nations and monarchs were thy thralls of yore:

Unto the grave's old womb forevermore
Hast thou betrayed the passion and the lust.

Fair as the moon of summer is thy face,
And mystical with cloudiness of hair. . . .
Only an eye, subornless by delight,

Shall find, within thy phosphorescent gaze,
Those caverns of corruption and despair
Where the Worm toileth in the charnel night.

Psalm to the Desert

1. The years have set thee apart, O desert: Silence and solitude are upon thee for the twiform sigil of the last oblivion.
2. Thy barrenness is bound about thee like iron; it cleaveth to thee as a girdle to the girdlestead;
3. Even as the skin upon a corpse, it tighteneth forever.
4. Thy womb is closen, the aperture thereof is filled with an obstipation of sand, and the coverture made strait with stone:
5. The sun is impotent thereon, no less than upon the womb of the centre.
6. Thy breasts are fallen, they are flat and rivelled; and the milk within them is marah:
7. Thou sucklest the viper, affording him a deadly life, and givest the adder and the crotalus to draw a replenishment of their venom;
8. Herpeton lies in the hollow between thy paps.
9. Thou art given as a bride to the abyss and a wife to the nether vast;
10. Who hath hold upon thy middle with immensitude for a closure of arms, and the mereness of ether for ineluctable clasping:
11. Thou art breathed upon with a bitter breath, and a voice of infinite suspiration; a wind is about thee for the sound of the terrible sighing of voidness.
12. Thy fate is riveted upon thee, thy doom is made fast with bolts of metal that was mined from beneath the nadir;
13. A curse is gone forth against thee, a ban hath been spoken by a voice that is stronger than the voice of the sun:
14. It hath said, Behold, thou art sterile, the black field of the bottom of the gulf, which is sown with a dust of constellations, shall bring forth sooner than thou;
15. Thy womb shall conceive but of death, the turning thereof shall be dissolution, and the seed of corruption;
16. Even till the time of the rending of stars and atoms, when the Worm shall lay hold on the heart of God for a final pasture;

17. When Chaos shall be taken from its place, and scattered upon the provinces of the suns;
18. When Hell shall heave, and bespew the empyrean with a fiery parbreak;
19. When the zenith shall be overflowed with a sea of molten adamant, and vastness filled with the sound of the cleaving of the nadir.

Inheritance

Of all the sovereignty thine eyes obtain,
Thy grant of vision from the royal sun,
And all thine appanage of lordly dream,
The dust, wherewith the worm is parcener,
Waits with perennial claim, nor will resign
Its right in thee. All glories and all gleams,
The seven splendors that inform the light,
And beauties immemorial as the moon,
Robing the barren world—all which thine eyes
Hold for inheritance, at length shall fill
The blindness and oblivion of the grave,
And leave it dark.

With dustiness and night
Upon thy mouth of starry proud desire,
With slumber for thy dreams, thou wilt repose,
Nor startle when the lazy, loitering worm
Is slow to leave the tavern of thy brain.

Memnon at Midnight

Methought upon the tomb-encumbered shore
I stood of Egypt's lone monarchal stream,
And saw immortal Memnon, throned supreme
In gloom as of that Memphian night of yore:
Fold upon fold purpureal he wore,
Beneath the star-borne canopy extreme—
Carven of silence and colossal dream,
Where waters flowed like sleep forevermore.

Lo, in the darkness, thick with dust of years,
How many a ghostly god around his throne,
With thronging wings that were forgotten Fames,
Stood, ere the dawn restore to ancient ears
The long-withholden thunder of their names,
And music stilled to monumental stone.

The City in the Desert

In a lost land, that only dreams have known,
Where flaming suns walk naked and alone;
Among horizons bright as molten brass,
And glowing heavens like furnaces of glass,
It rears with dome and tower manifold,
Rich as a dawn of amarant and gold,
Or gorgeous as the Phoenix, born of fire,
And soaring from an opalescent pyre
Sheer to the zenith. Like some anademe
Of Titan jewels turned to flame and dream
The city crowns the far horizon-light
Over the flowered meads of damassin. . . .
A desert isle of madreperl! wherein
The thurifer and opal-fruited palm
And heaven-thronging minarets becalm
The seas of azure wind. . . .

(*Note*: These lines were remembered out of a dream, and are given verbatim.)

The Blindness of Orion

So blind Orion, groping for the morn
With eyes uplift whereon forever hung
Infinite burden and suspense of night,
Had clomb the long and mountain-ending vast,
Led by the Cyclops. Many a dim ravine
Where serried pines were silent ere the dawn
And many a slope or terrace of the snow,
Pure as Pentelic marble for the tread
Of roseal-footed light, lay far behind
Still drowned in stagnant purples. Toiling up
Even to the very threshold of the heavens,
They heard the ascending eagles hail the sun
Round the forsaken throne of Phosphorus,
Until the morning's levin-colored ray
Lightened upon the Cyclops, and he paused,
And over him ethereal glory drave
To rouse the dreaming colors in the cloud,
To give the sea its immemorial green

And strike the towering cities into gold
Along the low horizon.

Then, at last,
On dark Orion groping for the suns,
From out the sole, the Apollonian source,
Returning vision flowed, and he had power
And privilege once more upon the light,
And might receive its seven ministers,
Even with gathering rays of stars remote,
And take the tithe of beauty proffered still
By terrene shapes and images—by forms
Of flowers and statues and of women dancing;
Of sapling laurels, ancient olives gnarled;
The noontide shapes of headlands and of clouds;
The meres that curve in darkening amaranth
Amid the sunset range; and seas and rivers
Straight-tided or with currents serpentine
Dividing variously their protean shores.

The Mirrors of Beauty

Beauty has many mirrors to ensphere
Her presence or her passing: orbs of dew;
Far-flooding Amazons with margents new;
The narrowing circlet of the desert mere;
Deep wells on which the ruby planets rear;
Blades from Damascus; gems of Xanadu;
And pools that hold a falcon-hovered blue
Or eves whereon the ghostly owlets veer.

Often, upon the solitary sea,
She lieth, ere the wind shall gather breath—
One with the reflex of infinity;
In oriels filled with some conflagrant sky
Her vision dwells, or in the ring-dove's eye,
Or the black crystal of the eyes of Death.

The Flight of Azrael

Scene: An immense and darkling plain, remotely lit by the sunset of the last day. Two demons, passing from the interstellar deep, have paused on an isolated hill-top.

FIRST DEMON

What world is this, all desolate and dim
Under the lone, phantasmagoric heavens
Great with hanging night? Yon luminance
Is lurid as the furnace-glare of hell,
Seen from the contiguity of gloom
Of a Cimmerian region. All the air
Flags heavily, as beneath the weight of wings
Invisible and evil—from the plain
No movement, save of shadows mustering
Beyond the heels of day.

SECOND DEMON

It is the Earth,
A hoary planet, old in wrath and woe
As any hell. Red pestilence and war
Have now refunded to the usuring wind
The breath of all its peoples; Azrael,
Delivering now the town and necropole
To one decay in night's abysmal vault,
Prepares him for departure. From afar,
Seest thou not the towering of his wings,
Like thunder on the sunset? Widening,
Those vans involve and stifle half the light
With bat-like folds and ribs: on the further stars,
Or worlds unknown of the outer infinite,
He now intends the darkness of his course;
On Algol's planets haply poised, he will
Make permanent the sable sun's eclipse,
Or round some vast Antarean satellite
His shadowed arc will broaden to a sphere,
Oblivion's black and perfect globe. . . . On Earth
He comes no more: the very worms have died
In the scarce-nibbled carrion; the thin wind
Will write man's epitaph in shifting sand,
And the pale unfading arabesques of frost
Adorn and fret his ghoul-forgotten tomb.

Duality

Thy soul is like a secret garden-close,
Where roots of cleft mandragoras enwreathe;
Where bergamot and fumitory breathe,
And ivy winds its flower with the rose.

The lolling weeds of Lethe, green or wan,
Exhale their fatal languors on the light;
From out infernal grails of aconite
Poisons and dews are proffered to the dawn.

Here, when the moon's phantasmal fingers grope
To find the marbles of a hidden tomb,
There sings the cypress-perchèd nightingale;

And all the silver-bellied serpents pale
Their ruby eyes amid the blossoms ope,
To lift and listen in the ghostly gloom.

Love Malevolent

I fain would love thee, but thy lips are fed
With poison-honey, hivèd in a skull;
They seem like scarlet poppies, beautiful
For delving roots, deep-clenchèd in the dead.

Thine eyes are coloured like the nightshade-flow'r. . . .
Blent in the opiate perfume of thy breath
Are dreams, and purple sleep, and scented death
For him that is thy lover for an hour.

Mandragora, within the graveyard grown,
Hath given thee its carnal root to eat,
And vipers, born and nurstled in a tomb,

From fawning mouths drip venom at thy feet;
Yet from thy lethal lips and thine alone,
Love would I drink, as dew from poison-bloom.

Exotique

Thy mouth is like a crimson orchid-flower
Whence perfume and whence poison rise unseen
To moons aswim in iris or in green,
Or mix with morning in an eastern bower.

Thou shouldst have known, in amaranthine isles,
The sunsets hued like fire of frankincense,
And noontides fraught with far-borne redolence,
The mingled spicery of purple miles.

Thy breasts, where blood and molten marble flow,
Thy warm white limbs, thy loins of tropic snow—
These, these, by which desire is grown divine,

Were made for dreams in mystic palaces,
For love and sleep and slow voluptuousness,
And summer seas afoam like foaming wine.

Alien Memory

Thy body like to rosy ivory,
    The fervours of thy beauty warm and bare,
    I knew them all, I know not when nor where,
In lands beside an amber-foaming sea.

Ah, once I found thee, lying by a palm
    Upon thy terraces of serpentine—
    Thy breast of dreams, voluptuous and divine
All given to the winds of myrrh and balm.

We saw the sun, a molten amethyst,
    Sink in the scented seas of foam and fire,
        And a slow night with ruby planets rise;

And all the night was curtain for our tryst,
        And all thine eager breast, thy burning thighs,
    And amorous arms a couch for my desire.

Fire of Snow

Pale fire of snow had lit the dusk for me:
Astray with mind half-consciously intent,
I had not thought the wood so imminent—
Pregnant with pine and sombre cypress-tree.
Darker than sleep, and mute with mystery
Like far-off death, where questing dreams are spent,
Their winding caverns deepened as I went
Therein, and paused in old expectancy.

* * *

Pale fire of snow had lit the dusk for me. . . .
But the black stillness held where once the wind
Had parted boughs in music, that the gleam
Of stars might enter; all was strangely blind,
Like midnight thickening 'neath the middle sea—
Filled with the silence of a time-slain dream.

In the Wind

Lo, in the wind what legions pass,
Phantom, innumerable, fleet;
Watching, I dream their pauseless feet
These lights that run upon the grass.

Lunar Mystery

O'er gardens lulled with ghostly light
In music leaned the languorous moon,
The burden of the murmured night.

Where amaranthine lilies wore,
In lofty pallor fully blown,
An ivory silence evermore,

Bemused, I saw the night's white song,
The flowers' moon-measured lullaby,
Its visible pale rune prolong.

Then, to my spelled, reluctant ear,
A whisper louder than the light
Pierced as from alien presence near;

Till half I deemed to shortly see
A silver seraph of the moon,
Or star-shape harping mystery.

But wingless yet the midnight seemed,
The garden footless to my gaze,
Save for a wind that briefly gleamed

Upon the pensive-pacèd hours,
And moonlight fluttering like a moth
Amid the swayed, enormous flowers.

Moon-Dawn

The hills, a-throng with swarthy pine,
Press up the pale and hollow sky,
And the squat cypresses on high
Reach from the lit horizon-line.

They reach, they reach, with gnarlèd hands—
Malignant hags, obscene and dark—
While the red moon, a demons' ark,
Is borne along the mystic lands.

The Mummy

From out the light of many a mightier day,
From Pharaonic splendor, Memphian gloom,
And from the night aeonian of the tomb
They brought him forth, to meet the modern ray,—
Upon his brow the unbroken seal of clay,
While gods have gone to a forgotten doom,
And desolation and the dust assume
Temple and cot immingling in decay

From out the everlasting womb sublime
Of cyclopean death, within a land
Of tombs and cities rotting in the sun,
He is reborn to mock the might of time,
While kings have built against Oblivion
With walls and columns of the windy sand.

Morning on an Eastern Sea

A silken sea, a sea of damassin,
With figured foam as flowers wove therein,
Where all the winds walk lightly. From afar—
Clean-carven on the skies of cinnabar—
The palmy isles like azure malachite,
Along the horizon for a time retard
A morning fraught with frankincense and nard,
And purple fires, and amber-scented light,
And flame like flame of perfumes. . .

Reclamation

Forevermore the Earth reclaims her own,
    Desire and vision, that have ventured far
    In prospect of the empyrean star,
Fail, meteor-like, upon the heavens lone:

Eyes that awhile were fain of ampler gloom,
    Or the blue suns of paradisean light
    With amaranthine worlds beyond the night,
Turn to the staring blindness of the tomb.

Afterglow

Rays upward streaming from the hidden sun,
    Far-sunken in the realm of Night,
Brim all the West and render beautiful
    Each sunset cloud and height.

So may some life, gone far beyond our ken,
    Send backward flowing beams of light—
An afterglow from darkness that shall make
    Its skyline fair and bright.

Nocturne

A silver sleep is on the vale;
The breathless pines are pale,
Where quiet shadows dream
By some departing stream.

With hands fantastical and still,
Upon the windless hill,
One cypress fain would hold
The moon of faded gold.

The Crucifixion of Eros

Because of thee immortal Love hath died:
Because thy wilful heart will not believe,
Thy hands and mine a thorny crown must weave,
And build a cross for Love the crucified.

Behold, how beautiful the limbs that bleed—
The limbs that bleed, O stubborn heart, for us!

Stilled are the lids so softly tremulous,
And mute the mouth of our eternal need. . . .

Though this thy fearful lips would now deny,
Love is divine and cannot wholly die:
Draw forth the nails thy tender hands have driven,

And we will know the mercy infinite,
Will find redemption in our own delight,
And in each other's heart the only heaven.

Suggestion

Upon the woven clouds, as on thy glowing hair,
The sunset dreams and dies in sombre, sullen gold—
In unforgotten flame that makes my soul despair:
I weep to-night, because the waning light is fair,
Upon the woven clouds of sombre, sullen gold.

Thy feet were wont to pass at evening on the flow'rs—
At evening, like the swift and silver-footed rain . . .
O! gardens that thy feet may never find again! . . .
Ever my heart must fail, when on the trodden flow'rs
Returns at summer eve the silver-footed rain.

Arabesque

Like arabesques of ebony,
The cypresses, in silhouette,
Fantastically cleave and fret
A moon of yellow ivory.

Like orient lamps the rays illume
A leafy pattern manifold,
And all the field is overscrolled
With curiously figured gloom.

Like arabesques of ebony,
Or like Arabian lattices,
For ever seem the cypresses,
Before a moon of ivory.

Belated Love

Ah, woe is me, for Love hath lain asleep,
Hath lain too long in some Circean close—
Till on his dreaming wings the ruined rose
Fell lightly, and the rose-red leaves were deep.

Ah, wellaway, for Love is overlate:
Far-wandering, alone, we know not where,
He found the white and purple poppies fair,
Nor heard the summer pass importunate.

Sweet Love, can we forgive thy loitering?
The golden summer, like a dream at dawn,
Changes, and from our kindled eyes is gone,

And leaves grey autumn. . . . We have heard thy wing
But with a sound of sighing; heart on heart,
In our own sighs we hear thy wing depart.

November Twilight

November's winy sunset leaves,
Deep in the silver heavens far,
One ruby-hearted star
That lit the summer's moon-forsaken eves.

Under its ray, remote, alone,
Ascends upon the ashen gloom
The ghostly faint perfume
From autumn's grey, forgotten roses flown.

Desolation

It seems to me that I have lived alone—
Alone, as one that liveth in a dream:
As light on coldest marble, or the gleam
Of moons eternal on a land of stone,
The days have been to me. I have but known
The silence of Thulean lands extreme—
A silence all-attending and supreme
As is the sea's enormous monotone.

Upon the waste no palmed mirages are,
But strange chimeras roam the steely light,

And cold parheila hang on hill and scaur
Where flowers of frost alone have bloomed. . . . I crave
The friendly clasp of finite arms, to save
My spirit from the ravening Infinite.

Coldness

Thy heart will not believe in love:
Therefore is love become to me
A dream resolved to mockery,
And death and life are less than love.

O, bright and beautiful as flame
Thy hair, and pale thy lips, and eyes
Like seas wherein the waning skies
Of autumn lie in paler flame.

Forevermore thy heart abides,
A dreaming crystal, pure and cold,
Amid whose visions manifold
No shape nor any shade abides.

Thy days are void and vain as death:
The moons and morrows weave for thee
A sleep of light eternally,
Where life is as a dream of death.

Chill as white jewels, or the moon,
And virginal as ice or fire,
Thou knowest life and life's desire
As a bright mirror knows the moon.

Lo, if thy heart believed in love,
It were not more nor less to me:
I know *thy* love a mockery,
And all my dreams less vain than love.

The Kingdom of Shadows

A crownless king who reigns alone,
I live within this ashen land,
Where winds rebuild from wandering sand
My columns and my crumbled throne.

My sway is on the men that were,
And wan sweet women, dear and dead;
Beside a marble queen, my bed
Is made within the sepulcher.

In gardens desolate to the sun,
Faring alone, I sigh to find
The dusty closes, dim and blind,
Where winter and the spring are one.

My shadowy visage, grey with grief,
In sunken waters walled with sand,
I see—where all mine ancient land
Lies yellow like an autumn leaf.

My silver lutes of subtle string
Are rust—but on the grievous breeze
I hear what sobbing memories,
And muted sorrows murmuring!

Across the broken monuments,
Memorial of the dreams of old,
The sunset flings a ghostly gold
To mock mine ancient affluence.

About the tombs of stone and brass
The silver lights of evening flee;
And slowly now, and solemnly,
I see the pomp of shadows pass.

Often, beneath some fervid moon,
With splendid spells I vainly strive
Dead loves imperial to revive,
And speak a heart-remembered rune—

But, ah, the lovely phantoms fail,
The faces fade to mist and light,
The vermeil lips of my delight
Are dim, the eyes are ashen-pale.

A crownless king who reigns alone,
I live within this ashen land,
Where winds rebuild from wandering sand
My columns and my crumbled throne.

Give Me Your Lips

Give me your lips:
Like to some scarlet fruit of Paradise,
That grew before the gates were barred,
They burn upon my eyes;
Or like to scarlet flow'rs,
Wherefrom a sweet and subtle poison drips;
Or crimson jewels, cold and hard,
That, kissed of my desire,
Shall magically melt to wine and fire—
To wine beyond the wine of earthly hours,—
To fire
More than the fire of heavens many-starred.

Give me your lips:
When you have laid your vermeil mouth on mine,
No draught, no anodyne,
Nor comb wherefrom the amber honey drips;
No marah drunk beneath the desert skies,
Nor all the green and bitter wine of seas;
No dews of Lethe nor of Paradise—
Not one, nor all of these,
Shall take away the taste of fire and wine
Your lips have left on mine.

Strangeness

O love, thy lips are bright and cold,
Like jewels carven curiously
To symbols of a mystery,
A secret lost ere time was old.

Like woven amber, finely spun,
Thy hair, enwoofed with golden light,
Remembers yet the flaming flight
Of some unknown archaic sun.

Thine eyes are crystals green and chill,
Wherein, as in a shifting sea,
Wan fires and drowning lusters flee
To starless deeps for ever still.

Fallen across thy dreaming face,
The dawn is made a secret thing,
Like flame of crimson lamps that swing
In midnight caverns dim with space.

Thy smile is like the furtive gleam
Of fleeing moon a traveler sees
Through closing arms of cypress-trees
In secret lines of night and dream.

Sphinx-like, unsolved eternally,
Thy beauty's riddle doth abide,
And love hath come, and love hath died,
Striving to read the mystery.

Thy face a dream the dawn illumes
Makes mild and marvelous the light—
As flame from lamp of chrysolite
Amid an altar's azure fumes.

Impression

The silver silence of the moon
Upon the sleeping garden lies;
The wind of evening dies
As in forgetful dreams a ghostly tune.

How white, how still the flowers are,
As carved of pearl and ivory!
The pines are ebony,
A sombre frieze on heavens pale and far.

Like mirrors made of lucid stone
The pools lie still and bright and cold,
Where moon and stars behold,
In some eternal trance, themselves alone.

The Exile

Against my heart your heart is closed; you bid me go:
What ways are left in all the world for love to know?
Desolate oceans, and the light of lonely plains,
Dead moons that wander in the wastes of ice and snow—

These, these I fain would see, and find the splendid bourn
Of sunset, or the brazen deserts of the morn,
That I might lose this ever-aching loneliness
In vaster solitude; and love be less forlorn,

Faring to seek with alien sun and alien star
The strange, the veiled horizons infinite and far;
Spaces of fire and night, the skies of steel and gold,
Or sunset-haunted seas where foamless islands are.

Ave atque Vale

Black dreams; the pale and sorrowful desire
Whose eyes have looked on Lethe and have seen,
Deep in the sliding ebon tide serene,
Their own vain light inverted; the vain lyre
That only tells of love and languishing;
Autumnal roses blind with rain; slow foam
From desert-sinking seas, with honeycomb
Of aconite and poppy—these I bring
With this my bitter, barren love to thee;
And from the grievous springs of memory,
Far in the great Maremma of my heart,
I proffer thee to drink; and on thy mouth,
With the one kiss wherein we meet and part,
Leave fire and dust from quenchless leagues of drouth.

The Tears of Lilith

O lovely demon, half-divine!
Hemlock and hydromel and gall,
Honey and aconite and wine
Mingle to make that mouth of thine—

Thy mouth I love: but most of all
It is thy tears that I desire—
Thy tears, like fountain-drops that fall
In gardens red, Satanical;

Or like the tears of mist and fire,
Wept by the moon, that wizards use
To secret runes when they require
Some silver philtre, sweet and dire.

Alexandrines

Knowing the weariness of dreams, and days, and nights,
The great and grievous vanity of joy and pain;
Frail loves that pass, where languors infinite remain,
Fervors and long despairs and desperate, brief delights;

Knowing how in the witless brains of them that were,
The drowsy, wiving worm hath prospered and hath died;
Knowing that, evermore, by moon and sun abide
The standing glooms made stagnant in the sepulcher;

Knowing the vacillant leaves that tremble, flame, and fall,
The sweetly-wasting rose, the dawns and stars that wane—
Knowing these things, the desolate heart and soul are fain
Of the one perfect sleep which filleth, foldeth all.

Autumnal

In all the pleasances where Love was lord,
Blossom the mournful immortelles alone;
The fallen roses crumble, and are blown,
A snow of red, about the barren sward.

The misty sun is grown a dimmer gold:
Only the leaves, the leaves forever seem
To tell and treasure, in a gorgeous dream,
The aureate fervor of the dawns of old.

Only for us remains the memory
Of sultry moons and summer suns that were;
And we have found, where fallen roses stir,
The immortelles that flower mournfully.

The Whisper of the Worm

1918–1920

A Vision of Lucifer

I saw a shape with human form and face,
If such should in apotheosis stand:
Deep in the shadows of a desolate land
His burning feet obtained colossal base,
And spheral on the lonely arc of space,
His head, a menace unto heavens unspanned,
Arose with towered eyes that might command
The sunless, blank horizon of that place.

And straight I knew him for the mystic one
That is the brother, born of human dream,
Of man rebellious at an unknown rod;
The mind's ideal, and the spirit's sun;
A column of clear flame, in lands extreme,
Set opposite the darkness that is God.

Sepulture

Deep in my heart, as in the hollow stone
And silence of some olden sepulcher,
Thy silver beauty lies, and shall not stir—
Forgotten, incorruptible, alone:
Though altars darken, and a wind be blown
From starless seas on beacon-fires that were—
Within thy tomb, with oils of balm and myrrh,
Forever burn the onyx lamps unknown.

And though the bleak Novembral gardens yield
Rose-dust and ivy-leaf, nor any flower
Be found through vermeil forest or wan field—
Still, still the asphodel and lotos lie
Around thy bed, and hour by silent hour,
Exhale immortal fragrance like a sigh.

Palms

Palms in the sunset of a languid summer land!
Sculpture of living green, on dreamy scarlet light
Dividing as a wall the twilight from the night!
How magically still and luminous they stand,

Inclining fretted leaves above some red lagoon—
Careless alike, in mystic and immense repose,
Of the flamingo-colored, flying sun that goes,
Or the slow coming of the lion-colored moon.

Mors

Sweeter the thought of death to me
Than love's own sleep or any dream;
Than starlight on some ebon stream
Or moonlight on the marble sea.

Like black and mummia-laden wine
My soul foredrains oblivion:
The bitter splendors of the sun
Resolved in Lethe's anodyne.

Love and desire and dead delight
And dead despair are shades that pass
As in a necromancer's glass
To mingle with the shades of night.

They pass. . . . The secret peace I crave
Like a black shroud enwraps me round—
Lost, and voluptuously drowned
In the dark languor of the grave.

Dissonance

The harsh, brief sob of broken horns; the sound
Of hammers, on some clanging sepulcher;
Lutes in a thunder-storm; a dulcimer
By sudden drums and clamoring bugles drowned;
Crackle of pearls, and gritting rubies, ground
Beneath an iron heel; the heavy whirr
Of battle-wheels; a hungry leopard's purr;
And sigh of swords withdrawing from the wound:—

All, all are in thy dreadful fugue, O life,
Thy dark, malign and monstrous music, spun
In hell, from a delirious Satan's dream! . . .
O! dissonance primordial and supreme—
The moan, the thunder, evermore at strife,
Beneath the unheeding silence of the sun!

Eidolon

Chryselephantine, clear as carven flame,
Before my gaze thy soul's eidolon stands,
As on the threshold of the frozen lands
A frozen sun forevermore the same.

All passion that the passive marbles make
Imperishable in their shining sleep
Is thine; and all the wan despairs that weep
With tears of ice and crystal, cannot break

The heart, which like a ruby white and rare,
In thy deep breast impenetrably gleams. . . .
More beautiful than any sphinx, and fair

As Aphrodite dead, thine image seems—
Guarding forever, in its golden eyes,
The treasure of intagliate memories.

Haunting

There is no peace amid the moonlight and the pines;
Deep in the windless gloom the lamplike thought of you
Abides; and ah, what burning memories pursue
My heart among the pallid marbles! . . . Night assigns

Your silver face for wardress of the doors of sleep;
Beyond the wilder bourns of dreamland flown, your eyes
Are amber planets on the ultimate lost skies;
Moonlike and dim, you wander ever in the deep

Which is the nethermost unknowable abyss
Of my own soul, and in its night your spirit lives. . . .
Shall I not find the very draught that Lethe gives
Salt with your tears, and sweet with savor of your kiss?

Image

Calm as a long-forgotten marble god who smiles,
Colossal, in the grim serenity of stone,
Upon the broken pillars lying all alone
Athwart the horizon's infinite and yellow miles;

Whom neither desert darkness nor the desert noon,
Nor dawns that render terrible the bare dead land;

Nor winds that wrap his mighty form in palls of sand,
Nor the Medusa of the dumb and stony moon,

Shall evermore dismay, nor lion, nor the lynx
With silken-sheathèd claws and eyes of golden glede;
Nor any griffin, from the gates of treasure freed
To roam the gulfs, nor any wild and wandering sphinx:—

Even thus, amid the waste of all fair things that were,
Of high marmoreal dreams immense and overthrown,
I wait forever, and about my face is blown
The sand of crumbling cenotaph and sepulcher.

In November

With autumn and the flaring leaves our love must end—
Ere flauntful spring shall mock thy tears and my despair
With blossoms red or pale, some April bride may wear:
Now, while the weary, grey, forgetful heavens bend

Above the grief and languor of the dying lands,
In one last kiss shall meet and mingle and expire
The muted, last, remembering sighs of our desire;
And on my face the flower-like burden of thy hands

Shall rest a little, and be taken tenderly,
And, ah, how lightly hence! And in thy golden eyes,
Thy love, and all the ashen glory of the skies,
Shall mingle, and as in a mirror lie for me.

Memorial

Thy mouth, whereof the worm was amorous,
Thy brows, whereon some waning moon had power,
Thy breasts, corruptible as any flower,
And all thy troubled beauty tremulous—

These, these, my careful love hath laid away,
And in the tomb its marble dreams have made,
Thou sleepest, by no dawn or noon betrayed
To the cold light of time's corrosive day.

Yes, till my brain and all the dreams thereof,
And mournful memories, are bitter mould,
Thou liest, lovelier with death and love,

Than any queen ensepulchered of old,
Whose balmy cerements, with a soft perfume,
Make sweet for aye the mausolean gloom.

A Precept

With words of ivory,
Of bronze, of ebony,
Of alabaster, marble, steel and gold,
The beauty of the visible is told.

How, how with these express
The unseen Loveliness—
Splendor and light and harmony and sound
The heart has felt, the sense has never found?

No shining words of stone—
Shadow and cloud alone—
These shall the poet seek eternally,
Whose lines would carve the mask of Mystery.

Requiescat in Pace

M.L.M.

White iris on thy bier,
With the white rose, we strew,
And lotus pale or blue
As moonlight on the orient mountain-snows.

Slumber, as they that sleep
In the slow sands unknown,
Or under seas that zone
With lulling foam the sealed, extremer lands.

Slumber, with songless birds
That sang, and sang to death,
Giving their gladder breath
To lonely winds in one melodious pang.

Sleep, with the golden queens
Of planets long forgot,
Whose fire-soft lips are not
Recalled by any sorcery of song.

Sleep, with the flowers that were,
And any leaf that fell
On field or flowerless dell
In autumns lost of memory and grief.

Pass, with the music flown
From ivory lyre, and lute
Of mellow string left mute
In cities desolate ere the dream of Tyre.

Pass, with the clouds that sank
In sunset turned to grey
On some Edenic day
For which the exiled years have ever yearned.

White iris on thy bier,
With the white rose, we strew,
And lotus pale or blue
As moonlight on the orient mountain-snows.

In Saturn

Upon the seas of Saturn I have sailed
To isles of high primeval amarant,
Where the flame-tongued, sonorous flowers enchant
The hanging surf to silence; all engrailed

With ruby-colored pearls, the golden shore
Allured me; but as one whom spells restrain,
For blind horizons of the sombre main
And harbors never known, my singing prore

I set forthrightly. Formed of fire and brass,
And arched with moons, immenser heavens deep
Were opened—till above the darkling foam,

With dome on cloudless adamantine dome,
Black peaks no peering seraph deems to pass
Rose up from realms ineffable as sleep!

Winter Moonlight

The silence of the silver night
Lies visibly upon the pines;
In marble flame the moon declines
Where spectral mountains dream in light.

And pale as with eternal sleep
The enchanted valleys, far and strange,
Extend for ever without change
Beneath the veiling splendors deep.

Carven of steel or fretted stone,
One stark and leafless autumn tree
With shadows made of ebony
Leans on the moon-ward field alone.

Inferno

Grey hells, or hells aglow with hot and scarlet flowers;
White hells of light and clamor; hells the abomination
Of breathless, deep, sepulchral desolation
Oppresses ever—I have known them all, through hours
Tedious as dead eternity; where timeless powers,
Leagued in malign, omnipotent persuasion—
Wearing the guise of love, despair and aspiration,
Forever drove through ashen fields and burning bowers

My soul that found no sanctuary. . . . For Lucifer,
And all the weary, proud, imperious, baffled ones
Made in his image, hell is anywhere: the ice
Of hyperboreal deserts, or the blowing spice
In winds from off Sumatra, for each wanderer
Preserves the jealous flame of sad, infernal suns.

The Whisper of the Worm

How long, O soul, hast parleyed with the worm—
Hearing how long the whisper subtle-sweet
From out the dust thy Sisyphean feet
Must darkly vex and travel for a term?

"Lie down with me: supreme and sole release
I proffer, from the weariness of things,
From ways where with no serpent-staff nor wings
Thou pantest still; I am the way of peace.

"Lie down with me, lie down, and thou shalt know
The secret known to slave and Pharaoh,
And win the final wisdom of the dead:

"Like couches amaranthine-piled and deep
Where love may lie, by pleasure laid asleep,
I make the mould or marble of thy bed."

The Chimera

O, who will slay the last chimera, Time?
Though Love and Death have many a cunning dart—
In spite of these, and close-wrought webs of Art,
And slumber, with a slow, Lethean lime—

Still, still he lives; and though thy feet attain
The lunar peaks of ice and crystal, he,
Some night of agonized eternity
With brazen teeth shall gnaw thy fettered brain.

Gorged with the dust of thrones and fanes destroyed—
With lidless eyes like moons of adamant,
And vaulted mouth emportalling the void,

He crouches like a passive sphinx before
Some temple-gate, or grinning, moves to grant
Thine entrance at the monarch's golden door.

Autumn Orchards

Templed beneath unmoving skies,
      From saffron unto red aspire
      The trees with unconsuming fire
Of Autumn's smokeless sacrifice.

While zephyrs tell her sacred name,
      I find a little time to kneel,
      Ere lightless Winter's silent heel
Stamp out the smouldering altar-flame.

Disillusionment

I used to dream, long, long ago,
That the clouds were marvelous white elephants
Journeying in droves to a far-off sacred city
That always made the sunset with the reflection of its altar-fires.

But now I am grown old and wise
And disillusioned,

And I know that the clouds are toy-animals for children,
And are made of cotton-batting,
Or at best are woven from a sort of mercerized wool,
And are always cut out
With patterns of tissue-paper.

Ode to Peace

Goddess, arise!
I invoke thee,
Thou Aphrodite of dammed-up gutters,
O Venus of sewers
Clogged by an accumulation of excrement,
Or of wells
Where someone has dumped a wagon-load of tin cans
And empty bottles;
And within whose waters
Dogs a month deceased,
And slowly decomposing cats,
Lie side by side in amicable corruption.
Arise, and languidly
As a prostitute disrobing for a cheap lover,
Remove thy chemise,
And lightly tossing it heavenward,
Net in its meshes the unnumbered dimes and nickels of the stars,
Together with the moon's moidore;
And take them all to settle up the booze-bills of thy devotees,
And to start a new account
At the corner saloon.

Antepast

The thought of death to me
Is like a well in some oasis dim—
Cool-gleaming, hushed, and hidden gratefully
Among the palms asleep
At silver evening on the desert's rim.

Or as a couch of stone,
Whereon, by moonlight, in a marble room,
Some fevered king reposes all alone—
So is the hope of sleep,
The inalienable surety of the tomb.

Ashes of Sunset

Who fares to find the sunset ere it fly,
Turning to light and fire the further west,
Shall have the veils of twilight for his quest,
And all the falling of an ashen sky.

On lands he shall not know, the splendor lies—
A pharos on some alienated shore,
In foam and purple lost forevermore,
Where dreams are kindled in remoter eyes.

At Sunrise

The moon declines in lonely gold
Among the stars of ashen-grey—
Veiling the pallors of decay
With clouds and glories, fold on fold.

Now, in a crystal interlude,
Stillness and twilight briefly rest,
Ere sudden gules illume the crest
Of peaks where solemn purples brood;

And from the low Favonian bourn
A sweet wind blows so lightly by
It seems the futile silver sigh
Breathed by the lingering moon forlorn.

Crepuscule

The sunset-gonfalons are furled
On plains of evening, broad and pale,
And woven athwart the waning world
The air is like a silver veil.

Into the thin and trembling gloom,
That holds a hueless warp of light,
The murmuring wind on a slow loom
Weaves the rich purples of the night.

The Melancholy Pool

Marked by that priesthood of the Night's misrule,
The shadow-cowled, imprecatory trees—

Cypress that guarded woodland secrecies
And graves that waited for delaying ghoul,
Nathless I neared the melancholy pool,
Chief care of all, but closelier sentinelled
By those whose roots were deepest in dead eld.
Where the thwart-woven boughs were wet and cool
As with a mist of poison, I drew near
To mark the tired stars peer dimly down
Through riven branches from the height of space,
And shudder in those waters with quick fear,
Where in black deeps the pale moon seemed to drown—
A haggard girl, with dead, despairing face.

Mirage

Deem ye the veiling vision will abide—
The marvel, and the glamor, and the dream
Which lies in light upon the barren world? . . .

The wings of Phoenix towering to the sun,
Nor opals, nor the morning foam, may hold
The hueful light that as from faery moons
Is mirrored on the sand; where many a time,
From fields that hem with golden asphodel
A river like a dragon coiled in light,
Rise to the noon the hovering minarets
And soaring walls of cities Ilion-like,
Till the dim winds are hung with palaces
Of orient madreperl.

For ever lost—
Like sunset on a land of old romance—
The splendor fails, and leaves the traveller
In bournless deserts flaunting to the day.

Mirrors

Mirrors of steel or silver, gold or glass antique!
Whether in melancholy marble palaces
In some long trance you drew the dreamy loveliness
Of Roman queens, or queens barbarical, or Greek:
Or, further than the bright and sun-pursuing beak
Of argosy might fare, beheld the empresses

Of lost Lemuria; or behind the lattices
Alhambran, have returned forbidden smiles oblique

Of wan mysterious women—mirrors, mirrors old,
Mirrors immutable, impassible as fate,
Your bosoms held the perished beauty of the past
Nearer than straining love might ever hope to hold;
And fleeing faces, lips too phantom-frail to last,
Found in your magic depth a life re-duplicate.

The Motes

I saw a universe today:
Through a disclosing bar of light
The motes were whirled in gleaming flight
That briefly dawned and sank away.

Each had its swift and tiny noon;
In orbit-streams I marked them flit,
Successively revealed and lit.
The sunlight paled and shifted soon.

Recompense

Ah, more to me than many days and many dreams,
And more than every hope, or any memory,
This moment, when thy lips are laid immortally
On mine, and death and time are shadows of old dreams.

Now all the crownless, ruined years have recompense:
In one supreme, undying hour of light and fire,
The many moons and suns have found their one desire—
When in the hour of love, all life has recompense.

Satiety

A weary Juan, smothered in boudoirs,
To sea-salt moors and air unwalled would turn,
And clasp, beneath the paneless moon or stars,
The naked farm-girl on a bed of fern.

Triple Aspect

Lo, for Earth's manifest monotony
Of ordered aspect unto sun and star,
And single moon, I turn to years afar
And ampler worlds ensphered in memory.

There, to the zoned and iris-varying light
Of three swift suns in heavens of vaster range,
Transcendent beauty knows a trinal change,
And dawn and eve are in the place of night.

There, long ago, in mornings ocean-green,
I saw vast deserts verdant with the sky,
Or under yellow noons wide waters lie
Like molten bronze that boiled with fires unseen.

Strange flowers that bloom but to an azure sun
I saw; and all complexities of light
That work fantastic magic on the sight
Wrought unimagined marvels one by one.

There, swifter shadows suffer gorgeous dooms—
Lost in an orange noon, an azure morn;
At twofold eve large, winged lights are born,
Towering to meet the dawn, or briefest glooms

Of chrysoberyl filled with alien stars
Draw from an emerald east to skies of gold.
Toward jasper waters leaning to behold,
Vague moons are lost amid great nenuphars.

Twilight on the Snow

Before the hill's high altar bowed,
The trees are Druids, weird and white,
Facing the vision of the light
With ancient lips to silence vowed.

No certain sound the woods aver,
Nor motion save of formless wings—
Filled with phantasmal flutterings,
With thronging gloom and shadow-stir.

Unseen, unheard, amid the dell
Lie all the winds that mantic trees
Have lulled with crystal warlockries
And bound about with Merlin-spell.

Fantasie

Enormous from the mountains' night,
  From silence, and the night of snow,
  The moon arises, lone and slow,
In mists of cold and crimson light.

Her monstrous orb incarnadine,
  A roc's-egg seems, that griffins bear
  Along the gulf of silver air,
And darkling valleys deep with pine.

Song of Sappho's Arabian Daughter

Dreaming, I said, "When she is come,
This desert garden that is me
For her shall offer mellowly
Its myrrh and its olibanum—
When she is come.

"The flowers of the moon for her
With blossoms of the sun shall bloom,
The fading roses breathe perfume,
The lightly fallen petals stir,
And sigh to her.

"Her presence, like a living wind
Each little leaf makes visible,
Shall enter there, or like the spell
(Upon the lulling leaves divined)
Of silent wind."

Alas! for she has come and gone,
And in the garden, green for her,
The flowers fall, the flowers stir
Only to winds of night and dawn:
For she has gone.

Forgetfulness

My life is less than any broken glass. . . .
My long and weary love, thy lips unwon—
All, all is turned to mere oblivion
With the grey flowers and the fallen grass
Of yesteryear. And on the winds that pass
Thy music and thy memory are one;
For thy wan face, desired above the sun,
Only some languid echo saith Alas. . . .

Love is no more, immemorially flown
As any leaf or petal. . . . But to me
The very fields are still, and strange, and lone;
The forest and the garden fail for breath,
Where the dumb heavens hold implacably
An autumn like the marble sleep of death.

Transcendence

To look on love with disenamored eyes;
To see with gaze relentless, rendered clear
Of hope or hatred, of desire and fear,
The insuperable nullity that lies
Behind the veils of various disguise
Which life or death may haply weave; to hear
Forevermore in flute and harp the mere
And all-resolving silence; recognize
The gules of autumn in the greening leaf,
And in the poppy-pod the poppy-flower:—
This is to be the lord of love and grief,
O'er time's illusion and thyself supreme,
As, half-aroused in some nocturnal hour,
The dreamer knows and dominates his dream.

To the Beloved

Green suns, and suns of garnet I have known—
Turning, with suns that mock the sapphire-gem,
The constellated moons that mirror them
To ever-changing opals. On the flown
Horizons I have followed, all alone,
To meadows of mirage the deserts hem,

And sought to break the ghostly, golden stem
Of roses of illusion, briefly blown
By evanescent wells. One after one
The outward ways of wonder I have trod
Through alien lives ineffable. But none
Hath held the troublous marvel and surprise
That gleams and trembles in thy slightest nod,
Or sleeps between thine eyelids and thine eyes.

Laus Mortis

The imperishable phantoms, Love and Fame,
Nor Beauty, burning on the mist and mire
A fugitive uncapturable fire,
Nor God, that is a darkness and a name—
Not these, not these my choric dreams acclaim,
But Death, the last and ultimate desire,
Great Death I praise with litany and lyre
And sombre prayer implacably the same.

O, incommunicable hope that lies
Deep in despair, as tapers that illume
Some fearful fane's arcanic, sacred gloom!
O, solace of all weary hearts and wise!—
The dream which Satan hath for anodyne,
Which is to God a sweet and secret wine.

The Traveller

O traveller, declare thy quest!
Thy hair is white with alien days
Thy dusty face and feet attest
The devious length of alien ways
O traveller declare thy quest!

"It is to seek mine ancient home—
My home that lies I know not where—
Restless forever I must roam
And find the horizons of despair
But nevermore my home."

Ombos

With hecatonstylon and hundred-gated wall,
With domes Titanical of copper heaped upon
Some wide horizon wan, where fiery heavens fall;

With climbing pyramid on pyramid exalt
In mythical basalt, within whose tomb is hid
Some bestial horror bid to ward the vault.

With fanes of monstrous form, in sombre granite hewn,
With towers to stab the moon, with pinnacles that storm
Like steely swords enorm the molten sun at noon.

The Absence of the Muse

O Muse, where loiterest thou? In any land
Of Saturn, lit with moons and nenuphars?
Or in what high metropolis of Mars—
Hearing the gongs of dire, occult command,
And bugles blown from strand to unknown strand
Of continents embattled in old wars
That primal kings began? Or on the bars
Of ebbing seas in Venus, from the sand
Of shattered nacre with a thousand hues,
Dost pluck the blossoms of the purple wrack
And roses of blue coral for thy hair?
Or, flown beyond the roaring Zodiac,
Translatest thou the tale of earthly news
And earthly songs to singers of Altair?

Quest

All beneath a wintering sky,
Follow the wastrel butterfly;
With vermilion leaf or bronze—
Tatters of gorgeous gonfalons—
With the winds that always hold
Echo of clarions lost and old—
We must hasten, hasten on
Toward the azure world withdrawn,
We must wander, wander so
Where the ruining roses go;
Where the poplar's pallid leaves

Drift among the gathered sheaves
In that harvest none shall glean;
Where the twisted willows lean
In their strange, tormented woe,
Seeing, on the streamlet's flow,
Half their fragile leaves depart;
Where the secret pines at heart,
High, funereal, vespertine,
Guard eternal sorrows green:—
We shall follow, we shall find
Haply, ere the light is blind,
The moulded place where Beauty lay,
Moon-beheld until the day,
In the woven windlestrae;
Or the pool of tourmaline,
Rimmed with golden reeds, that was
In the dawn a tiring-glass
For her undelaying mien.

Ever wander, wander so,
Where the ruining roses go;
All beneath a wintering sky,
Follow the wastrel butterfly.

Symbols

No more of gold and marble, nor of snow
And sunlight and vermilion, would I make
My vision and my symbols, nor would take
The auroral flame of some prismatic floe.
Nor iris of the frail and lunar bow,
Flung on the shafted waterfalls that wake
The night's blue slumber in a shadowy lake.
To body forth my fantasies, and show
Communicable mystery, I would find,
In adamantine darkness of the earth,
Metals untouched of any sun; and bring
Black azures of the nether sea to birth—
Or fetch the secret, splendid leaves, and blind
Blue lilies of an Atlantean spring.

Heliogabalus

I

He, the supreme idealist of Sin,
Through scarlet days a white perfection sought—
To make of lyric deed and lyric thought
One music of perverse accord, wherein
The songless blatancy and banal din
Of all the world should perish: he had wrought
From Vice a pure, Pentelic Venus, fraught
With lines of light and terror, that should win
The plaudits of the stars. . . . But prevalent
For him, above the achievable desire,
And Life perfectible by Sin and Art,
Such lusts as leave the Titans impotent
Allured, and Life and Sin, in worlds apart,
Were fair with suns of quintessential fire.

II

For him the mystery whose name is Love
Took many veils and vestures, haunting him
Through subtle, chill, uncertain loin and limb
Of lesbians pale as Aphrodite's dove;
Or in the doubtful thighs and bosom of
Hermaphroditus, fugitive and dim;
Or his own face, on autumn pools aswim
Through windless shadows of a golden grove.

The vestal moon, the violating sun,
For him were made Love's metamorphoses;
Till, flown from these, as from the forms of old,
The god was gone in worlds beyond access,
With flame-ensculptured bosom found of none,
And eyes too bright with inenarrable gold.

The Hope of the Infinite

My hope is in the unharvestable deep
That shows with eve the treasure of the stars
To mournful kings behind their palace-bars,
And wanderers outworn, and boys who weep
A shattered bauble—or above the sleep

Of headsmen, and of men condemned to die,
Pours out the moon's white mercy from on high
Or hides with clement gloom the hours that creep
Like death-worms to the grave. . . . And I have ta'en,
From storming seas by sunset glorified,
Or from the dawn of ashen wastes and wide,
Some light re-gathered from the lamps that wane,
And promise of a translunary Spain
Where loves forgone and forfeit dreams abide.

Flamingoes

On skies of tropic evening, broad and beryl-green,
Above a tranquil sea of molten malachite,
With flare of scarlet wings, in long and level flight,
The soundless, fleet flamingoes pass to isles unseen.

They pass and disappear, where darkening palms indent
The horizon, underneath some high and tawny star—
Lost in the sunset gulfs of glowing cinnabar
Where sinks the painted moon with prows of orpiment.

Rosa Mystica

The secret rose we vainly dream to find
Was blown in grey Atlantis long ago,
Or in old summers of the realms of snow
Its attar lulled the pole-arisen wind;
Or once its broad and breathless petals pined
In gardens of Persepolis, aglow
With fiery-sworded sunlight and the slow
Red waves of sand, invincible and blind.

On orient isles or isles hesperian,
Through mystic days ere mortal time began,
It flowered above the ever-flowering foam;
Or, legendless, in lands of yesteryear,
It flamed among the violets—near, how near
To unenchanted fields and hills of home!

For a Wine-Jar

When cup by cup the wine-bearer shall pour
For Omar and his guest my golden store,
Till only slow, black, sullen dregs remain—
Make haste, and fill me to the brim once more.

To Omar Khayyam

Omar, within thy scented garden-close,
When passed with eventide
The starward incense of the waning rose—
Too precious to abide
After the glad and golden death of spring—
Omar, thou heardest then,
Above the world of men,
The mournful rumor of an iron wing,
The sough and sigh of desolating years,
Whereof the wind is as the winds that blow
Out of a lonesome land of night and snow
Where timeless winter weeps with frozen tears;
And in thy bodeful ears
The brief and tiny lisp
Of petals curled and crisp,
Fallen at eve in Persia's mellow clime,
Was mingled with the mighty sound of time.

Omar, thou knewest well
How the fair days are sorrowful and strange
With time's inexorable mystery
And terror ineluctable of change:
Upon thine eyes the bleak and bitter spell
Of vision, thou didst see,
As in a magic glass,
The moulded mists and painted shadows pass—
The ghostly pomps we name reality;
And, lo, the level field,
With broken fane and throne
And dust of old, unfabled cities sown,
In unremembering years was made to yield,

From out the shards of Power,
The pillars frail and small
That lift for capital
The blood-like bubble of the poppy-flower;
And crowns were crumbled for the airy gold
The crocus and the daffodil should hold
As inalienable dower.
Before thy gaze the sad unvaried green
The cypresses like robes funereal wear,
Was woven on the gradual looms of air
From threadbare silk and tattered sendaline
That clothed some ancient queen;
And from the spoilt vermilion of her mouth
The myrtles rose, and from her ruined hair
And eyes that held the summer's ardent drouth
In blown, disrooted bowers;
And amber limbs and breast
Through ancient nights by sleepless love oppressed,
Or by the iron flight of loveless hours.

Knowing the weary wisdom of the years,
The empty truth of tears;
The suns of June that with some great excess
Of ardor slay the unabiding rose;
And grey-haired winter, wan and fervorless,
For whom no flower grows;
Seeing the paradisal bloom that pales
On orient snows untrod
In magic morns that grant,
Across a land of common green and grey,
The disenchanted day;
Knowing the gulf-deep veils
And walls of adamant
That ward the darkling verities of God—
Knowing these things, ah, surely thou wert wise
To kiss on ardent breast and avid mouth
Some girl whose eyes
Were golden with the sun-belovèd south—
To pluck the rose and drain the rose-red wine
In gardens half-divine;
Before the broken cup
Be filled and covered up
In dusty seas of everlasting drouth.

Beyond the Great Wall

Beyond the far Cathayan wall,
A thousand leagues athwart the sky,
The scarlet stars and mornings die,
The gilded moons and sunsets fall.

Across the sulphur-colored sands
With bales of silk the camels fare,
Harnessed with vermeil and with vair,
Into the blue and burning lands.

And ah, the song the drivers sing
To while the desert leagues away—
A song they sang in old Cathay
Ere youth had left the eldest king,

Ere love and beauty both grew old
And wonder and romance were flown
On irised wings to worlds unknown,
To stars of undiscovered gold.

And I their alien words would know,
And follow past the lonely wall
Where gilded moons and sunsets fall,
As in a song of long ago.

Ennui

My days are as a garden, where the dust
Of Dead Sea fruit in summer sows the ground,
And bows vermilion lilies heavy-crowned,
Or fills the myriad mouths of sleepy lust
The poppies raise . . . And emptied secretly,
Dull ashes from the urns of all the dead
Have sealed the fountain and the fountain-head,
And pall-wise draped the pine and myrtle-tree . . .

I am becalmed on some lethean main,
Long-implicate in airs of clinging grey,
In mists of muffled light and moons undone,—
Full torpidly my soul remembers pain,
And love itself as islands far away,
Refulgent with the incredible red sun.

In Lemuria

Rememberest thou? Enormous gongs of stone
Were stricken, and the storming trumpeteers
Acclaimed my deed to answering tides of spears,
And spoke the names of monsters overthrown—
Griffins whose angry gold, and fervid store
Of sapphires wrenched from mountain-plungèd mines—
Carnelians, opals, agates, almandines,
I brought to thee some scarlet eve of yore.

In the wide fane that shrined thee Venus-wise,
The fallen clamors died. . . . I heard the tune
Of tiny bells of pearl and melanite,
Hung at thy knees, and arms of dreamt delight;
And placed my wealth before thy fabled eyes,
Pallid and pure as jaspers from the moon.

Solution

The ghostly fire that walks the fen,
Tonight thine only light shall be;
On lethal ways thy soul shall pass,
And prove the stealthy, coiled morass
With mocking mists for company.

On roads thou goest not again,
To shores where thou hast never gone,
Fare onward, though the shuddering queach
And serpent-rippled waters reach
Like seepage-pools of Acheron

Beside thee; and the twisted reeds,
Close-raddled as a witch's net,
Enwind thy knees, and cling and clutch
Like wreathing adders; though the touch
Of the blind air be dank and wet

As from a wounded Thing that bleeds
In cloud and darkness overhead—
Fare onward, where thy dreams of yore
In splendor drape the fetid shore
And pestilential waters dead.

And though the toads' irrison rise
Like grinding of Satanic racks,
And spectral willows, gaunt and grey,
Gibber along thy shrouded way,
Where vipers lie with livid backs

And watch thee with their sulphurous eyes—
Fare onward, till thy feet shall slip
Deep in the sudden pool ordained,
And all the noisome draught be drained
That turns to Lethe on the lip.

The Ghoul and the Seraph

Scene: A cemetery by moonlight. The Ghoul emerges from the shade of a cypress and sings.

THE SONG

The Pestilence is on the wing!
Behold! the sweet and crimson foam
Upon the lips of churl and king!
No worm but hath a feastful home:
The Pestilence is on the wing!

Even now his kiss incarnadines
The brows of maiden, queen and whore;
The nun to him her cheek resigns;
Wan lips were never kissed before,
His ancient kiss incarnadines.

Good cheer to thee, white worm of death!
The priest within the brothel dies,
The bawd hath sickened from his breath!
In grave half-dug the digger lies:
Good cheer to thee, white worm of death!

The Seraph appears from among the trees, half walking, half flying, with wings whose iris the moonlight has rendered faint, and pauses at sight of the Ghoul.

THE SERAPH

What gardener in crudded fields of hell,
Or scullion of the Devil's house, art thou—
To whom the filth of Malebolge clings,

And reek of horrid refuse? Thou art gnurled
And black as any Kobold from the mines
Where demons delve for orichalch and steel
To forge the infernal racks! Upon thy face,
Detestable and evil as might haunt
The last delirium of a dying hag,
Or necromancer's madness, fall thy locks
Like sodden reeds that trail in Acheron
From shores of night and horror; and thy hands,
Like roots of cypresses uptorn in storm
That still retain their grisly provender,
Make the glad wine and manna of the skies
Turn to a qualmish sickness in my veins.

THE GHOUL

And who art thou?—some white-faced fool of God,
With wings that emulate the giddy bird,
And bloodless mouth for ever filled with psalms
In lieu of honest victuals! . . . Askest thou
My name? I am the ghoul Necromalor:
In new-made graves I delve for sustenance,
As man within his turnip-fields; I take
For table the uprooted slab, that bears
The words, "In Pace;" black and curdled blood
Of cadávers is all my cupless wine—
Slow-drunken, as the dainty vampire drinks
From pulses oped in never-ending sleep.

THE SERAPH

O, foulness born as of the ninefold curse
Of dragon-mouthed Apollyon, plumed with darts
And armed with horns of incandescent bronze!
O, dark as Satan's nightmare, or the fruit
Of Belial's rape on hell's black hippogriff!
What knowest *thou* of Paradise, where grow
The gardens of the manna-laden myrrh,
And lotos never known to Ulysses,
Whose fruit provides our long and sateless banquet?
Where boundless fields, unfurrowed and unsown,
Supply for God's own appanage their foison
Of amber-hearted grain, and sesame
Sweeter than nard the Persian air compounds

With frankincense from isles of India!
Where flame-leaved forests infinitely teem
With palms of tremulous opal, from whose tops
Ambrosial honies fall forevermore
In rains of nacred light! Where rise and rise,
Terrace on hyacinthine terrace, hills
Hung with the grapes that drip cerulean wine,
One draught whereof dissolves eternity
In bliss oblivious and supernal dream!

THE GHOUL

To all the meat their bellies most commend,
To all the according wine. For me, I wot,
The cates whereof thou braggest were as wind
In halls where men had feasted yesterday,
Or furbished bones the full hyena leaves.
Tiger and pig have their apportioned glut,
Nor lacks the shark his provender; the bird
Is nourished with the worm of charnels; man,
Or the grey wolf, will slay and eat the bird,
Till wolf and man be carrion for the worm.
What wouldst thou? As the elfin lily does,
Or as the Paphian myrtle, pale with love,
I draw me from the unreluctant dead
The rightful meat my belly's law demands.
Eaters of death are all: Life shall not live,
Save that its food be death: no atomy
In any star, nor heaven's remotest moon
But hath a billion billion times been made
The food of insatiable life, and food
Of death insatiate: for all is change—
Change, that hath wrought the chancre and the rose,
And wrought the star, and wrought the sapphire-stone,
And lit great altars, and the eyes of lions—
Change, that hath made the very gods from slime
Drawn from the pits of Python, and will fling
Gods and their builded heavens back again
To slime. The fruits of archangelic light
Thou braggest of, and grapes of azure wine,
Have been the dung of dragons and the blood
Of toads in Phlegethon: each particle
That is their splendor, clomb in separate ways

Through suns and worlds and cycles infinite—
Through burning brume of systems unbegun,
And manes of long-haired comets, that have lashed
The night of space to fury and to fire;
And in the core of cold and lightless stars,
And in immalleable metals deep,
Each atomy hath slept, or known the slime
Of cyclopean oceans turned to air
Before the suns of Ophiuchus rose;
And they have known the interstellar night,
And they have lain at root of sightless flowers
In worlds without a sun, or at the heart
Of monstrous-eyed and panting flowers of flesh,
Or eon-blooming amaranths of stone;
And they have ministered within the brains
Of sages and magicians, and have served
To swell the pulse of kings and conquerors,
And have been privy to the hearts of queens.

The Ghoul turns his back on the Seraph, and moves away, singing.

THE SONG

O condor, keep thy mountain-ways
Above the long Andean lands;
Gier-eagle, guard the eastern sands
Where the forsaken camel strays:
Beetle and worm and I will ward
The lardered graves of lout and lord.

Oh, warm and bright the blood that lies
Upon the wounded lion's trail!
Hyena, laugh, and jackal, wail,
And ring him round, who turns and dies!
Beetle and worm and I will ward
The lardered graves of lout and lord.

Arms of a wanton girl are good,
Or hands of harp-player and knight:
Breasts of the nun be sweet and white,
Sweet is the festive friar's blood.
Beetle and worm and I will ward
The lardered graves of lout and lord.

Tempus

O lethal Acheron gliding ever
In stealth between her mouth and mine,
Between our avid limbs, however
Closely these may cleave and twine,

O stanchless time, when shall we stay
Thy flowing with a straiter kiss,
With tighter hands retain the day
That trickles down the old abyss?

The Dials

Thy gnomons, O Time, are many and multiform:
Ever and ever, on the path of the pursuing sun,
They trace in elusive shadow the irresolvable phantom of night.

Silhouette

Fronting the sunset's molten sea
    The pines rear sombre, motionless,
As if to watch those splendid tides
    Ebb westward past their ken or guess.

Sharply they cleave the breathless air
    Each tree a poignant silhouette.
Black outposts of the night they seem
    Athwart the dying daylight set.

To Whom It May Concern

Your soul is a dead chicken lying on a city dump,
Inert and limp and sprawling,
Amid a rotten chaos of inassortable remnants,
Of rain-soaked whisky-cartons and soiled brassieres and worn-out tires
        and Sunday suits full of defunct moths
And maybe a blue box or two
Labelled Kotex.

Pegasus will shun your proximity,
All the golden wyverns will avoid you,
Veering to other skies and more savory systems,
And hippogriffs will never come to nuzzle you

With purple-spotted noses of nacarat and cyanine:
Even the ghouls will sniff and pass you by. . . .
But rats will come. . . .

Speculation

All the world is green and sad . . .
If I were a little frog,
Sitting on a lily-pad
In a cool and splashy bog,
Would the world be green and glad?

Ode to Aphrodite

Empress who hast the fertile stars in fee,
And toiling worlds to serve thy dread desire!
Who guard'st thine empery,
In deep on sullen deep,
With watchful suns of infatiguéd fire!
Not with the Lesbian lyre
I sing, and not of easeful love and sleep,—
Of arms and breasts that tire,
In brief, ecstatic throes,
On bed of shattered rose;
And not as they that worshipped thee of old,
I call on thine incomparable name,
And with no blasphemies of praise or blame:
Before thy hidden throne,
And thy veiled face, impassible, I hold
This iron harp of stridors manifold,—
And telling thy termless fame,
In strophes durable as graven stone,
And loud as stricken gold!

The Oracle

Life and time are changeful mist
    Of a never-changing sea;
    Death is also Vanity,
Said the Master Ironist.

A Memory

Remember'st thou that day, my sweet,
A thousand years agone,
When from the desert's glare and heat
I came at set of sun,
To where with towers agleam,
Bagdad lay by the Tigris stream?

And I had ridden long and far
Over the sands to thee
Thy face as a guiding star,
Beckoning ever to me.
The burning miles were naught
Beloved, with thee in my thought.

For I was a Bedouin bold and swart
A robber and outlaw—
Chief of a band, and thou, my heart,
Child of a proud pasha.

Unto the garden at eve I went,
Where weary was the air
With rose and jasmine subtly blent,
And found thee waiting there.

Lo! Like the moon thou seemed to me
Coming to light my dusk.
Aye, gloom and darkness fled from thee
With breath of myrrh and musk,
And lovelit eyes and face,
Thou camest to my warm embrace.

To a Northern Venus

I would not have you anywhere,
Save in some interspace of pines,
When the blue flame of day declines
On altars of the solemn air;

And all the woodland, warm with spice,
As from a hundred censers flown,
Hierophantic, weird, unknown,
Seems to await a sacrifice.

O, come and cast your veils aside!

No robe but does your beauty wrong:
This pilgrim Love, he hath not long
Between your foam-white breasts to bide.

Ah, paler for the shadows green
That gather to your subtler form,
And waver on your lifted arm,
Like riven veils obscurely seen;

And fairer with your ashen hair
Enkindled by the sudden ray
Which is the backward glance of day
From oubliettes of burning air—

Come, child of Friga, made for love,
And let my arms your girdle be,
And give your pallid loins to me,
And all the secret fires thereof.

In Alexandria

Your body was an altar of delight,
With almond petals strewn,
Whereat we worshipped in the shrine of night.

Pale as the vernal moon,
You gave our lips your languid bosom bare
And limbs that seemed to swoon.

Faintly, from drooping feet to trailing hair,
You trembled with our kisses
Numberless as the flowers fallen there.

Through Love's unknown abysses
Your lovers twain were wafted far with you,
While in strange triune blisses,

Deeper than death, we died and lived anew.

The Incubus of Time

Ill days and dolorous nights and years accurst—
The increase of evil, that is twin to life;
Weariness of re-animated strife,
And love, renewing with the selfsame thirst
The same delight—a drunken Tantalus;

And the thousand-chorded monotones of pain
Irresolubly played and played again
On broken souls and bodies ruinous.

I would the world and all its leaden woe,
Its ennui, like incumbent tombs of stone,
And time's each minute, as an iron clod,
Were bound about the monstrous throat of God,
And He were drawn in deathless overthrow
To some blind nadir of the voids unknown.

Amor Aeternalis

O Love, thou Judas of the martyred soul!
Thou pandar to the painted harlot, Life!
The rankest lies wherewith thy heart is rife
Too fulsomely illume thy lips' red scroll,
Whereon is writ the secret of our dole,
Of mortal woes immortalized by thee,
And wisdom, through thine olden perfidy,
Drawn back to life from some Lethean shoal.

Away! I know the weariness and fever—
Kisses compounded of the world's old dust
With fire that feeds the seventh hell for ever!
The grave shall keep a gentler couch than thine,
Though round my heart the roots of nettles twine,
Wreathed in the ancient attitude of lust.

The Hashish-Eater

1920

The Hashish-Eater; or, The Apocalypse of Evil

Bow down: I am the emperor of dreams;
I crown me with the million-colored sun
Of secret worlds incredible, and take
Their trailing skies for vestment when I soar,
Throned on the mounting zenith, and illume
The spaceward-flown horizon infinite.
Like rampant monsters roaring for their glut,
The fiery-crested oceans rise and rise,
By jealous moons maleficently urged
To follow me for ever; mountains horned
With peaks of sharpest adamant, and mawed
With sulphur-lit volcanoes lava-langued,
Usurp the skies with thunder, but in vain;
And continents of serpent-shapen trees,
With slimy trunks that lengthen league by league,
Pursue my flight through ages spurned to fire
By that supreme ascendance; sorcerers,
And evil kings, predominantly armed
With scrolls of fulvous dragon-skin whereon
Are worm-like runes of ever-twisting flame,
Would stay me; and the sirens of the stars,
With foam-like songs from silver fragrance wrought,
Would lure me to their crystal reefs; and moons
Where viper-eyed, senescent devils dwell,
With antic gnomes abominably wise,
Heave up their icy horns across my way.
But naught deters me from the goal ordained
By suns and eons and immortal wars,
And sung by moons and motes; the goal whose name
Is all the secret of forgotten glyphs
By sinful gods in torrid rubies writ
For ending of a brazen book; the goal
Whereat my soaring ecstasy may stand
In amplest heavens multiplied to hold
My hordes of thunder-vested avatars,
And Promethèan armies of my thought,
That brandish claspèd levins. There I call
My memories, intolerably clad

In light the peaks of paradise may wear,
And lead the Armageddon of my dreams
Whose instant shout of triumph is become
Immensity's own music: for their feet
Are founded on innumerable worlds,
Remote in alien epochs, and their arms
Upraised, are columns potent to exalt
With ease ineffable the countless thrones
Of all the gods that are or gods to be,
And bear the seats of Asmodai and Set
Above the seventh paradise.

Supreme
In culminant omniscience manifold,
And served by senses multitudinous,
Far-posted on the shifting walls of time,
With eyes that roam the star-unwinnowed fields
Of utter night and chaos, I convoke
The Babel of their visions, and attend
At once their myriad witness. I behold
In Ombos, where the fallen Titans dwell,
With mountain-builded walls, and gulfs for moat,
The secret cleft that cunning dwarves have dug
Beneath an alp-like buttress; and I list,
Too late, the clang of adamantine gongs
Dinned by their drowsy guardians, whose feet
Have felt the wasp-like sting of little knives
Embrued with slobber of the basilisk
Or the pale juice of wounded upas. In
Some red Antarean garden-world, I see
The sacred flower with lips of purple flesh,
And silver-lashed, vermilion-lidded eyes
Of torpid azure; whom his furtive priests
At moonless eve in terror seek to slay
With bubbling grails of sacrificial blood
That hide a hueless poison. And I read
Upon the tongue of a forgotten sphinx,
The annulling word a spiteful demon wrote
In gall of slain chimeras; and I know
What pentacles the lunar wizards use,
That once allured the gulf-returning roc,
With ten great wings of furlèd storm, to pause

Midmost an alabaster mount; and there,
With boulder-weighted webs of dragons' gut
Uplift by cranes a captive giant built,
They wound the monstrous, moonquake-throbbing bird,
And plucked from off his saber-taloned feet
Uranian sapphires fast in frozen blood,
And amethysts from Mars. I lean to read
With slant-lipped mages, in an evil star,
The monstrous archives of a war that ran
Through wasted eons, and the prophecy
Of wars renewed, which shall commemorate
Some enmity of wivern-headed kings
Even to the brink of time. I know the blooms
Of bluish fungus, freaked with mercury,
That bloat within the craters of the moon,
And in one still, selenic hour have shrunk
To pools of slime and fetor; and I know
What clammy blossoms, blanched and cavern-grown,
Are proffered to their gods in Uranus
By mole-eyed peoples; and the livid seed
Of some black fruit a king in Saturn ate,
Which, cast upon his tinkling palace-floor,
Took root between the burnished flags, and now
Hath mounted and become a hellish tree,
Whose lithe and hairy branches, lined with mouths,
Net like a hundred ropes his lurching throne,
And strain at starting pillars. I behold
The slowly-thronging corals that usurp
Some harbor of a million-masted sea,
And sun them on the league-long wharves of gold—
Bulks of enormous crimson, kraken-limbed
And kraken-headed, lifting up as crowns
The octiremes of perished emperors,
And galleys fraught with royal gems, that sailed
From a sea-fled haven.

Swifter and stranger grow
The visions: now a mighty city looms,
Hewn from a hill of purest cinnabar
To domes and turrets like a sunrise thronged
With tier on tier of captive moons, half-drowned
In shifting erubescence. But whose hands

Were sculptors of its doors, and columns wrought
To semblance of prodigious blooms of old,
No eremite hath lingered there to say,
And no man comes to learn: for long ago
A prophet came, warning its timid king
Against the plague of lichens that had crept
Across subverted empires, and the sand
Of wastes that cyclopean mountains ward;
Which, slow and ineluctable, would come
To take his fiery bastions and his fanes,
And quench his domes with greenish tetter. Now
I see a host of naked giants, armed
With horns of behemoth and unicorn,
Who wander, blinded by the clinging spells
Of hostile wizardry, and stagger on
To forests where the very leaves have eyes,
And ebonies like wrathful dragons roar
To teaks a-chuckle in the loathly gloom;
Where coiled lianas lean, with serried fangs,
From writhing palms with swollen boles that moan;
Where leeches of a scarlet moss have sucked
The eyes of some dead monster, and have crawled
To bask upon his azure-spotted spine;
Where hydra-throated blossoms hiss and sing,
Or yawn with mouths that drip a sluggish dew
Whose touch is death and slow corrosion. Then
I watch a war of pygmies, met by night,
With pitter of their drums of parrot's hide,
On plains with no horizon, where a god
Might lose his way for centuries; and there,
In wreathèd light and fulgors all convolved,
A rout of green, enormous moons ascend,
With rays that like a shivering venom run
On inch-long swords of lizard-fang.

Surveyed
From this my throne, as from a central sun,
The pageantries of worlds and cycles pass;
Forgotten splendors, dream by dream, unfold
Like tapestry, and vanish; violet suns,
Or suns of changeful iridescence, bring
Their rays about me like the colored lights

Imploring priests might lift to glorify
The face of some averted god; the songs
Of mystic poets in a purple world
Ascend to me in music that is made
From unconceivèd perfumes and the pulse
Of love ineffable; the lute-players
Whose lutes are strung with gold of the utmost moon,
Call forth delicious languors, never known
Save to their golden kings; the sorcerers
Of hooded stars inscrutable to God,
Surrender me their demon-wrested scrolls,
Inscribed with lore of monstrous alchemies
And awful transformations.

If I will,
I am at once the vision and the seer,
And mingle with my ever-streaming pomps,
And still abide their suzerain: I am
The neophyte who serves a nameless god,
Within whose fane the fanes of Hecatompylos
Were arks the Titan worshippers might bear,
Or flags to pave the threshold; or I am
The god himself, who calls the fleeing clouds
Into the nave where suns might congregate
And veils the darkling mountain of his face
With fold on solemn fold; for whom the priests
Amass their monthly hecatomb of gems—
Opals that are a camel-cumbering load,
And monstrous alabraundines, won from war
With realms of hostile serpents; which arise,
Combustible, in vapors many-hued
And myrrh-excelling perfumes. It is I,
The king, who holds with scepter-dropping hand
The helm of some great barge of orichalchum,
Sailing upon an amethystine sea
To isles of timeless summer: for the snows
Of hyperborean winter, and their winds,
Sleep in his jewel-builded capital,
Nor any charm of flame-wrought wizardry,
Nor conjured suns may rout them; so he flees,
With captive kings to urge his serried oars,
Hopeful of dales where amaranthine dawn

Hath never left the faintly sighing lote
And lisping moly. Firm of heart, I fare
Impanoplied with azure diamond,
As hero of a quest Achernar lights,
To deserts filled with ever-wandering flames
That feed upon the sullen marl, and soar
To wrap the slopes of mountains, and to leap
With tongues intolerably lengthening
That lick the blenchèd heavens. But there lives
(Secure as in a garden walled from wind)
A lonely flower by a placid well,
Midmost the flaring tumult of the flames,
That roar as roars a storm-possessèd sea,
Implacable for ever; and within
That simple grail the blossom lifts, there lies
One drop of an incomparable dew
Which heals the parchèd weariness of kings,
And cures the wound of wisdom. I am page
To an emperor who reigns ten thousand years,
And through his labyrinthine palace-rooms,
Through courts and colonnades and balconies
Wherein immensity itself is mazed,
I seek the golden gorget he hath lost,
On which, in sapphires fine as orris-seed,
Are writ the names of his conniving stars
And friendly planets. Roaming thus, I hear
Like demon tears incessant, through dark ages,
The drip of sullen clepsydrae; and once
In every lustrum, hear the brazen clocks
Innumerably clang with such a sound
As brazen hammers make, by devils dinned
On tombs of all the dead; and nevermore
I find the gorget, but at length I find
A sealèd room whose nameless prisoner
Moans with a nameless torture, and would turn
To hell's red rack as to a lilied couch
From that whereon they stretched him; and I find,
Prostrate upon a lotus-painted floor,
The loveliest of all belovèd slaves
My emperor hath, and from her pulseless side
A serpent rises, whiter than the root
Of some venefic bloom in darkness grown,

And gazes up with green-lit eyes that seem
Like drops of cold, congealing poison.

Hark!
What word was whispered in a tongue unknown,
In crypts of some impenetrable world?
Whose is the dark, dethroning secrecy
I cannot share, though I am king of suns,
And king therewith of strong eternity,
Whose gnomons with their swords of shadow guard
My gates, and slay the intruder? Silence loads
The wind of ether, and the worlds are still
To hear the word that flees mine audience.
In simultaneous ruin, all my dreams
Fall like a rack of fuming vapors raised
To semblance by a necromant, and leave
Spirit and sense unthinkably alone
Above a universe of shrouded stars
And suns that wander, cowled with sullen gloom,
Like witches to a Sabbath. . . . Fear is born
In crypts below the nadir, and hath crawled
Reaching the floor of space, and waits for wings
To lift it upward like a hellish worm
Fain for the flesh of cherubim. Red orbs
And eyes that gleam remotely as the stars,
But are not eyes of suns or galaxies,
Gather and throng to the base of darkness; a flame
Behind some black, abysmal curtain burns,
Implacable, and fanned to whitest wrath
By raisèd wings that flail the whiffled gloom,
And make a brief and broken wind that moans
As one who rides a throbbing rack. There is
A Thing that crouches, worlds and years remote,
Whose horns a demon sharpens, rasping forth
A note to shatter the donjon-keeps of time,
Or crack the sphere of crystal. All is dark
For ages, and my tolling heart suspends
Its clamor as within the clutch of death
Tightening with tense, hermetic rigors. Then,
In one enormous, million-flashing flame,
The stars unveil, the suns remove their cowls,
And beam to their responding planets; time

Is mine once more, and armies of its dreams
Rally to that insuperable throne
Firmed on the zenith.

Once again I seek
The meads of shining moly I had found
In some anterior vision, by a stream
No cloud hath ever tarnished; where the sun,
A gold Narcissus, loiters evermore
Above his golden image. But I find
A corpse the ebbing water will not keep,
With eyes like sapphires that have lain in hell
And felt the hissing coals; and all the flowers
About me turn to hooded serpents, swayed
By flutes of devils in lascivious dance
Meet for the nod of Satan, when he reigns
Above the raging Sabbath, and is wooed
By sarabands of witches. But I turn
To mountains guarding with their horns of snow
The source of that befoulèd rill, and seek
A pinnacle where none but eagles climb,
And they with failing pennons. But in vain
I flee, for on that pylon of the sky
Some curse hath turned the unprinted snow to flame—
Red fires that curl and cluster to my tread,
Trying the summit's narrow cirque. And now
I see a silver python far beneath—
Vast as a river that a fiend hath witched
And forced to flow reverted in its course
To fountains whence it issued. Rapidly
It winds from slope to crumbling slope, and fills
Ravines and chasmal gorges, till the crags
Totter with coil on coil incumbent. Soon
It hath entwined the pinnacle I keep,
And gapes with a fanged, unfathomable maw
Wherein great Typhon and Enceladus
Were orts of daily glut. But I am gone,
For at my call a hippogriff hath come,
And firm between his thunder-beating wings
I mount the sheer cerulean walls of noon
And see the earth, a spurnèd pebble, fall—
Lost in the fields of nether stars—and seek

A planet where the outwearied wings of time
Might pause and furl for respite, or the plumes
Of death be stayed, and loiter in reprieve
Above some deathless lily: for therein
Beauty hath found an avatar of flowers—
Blossoms that clothe it as a colored flame
From peak to peak, from pole to sullen pole,
And turn the skies to perfume. There I find
A lonely castle, calm, and unbeset
Save by the purple spears of amaranth,
And leafing iris tender-sworded. Walls
Of flushèd marble, wonderful with rose,
And domes like golden bubbles, and minarets
That take the clouds as coronal—these are mine,
For voiceless looms the peaceful barbican,
And the heavy-teethed portcullis hangs aloft
To grin a welcome. So I leave awhile
My hippogriff to crop the magic meads,
And pass into a court the lilies hold,
And tread them to a fragrance that pursues
To win the portico, whose columns, carved
Of lazuli and amber, mock the palms
Of bright Aidennic forests—capitalled
With fronds of stone fretted to airy lace,
Enfolding drupes that seem as tawny clusters
Of breasts of unknown houris; and convolved
With vines of shut and shadowy-leavèd flowers
Like the dropt lids of women that endure
Some loin-dissolving ecstasy. Through doors
Enlaid with lilies twined luxuriously,
I enter, dazed and blinded with the sun,
And hear, in gloom that changing colors cloud,
A chuckle sharp as crepitating ice
Upheaved and cloven by shoulders of the damned
Who strive in Antenora. When my eyes
Undazzle, and the cloud of color fades,
I find me in a monster-guarded room,
Where marble apes with wings of griffins crowd
On walls an evil sculptor wrought; and beasts
Wherein the sloth and vampire-bat unite,
Pendulous by their toes of tarnished bronze,
Usurp the shadowy interval of lamps

That hang from ebon arches. Like a ripple
Borne by the wind from pool to sluggish pool
In fields where wide Cocytus flows his bound,
A crackling smile around that circle runs,
And all the stone-wrought gibbons stare at me
With eyes that turn to glowing coals. A fear
That found no name in Babel, flings me on,
Breathless and faint with horror, to a hall
Within whose weary, self-reverting round,
The languid curtains, heavier than palls,
Unnumerably depict a weary king
Who fain would cool his jewel-crusted hands
In lakes of emerald evening, or the fields
Of dreamless poppies pure with rain. I flee
Onward, and all the shadowy curtains shake
With tremors of a silken-sighing mirth,
And whispers of the innumerable king,
Breathing a tale of ancient pestilence
Whose very words are vile contagion. Then
I reach a room where caryatides,
Carved in the form of voluptuous Titan women,
Surround a throne of flowering ebony
Where creeps a vine of crystal. On the throne
There lolls a wan, enormous Worm, whose bulk,
Tumid with all the rottenness of kings,
Overflows its arms with fold on creasèd fold
Obscenely bloating. Open-mouthed he leans,
And from his fulvous throat a score of tongues,
Depending like to wreaths of torpid vipers,
Drivel with phosphorescent slime, that runs
Down all his length of soft and monstrous folds,
And creeping among the flowers of ebony,
Lends them the life of tiny serpents. Now,
Ere the Horror ope those red and lashless slits
Of eyes that draw the gnat and midge, I turn
And follow down a dusty hall, whose gloom,
Lined by the statues with their mighty limbs,
Ends in a golden-roofèd balcony
Sphering the flowered horizon.

Ere my heart
Hath hushed the panic tumult of its pulses,

I listen, from beyond the horizon's rim,
A mutter faint as when the far simoon,
Mounting from unknown deserts, opens forth,
Wide as the waste, those wings of torrid night
That shake the doom of cities from their folds,
And musters in its van a thousand winds
That, with disrooted palms for besoms, rise,
And sweep the sands to fury. As the storm,
Approaching, mounts and loudens to the ears
Of them that toil in fields of sesame,
So grows the mutter, and a shadow creeps
Above the gold horizon like a dawn
Of darkness climbing zenith-ward. They come,
The Sabaoth of retribution, drawn
From all dread spheres that knew my trespassing,
And led by vengeful fiends and dire alastors
That owned my sway aforetime! Cockatrice,
Python, tragelaphus, leviathan,
Chimera, martichoras, behemoth,
Geryon, and sphinx, and hydra, on my ken
Arise as might some Afrit-builded city
Consummate in the lifting of a lash
With thunderous domes and sounding obelisks
And towers of night and fire alternate! Wings
Of white-hot stone along the hissing wind
Bear up the huge and furnace-hearted beasts
Of hells beyond Rutilicus; and things
Whose lightless length would mete the gyre of moons—
Born from the caverns of a dying sun—
Uncoil to the very zenith, half-disclosed
From gulfs below the horizon; octopi
Like blazing moons with countless arms of fire,
Climb from the seas of ever-surging flame
That roll and roar through planets unconsumed,
Beating on coasts of unknown metals; beasts
That range the mighty worlds of Alioth rise,
Afforesting the heavens with multitudinous horns
Amid whose maze the winds are lost; and borne
On cliff-like brows of plunging scolopendras,
The shell-wrought towers of ocean-witches loom;
And griffin-mounted gods, and demons throned
On sable dragons, and the cockodrills

That bear the spleenful pygmies on their backs;
And blue-faced wizards from the worlds of Saiph,
On whom Titanic scorpions fawn; and armies
That move with fronts reverted from the foe,
And strike athwart their shoulders at the shapes
Their shields reflect in crystal; and eidola
Fashioned within unfathomable caves
By hands of eyeless peoples; and the blind
Worm-shapen monsters of a sunless world,
With krakens from the ultimate abyss,
And Demogorgons of the outer dark,
Arising, shout with dire multisonous clamors,
And threatening me with dooms ineffable
In words whereat the heavens leap to flame,
Advance upon the enchanted palace. Falling
For league on league before, their shadows blight
And eat like fire the amaranthine meads,
Leaving an ashen desert. In the palace
I hear the apes of marble shriek and howl,
And all the women-shapen columns moan,
Babbling with terror. In my tenfold fear,
A monstrous dread unnamed in any hell,
I rise, and flee with the fleeing wind for wings,
And in a trice the wizard palace reels,
And spiring to a single tower of flame,
Goes out, and leaves nor shard nor ember! Flown
Beyond the world upon that fleeing wind
I reach the gulf's irrespirable verge,
Where fails the strongest storm for breath, and fall,
Supportless, through the nadir-plungèd gloom,
Beyond the scope and vision of the sun,
To other skies and systems.

In a world
Deep-wooded with the multi-colored fungi
That soar to semblance of fantastic palms,
I fall as falls the meteor-stone, and break
A score of trunks to atom-powder. Unharmed
I rise, and through the illimitable woods,
Among the trees of flimsy opal, roam,
And see their tops that clamber hour by hour
To touch the suns of iris. Things unseen,

Whose charnel breath informs the tideless air
With spreading pools of fetor, follow me,
Elusive past the ever-changing palms;
And pittering moths with wide and ashen wings
Flit on before, and insects ember-hued,
Descending, hurtle through the gorgeous gloom
And quench themselves in crumbling thickets. Heard
Far off, the gong-like roar of beasts unknown
Resounds at measured intervals of time,
Shaking the riper trees to dust, that falls
In clouds of acrid perfume, stifling me
Beneath an irised pall.

Now the palmettoes
Grow far apart, and lessen momently
To shrubs a dwarf might topple. Over them
I see an empty desert, all ablaze
With amethysts and rubies, and the dust
Of garnets or carnelians. On I roam,
Treading the gorgeous grit, that dazzles me
With leaping waves of endless rutilance,
Whereby the air is turned to a crimson gloom
Through which I wander blind as any Kobold;
Till underfoot the grinding sands give place
To stone or metal, with a massive ring
More welcome to mine ears than golden bells
Or tinkle of silver fountains. When the gloom
Of crimson lifts, I stand upon the edge
Of a broad black plain of adamant that reaches,
Level as windless water, to the verge
Of all the world; and through the sable plain
A hundred streams of shattered marble run,
And streams of broken steel, and streams of bronze,
Like to the ruin of all the wars of time,
To plunge with clangor of timeless cataracts
Adown the gulfs eternal.

So I follow
Between a river of steel and a river of bronze,
With ripples loud and tuneless as the clash
Of a million lutes; and come to the precipice
From which they fall, and make the mighty sound

Of a million swords that meet a million shields,
Or din of spears and armor in the wars
Of half the worlds and eons. Far beneath
They fall, through gulfs and cycles of the void,
And vanish like a stream of broken stars
Into the nether darkness; nor the gods
Of any sun, nor demons of the gulf,
Will dare to know what everlasting sea
Is fed thereby, and mounts forevermore
In one unebbing tide.

What nimbus-cloud
Or night of sudden and supreme eclipse,
Is on the suns of opal? At my side
The rivers run with a wan and ghostly gleam
Through darkness falling as the night that falls
From spheres extinguished. Turning, I behold
Betwixt the sable desert and the suns,
The poisèd wings of all the dragon-rout,
Far-flown in black occlusion thousand-fold
Through stars, and deeps, and devastated worlds,
Upon my trail of terror! Griffins, rocs,
And sluggish, dark chimeras, heavy-winged
After the ravin of dispeopled lands,
And harpies, and the vulture-birds of hell,
Hot from abominable feasts, and fain
To cool their beaks and talons in my blood—
All, all have gathered, and the wingless rear,
With rank on rank of foul, colossal Worms,
Makes horrent now the horizon. From the van
I hear the shriek of wyvers, loud and shrill
As tempests in a broken fane, and roar
Of sphinxes, like relentless toll of bells
From towers infernal. Cloud on hellish cloud
They arch the zenith, and a dreadful wind
Falls from them like the wind before the storm,
And in the wind my riven garment streams
And flutters in the face of all the void,
Even as flows a flaffing spirit, lost
On the pit's undying tempest. Louder grows
The thunder of the streams of stone and bronze—
Redoubled with the roar of torrent wings

Inseparably mingled. Scarce I keep
My footing in the gulfward winds of fear,
And mighty thunders beating to the void
In sea-like waves incessant; and would flee
With them, and prove the nadir-founded night
Where fall the streams of ruin. But when I reach
The verge, and seek through sun-defeating gloom
To measure with my gaze the dread descent,
I see a tiny star within the depths—
A light that stays me while the wings of doom
Convene their thickening thousands: for the star
Increases, taking to its hueless orb,
With all the speed of horror-changèd dreams,
The light as of a million million moons;
And floating up through gulfs and glooms eclipsed
It grows and grows, a huge white eyeless Face
That fills the void and fills the universe,
And bloats against the limits of the world
With lips of flame that open. . . .

The Infinite Quest

1920–1922

The Dream

It was a nest of horror, whimsy-wrought
With orts and shreds from old abysses caught;
An eyrie swung on swift ulterior awe,
Tangled on summits of mysterious thought.

Grotesque and vague, I watch the vision shift—
A bubble that a Titan's breath might lift,
Who drowns in seas more dark than his despair,
Fabrics of iron hue, whirling adrift,

Or like pellucid crystals dropt from hands
Of toying Gods, that fire my shadow-lands—
Then, like a sphere exalted past the sun,
It bursts!—while thought in eager question stands.

Conscious of gulfs down which I dare not gaze,
I grope on faltering and imperiled ways
To shores where hoary mountains dance and roar,
And silent oceans lie as in amaze.

The flames that wait against the End of things
Flutter and verge unto my wanderings.
Past numb and blanching regions loved of Death,
Aback I flee, floating on lifeless wings—

Past midnight deserts full of sorceries,
Yet levin-lit and bare as breathless seas,
Dreading the tiger-crough of ghastly Shapes
Alert in the wilds of dim eternities.

Now, in a trice, it seems that Time is done:
Light still endures, whose touch I may not shun;
Though at my back I hear the lips of Night
Puff out the flaring beacon of the sun.

Upon a barren blink I reel to see
The lower Dark—while, thundering over me,
Dawn hurls therein the cinders of dead stars,
And shells of worlds that rattle emptily.

Requiescat

What was Love's worth,
Who lived with roses?—
Love that is earth,
And with earth reposes!

What was Love's wonder?—
Scent of the flowers
After the thunder,
Thunder, and showers!

What were the breathless
Words that he said?—
Love that was deathless,
Love that is dead! . . .

Echo hath taken
The song, and flown;
None shall awaken
Music and moan.

Buds and the flower,
All that Love found,
Last but an hour,
Strewn on his mound.

To Nora May French

Importunate, the lion-throated sea,
Blind with the mounting foam of winter, mourns
To cliffs where cling the wrenched and labored roots
Or cypresses, and blossoms granite-grown
Lose in the gale their tattered petals, cast
On bleak, tumultuous cauldrons of the tide
Where fell thine ashes. Past the cobalt bay
The morning dunes a dust of marble seem—
Wrought from primeval fanes to Beauty reared,
And shattered by some vandal Titan's mace
To more than time's own ruin. Woods of pine
Above the dunes in Gothic gloom recede,
And climb the ridge that arches to the north
Long as a lolling dragon's chine. The gulls,

Like ashen leaves far off upon the wind,
Flutter above the broad and smouldering sea
That lightens with the fire-white foam. But thou,
Of whom the sea is urn and sepulcher,
Who hast thereof a blown tumultuous sleep
And stormy peace in gulfs impacable—
What carest thou if Beauty loiter there,
Clad with the crystal noon? What carest thou
If sharp and sudden balsams of the pine
Mingle for her in the air's bright thurible
With keener fragrance proffered by the deep
From riven gulfs resounding? . . . Knowest thou
What solemn shores of crocus-colored light,
Reared by the sunset in its realm of change,
Will mock the dream-lost isles that sirens ward,
And charm the icy emerald of the seas
To unabiding iris? Knowest thou
The waxing of the wan December foam—
A thunder-cloven veil that climbs and falls
Upon the cliffs forevermore?
      Thou art still
As they that sleep in the eldest pyramid—
Or mounded with Mesopotamia
And immemorial deserts! Thou hast part
In the wordless, dumb conspiracy of death—
Silence wherein the warrior kings accord
And all the wrangling seers! If now thy voice
In any wise return, and word of thee,
It is a lost, incognizable sigh
Upon the wind's oblivious woe, or blown,
Antiphonal, from wave to plangent wave,
In the vast unhuman sorrow of the main
On tides that lave the city-laden shores
Of lands wherein the eternal vanities
Are served at many altars; tides that wash
Lemuria's unfathomable walls,
And idly sway the weed-involvèd oars
Rotting amid the moles of orichalchum
In deep Atlantis; tides resurgent ever
From coral-coffered bones of all the drowned,
And sunless tombs of pearl that krakens guard.

II

As none shall roam the sad Leucadian rock
Above the sea's immitigable moan,
But in his heart a song that Sappho sang,
And flame-like murmur of the muted lyres
That time has not extinguished, and the cry
Of nightingales two thousand years ago
Shall mix with those remorseful chords that break
To endless foam and thunder; and he learn
The unsleeping woe that lives in Mytelene
Till wave and deep are dumb with ice, and rime
Has paled the rose for ever—even thus,
Daughter of Sappho, passion-souled and fair,
Whose face the lutes of Lesbos would have sung
And white Erinna followed—even thus
The western wave is eloquent of thee,
And half the wine-like fragrance of the foam
Is attar of thy spirit, and the pines,
From breasts of darkling, melancholy green,
Release remembered echoes of thy song
To airs importunate. No wraith of fog,
Twice-ghostly with the Hecatean moon,
Nor rack of blown, phantasmal spume shall rise,
But I will dream thy spirit walks the sea,
Unpacified with Lethe. Thou art grown
A part of all sad beauty, and my soul
Has found thy buried sorrow in its own,
Inseparable for ever. Moons that pass
Immaculate, to solemn pyres of snow,
And meres whereon the broken lotus dies,
Are kin to thee, as wine-lipped autumn is,
With suns of swift irreparable change,
And lucid evenings eager-starred. Of thee
The pearlèd fountains tell, and winds that take
In one white swirl the petals of the plum
And leave the branches lonely. Royal blooms
Of the magnolia, pale as beauty's brow,
And foam-white myrtles, and the fiery, bright
Pomegranate-flowers, will subtly speak of thee
While spring has speech and meaning. Music has
Her fugitive and uncommanded chords,
That thrill with tremors of thy mystery,

Or turn the void thy fleeing soul has left
To murmurs inenarrable, that hold
Epiphanies of blind, conceiveless vision,
And things we dare not know, and dare not dream.

(*Note:* Nora May French, one of the most gifted women-poets of America, died by her own hand at Carmel in 1907. Her ashes were strewn into the sea from Point Lobos.)

Psalm

My beloved is a well of clear waters,
To which I have come at noontide,
From the land of the Abomination of Desolation
From the lion-dreaded waste,
Where nothing dwelleth but the inconsolable crying of an evil wind,
And the wandering realms and cities of the wide mirage;
Where no one passeth except the sun,
Who walked like a terrible god through the hell of the brazen skies;
And the dreadful cohorts of the constellations,
Who pass remote in alien years,
And clad with icy azures of unattainable distance.

My beloved is a singing fountain,
Set in a wide oasis,
Between the frondage of the fruitful palm,
And the branches of the flowering myrtle:
The wind that bloweth thereon,
Hath lain in a vale of cassia and myrrh,
And caressed the vermilion blossoms of the pomegranate,
Whose red is the red of the lips of Astarte;
A thousand nightingales are gathered there,
From all the gardens of lost romance;
And plots of purple and silver lilies,
More beautiful than the meadows of mirage,
Revive the flowers of Sabean queens,
And the blossoms worn by all the princesses of legend. . . .
Ah, suffer me to dwell
Thereby, and forget the gilded cities of desire,
The domes of spectral gold,
That fled from horizon to horizon
Before me, and left my feet in the sinking vales and shifting plains
of the desert,

Whose waters are green with corruption,
And bitter with the dust and ashes of death.
Ah, suffer me to sleep
In the balsam-laden shadows of the palm and myrtle,
By the ever-springing fountain!

A Psalm to the Best Beloved

Thou comfortest me with the manna of thy love,
And the kisses of thy mouth are wine and sustenance;
They are grateful as fruit
In lonely orchards by the wayside of a ruinous land,
They are sweet as the purple grapes
On parching hills that confront the autumnal desert,
Or apples that the mad simoom hath spared
In a garden with walls of syenite.
Thy loosened hair is a veil
For the weariness of mine eyes and eyelids,
Which have known the redoubled sun
In a desert valley with slopes of the dust of white marble,
And have gazed on the mounded salt
In the marshes of a lake of dead waters.
Thy body is a secret Eden
Fed with lethean springs,
And the touch of thy flesh is like to the savor of lotos.
In thy hair is a perfume of ecstasy,
And a perfume of sleep;
Between thy thighs is a valley of delight,
And a valley of peace.

Cleopatra

Thy beauty is the warmth and languor of an orient autumn,
Caressing all the senses—
With light from skies of heavy azure,
With perfume from blossoms large as thuribles,
That hang in the berylline dusk of palms;
With the balmy kiss of wind and wave beneath Canopus;
And the songs of exotic birds
That pass in vermilion-flashing flight from isle to isle
On an ocean of lazuli.
O, sweetness in the inmost sense,

As of blood-red fruits that have grown by the waters of Lethe,
Or fragrance of purple lilies crushed in a cypress-grove
By the sleeping limbs of Eros! . . .
Thou pervadest me with thy love
As the dawn pervadeth a valley among mountains,
Or as sunset filleth the amaranth-colored sea;
The desire of thy heart is upon me
Like a summer wind from Cythera,
Where Venus lies among the tiger-lilies
By a pool whose waters are fed from secret springs;
I inhale thy love
As the breath of hidden gardens of purple and scarlet,
Where Circe trails a gown
Whose colors are the reddening gold of flame
And the azure of the skies of autumn.

Nightfall

Low on the lilac breast of eve
The yellow rose of sunset lies . . .
Beneath my cheek, with little sighs,
I feel thy happy bosom heave.

Ah, darling, let the sun depart,
And night usurp the western hills!
A dearer flame thy bosom fills
And clearer suns are in my heart.

Love hath no need of other light:
Thy kisses on my lips and eyes,
Are like the dawn in Paradise
That burns upon the lidded sight.

Our bodies find an ecstasy,
A deepening rapture, soft and fair,
Like the blue seas and roseal air
About the isles of Faëry . . .

Thine ardent limbs are mine to hold;
From brow to breast, from knee to side,
My kisses and caresses glide
Like unseen flames of red and gold.

Ecstasy

Blind with your softly fallen hair,
I turn me from the twilight air;
And, ah, the wordless tale of love
My lips upon your lips declare!

High stars are on the shadowy south—
Unseen, unknown: the urgent drouth
Of desolate years in one deep kiss
Would drain the sweetness of your mouth.

Our straining arms that clasp and close
Ache with an ecstasy that grows,
And passion in our secret veins,
Like burning amber, glows and glows.

This love is sweet to have and hold,
Better than sandalwood or gold,
After the barren, bitter loves,
The mad and mournful loves of old.

This love is fortunate and fair,
Behind its veil of fallen hair;
This love has soft and clinging arms,
And a kind bosom, warm and bare.

Secret Love

Hung round with heavy silence fold on fold,
Thy love, within my veiled and votive heart,
Is like a darkling Venus, shrined apart
In some lost city legendless and old
Whose mobled walls and domes of blinded gold
Lapse in the sands of Syria: none may start
The antique doors, and tapestries of art
Where all the lost luxurious dreams are told,

To see, within a spikenard-scented room,
The gleam of clear marmoreal breast and limb—
The goddess, with her crescent mouth upturned
To meet the kiss of Adon in the gloom;
Her loins grow languid with a dream of him
For whom their pale Pentelic altar burned.

The Hidden Paradise

Our passion is a secret paradise—
Eden of lotos and the fruitful date,
With silence walled and held undesecrate
By man or prying seraph: we are wise

As any god and goddess, who have wrung
From roseal fruitage of a bough forbidden
The happy wine we drink, we drink unchidden,
Deep in the vales where vernal leaves are young,

And the first poppies loiter. . . . Though the breath
Of all the gods a bolted storm prepare,
Till blood-red gloom of thunders blind the sun,

Shall we not turn with clinging kisses there,
And, laughing, quaff some dreamless wine of death—
Triumphant still, in mere oblivion?

The Infinite Quest

In years no vision shall aver,
In lands no dream may name,
Toward alien things what longings were,
And thence what languors came!

For each horizon straitly sought,
With fealty to the stars,
What death or weariness was bought,
What bitterness, what bars?

I waken unto years afar,
And find the quest made new
In Earth, that was perchance a star
Unto my former view.

Exotic Memory

Thy body bright as wine-washed ivory,
Thy fervid charms, bare as the moon is bare,
I knew them all (I know not when nor where)
In lands beside some amber-foaming sea.

On a terrace crowned with terebinth and palm
I found thee lying, languid and supine,

Thy breast of dreams voluptuous and divine
All given to the winds of myrrh and balm.

We saw the sun, a molten amethyst,
Sink in the scented ocean's foam and fire
And a slow night with ruby planets rise;

And all the night's black temple walled our tryst,
Where, with libations and with liturgies,
We served the burning altars of desire.

Satiety

Dear you were as is the tree of Being
To the happy dead in heaven's bowers. . . .
Whence and what, this evil spell that flings me
Forth from love with loveless eyes unseeing?

Fair you were as nymph or queen of vision,
Bosomed like the succubi of dreams. . . .
All your beauty turns to sad, ironic
Weariness, and sorrowful derision.

Lo, of what avail our spent caresses—
Kisses that set the summer night aflame? . . .
Mute, enormous languor without cause—
What is this my autumn heart confesses?

All your breast was fragrant like the flowers
Of the grape on hills toward the south. . . .
Love is acrid now like staling asters
Sodden with the rain of autumn hours.

Fawn-Lilies

White lilies frail and cold,
With hearts of elfin gold!
Briefer than all brief things your hidden bloom,
Beneath the sombre grove—
Mournful, and dear, and fair as hapless love,
Foreknowing all the nearness of its doom.

White lilies cool and shy,
Deliciously ye die,
Before the vesper dews of any morrow!

But now, on windless air,
Your perfume lies, fresh as a woman's hair,
And faint as myrrh the dreams of noon would borrow.

White lilies cold and wan
As hands of swooning love—
As the fair throat whereon
My kisses clomb, to find her mouth's lit flame!—
Ye die, and cannot say
Who passed beneath the April pines to-day:
And you alone have heard our hidden love,
And known her flow'r-soft name.

Artemis

In the green and flowerless garden I have dreamt,
Lying beneath perennial moons apart,
Whose cypress-builded bowers
And ivy-plighted myrtles none shall part;

In the funereal maze of larch and laurel,
Across white lawns, athwart the spectral mountains,
Seen through the sighing haze
Of all the high and moon-suspended fountains,

With feet enshaded by the fruitless green
Of summer trees that bear no summer blossom;
With wintry lusters laid
Upon the mounded marble of thy bosom,

Thou dost await, O mournful, enigmatic
Image of love-bewildered Artemis,
Whose tender lips too late,
Or all too soon, have sought the wounding kiss.

Plum-Flowers

On boughs a-tremble with the rain,
The blown white flowers of the plum
Their fragile hold awhile retain.

And though tempestuous tears have come
Between us, and a startled moan
From mouths that kisses have made dumb—

Still, still, the gentler tears atone,
And still we keep our April love,
Like poising petals all unflown.

Chance

Bow down before the daemon of the world—
This monstrous god, half-idiot and half-ape,
With fumbling hands omnipotent to shape
A harlot's breast or build great altars. Hurled
From the lost sun to sunless hell, or whirled
Back to their heaven with equal jest and jape,
All other gods shall nevermore escape
His will that once begot them. Wars unfurled
With banners blown like ever-wandering fires
From realm to realm conflagrant, or the play
Of coupling mice or monsters, wake alway
To his dominion. Darkly born thereof,
The troubling atoms teem to stars and byres,
The leper's flesh, the white flesh of thy love.

Union

As the fumes of myrrh that mix with the odour of sandalwood
In a temple sacred to the goddess Lakme;
As moonlight mingled with starlight
In the lucent azure of an autumn lake;
As the sunset-rays of gold and crimson
That interlace on a couch of purple cloud—
Even so, Beloved,
Hath my love mingled with thine—
Even so, our souls are one,
Like two winds that meet in a valley of rose and lotus,
And fall to rest, uniting
As the still and fragrant air that lingers
On a bed of falling petals.

Song

I bring my weariness to thee,
My bitter dreams I bring;
Love with a wounded wing,

And life consumed of memory
I bring to thee.

The haven of thy happy breast—
Of this my dreams are fain:
For all my weary pain
In all the world there is no rest
But on thy breast.

Love Is Not Yours, Love Is Not Mine

Love is not yours, love is not mine:
It is the tranquil twilight heaven
Through which our pauseless feet are driven
Into the vast and desert noon.

Love is not mine, love is not yours:
It is a flying fire that passes,
Perishing on the blind morasses
After the frail and perished moon.

Poplars

Against the pale autumnal air,
The golden poplars burn and flare.

And golden lamps are lit for me,
Deep in the vaults of memory.

Forevermore the poplars rise
To light the lands where Beauty dies;

Where roses fail, and asters fade,
And lilies in the dust are laid.

And in my heart the lamps illume
A queenly couch of love and doom.

And one who lies in silence there,
Forever dead, forever fair,
With leaves and asters in her hair.

The Fugitives

Act I. Scene I.

A grassy meadow, by a lily-laden stream, within sight of Alnephrom, the capital of Poseidonis. Aviol, a girl of twelve, and the boy Cartha, a year or two older, approach from opposite sides of the mead[ow] and meet at the wat[er's e]dge. Aviol sings[:]

The Song of Aviol

Past the flown horizon's wall
And the flight of any wind—
Where the sunken sunsets fall,
Lies the land that Love would find.

There, among the magic palms,
They that flee the mists of sorrow
Watch their woe on wingèd balms
Borne and lost ere any morrow.

There, in vales of deathless lote,
Love is made the Dream Eternal—
One with all the myrrhs that float
'Neath the halted sun hesternal.

Land that kings may not discover,
Deep within the mystic west!
Only lover comes with lover
Through the fens where dragons nest.

They that seek it, summer-hearted,
Must outwing the winter swallow—
Far too far in realms uncharted
For the jealous gods to follow.

Past the flown horizon's wall
And the flight of any wind—
Where the sunken sunsets fall,
Lies the land that Love would find.

Song

Vagrant from the realms of rose,
Love has flown where no man knows:
Though your fleetest witch should bind
With her hair the April wind,
Love is still to seek and find.

Though your eldest necromant
Raise again with solemn chant
All the ghostly girls of yore,
Crowned with blossoms thin and frore,
Vagrant love returns no more.

Though the sirens sing for him
On ulterior isles made dim
With the foam of ultimate seas,
All beyond the Hesperides,
Love shall pass unseen of these.

Though you find in fields of morn
Blossoms of their dews forlorn,
And the grieving grasses bent
By the latest way he went,
Errant still and uncontent;

Though you seek from door to door
Through the city's wrath and roar;
Scan the phantom faces wan
Of the masquers mute with dawn—
Always love has come—and gone.

Though a lonely trail you tread,
Past the rim of autumn's red,
Ending on the moonlit snows—
Love has flown where no man knows,
Vagrant from the realms of rose.

The Love-Potion

Sluggish drops of sullen balm;
Blood-red wine from fruits of bane,
Subtly mixed with polar snows
Melted in a harlot's palm;
Attar from the firstling rose
On the grave of lovers slain:—

Featly find and featly bring
These, to make the magistral
Fraught with clear, unholy fire,
That shall end the languishing
Of a queen, and rouse desire
In a heart funereal.

The Song of Cartha

Queen, whose perilous bosom bare
Was the field of love's emprise,
I would hush my weary sighs
In the silence of thy hair.

In my heart thy kisses wrought
Raptures of the fabled faun;
Seal my lids before the dawn
With thy lips, and lift them not.

Queen, whose breasts were mine to keep
Through the moon-abandoned night,
Languid love and dead delight
In thine arms are fain to sleep.

Chant of Autumn

Like the voice of a golden star,
Heard from afar,
Perishing beauty calls
Out of the mist and rain;
Like the song of a silver wind
When the night is blind,
Murmuring music falls,
Never to rise again.

Voice of the leaves that die,
Whisper and sigh
Of ruinous gardens waning
Rose by ungathered rose.
Dolor of pines immortal,
That guard the portal
Of a lonely mead retaining
Blossoms that no man knows!

Voices of love and the autumn sun,
In my heart ye are one!
Fairer the petals that fall,
Dearer the beauty that dies,
And the pyres of autumn burning,
Than a thousand springs returning. . . .
O, perishing loves that call
In my heart and the hollow skies!

A Fragment

Autumn far off in memory,
That saw the crisping myrtles fade! . . .
Eons agone, my tomb was made
Beside the moon-constrainèd sea.

Ah, wonderful its portals were!
With carven doors of chrysolite
And walls of sombre syenite
They wrought mine olden sepulcher.

About the griffin-guarded plinth,
White blossoms crowned the scarlet vine,
And burning orchids opaline
Illumed the palm and terebinth.

On friezes of mine ancient fame
The cypress wrought its writhen shade,
And through the boughs the ocean made
Moresques of blue and fretted flame.

Poet or prince, I may not know
My perished name, nor bring to mind
Years that are one with dust and wind,
Nor songless love and tongueless woe—

Only the tomb they made for me,
With carven doors of chrysolite
And walls of sombre syenite
Beside the moon-constrainèd sea.

Enchanted Mirrors

1923–1926

Selenique

Perfect, marmoreal, curved and carven statue-wise,
Your hard immaculate beauty dulls the sharpness of desire,
And chills it to a changeless passion—
A frozen passion bright and pallid
And clear as is the ghostly fervor of the moon's white fire.
And all the dreams of you are lunar dreams—
Such bright and hueless visions as are born
Of moonset on autumnal meres forlorn,
Where the white lotus lingers,
Unstirred with full and fragile petals overblown
That the least wave would loosen
And shatter like the touch of fingers;
While the high clouds upon the western hills
Rest immobile as towering palaces
And mausoleums wrought of dim fantastic stone.

Semblance

Love was the flight of a crimson bird
Across the forest of your soul,
Where cypress-leaf and cypress-bole,
By mordant airs of autumn stirred,
Sigh with a long and sea-like word.

Joy was the burning heart-red bloom
A fair and wandering witch let fall
At twilight from her coronal,
Where mottling ivies mesh the tomb
Lost in a laurel-given gloom.

Time is the drip of fountain-spray
Upon the unbroken sword you flung
Amid the pouting poppies young
In a lost garden far away
Where the white girls of Circe lay.

Life is a house of painted stone
Reflected in a sunless lake,
Where drowning domes and turrets shake
In the black winds for ever blown
From shoreless tides no sail has known.

Grief is the mirror-builded hall
Wherein you roam eternally,
Seeking the ghost you shall not see—
In sorrow half-sardonical—
And meet yourself at every wall.

Change

For pity, not for love
(Because you loved me so)
With undesirous lips
I kissed you long ago.

You were not over-fair;
And surely it is strange
Your memory should return,
Touched with this fairer change.

For now at whiles I meet
In eves of weariness
Your sweetly watchful eyes
That know my still distress;

And turn to feel your lips
Laid soothly on my hair—
Your half-forgotten lips,
Grown strangely dear and fair.

Who knows?—if you should come
This shifting heart to prove,
Yours might the pity be,
And mine the pitied love.

Don Juan Sings

Lightly kiss and lightly pass
Ere the sleeping Love shall wake;
Nimble-footed, lean and take
Blossoms from a blind morass.

Past the dragon coiled in slumber,
Steal, and filch his guarded gold,
Taking all your hands may hold
And your hasty glances number.

Shadowy breasts and breasts of snow
Bear the rounded fruits of pleasure:
Taste them all, nor seek to treasure
Aught that turns to dust and woe.

Sombre locks and tresses fair,
In them all your fingers tangle;
Leave them lest your heart should strangle
In a noose of woman's hair.

The Nymph

Last night I was a vagrant faun:
I followed through the woods of dream
Where singing dryads led me on
By glimpses of a singing stream.

Half-seen beneath the broken moon,
Where lace of shadows fell and shifted,
Their wanton shoulders warm with June
Aroused me like a breast uplifted.

With limbs that fled, and faces turning,
And lips where song and laughter blent,
They passed, and I, in questful yearning,
After them with the shadows went.

Ah, clinging weariness that came
To clog at last my lonely feet!
Despairing of the hapless game,
I flung me in a still retreat;

And there, amid the ferns that kept
Her clear and veilless thighs from view,
I found a smiling nymph who slept—
And, lo, the sleeping nymph was you!

By the River

I deemed the golden nymphs were gone,
And pausing by the river, mused
On naiads and the forest-faun,
And idly broke the bronzing reeds
The lips of Pan would once have used.

Upon the willow-fretted stream
I watched the ripples fall and melt
Like amorous laughter in a dream,
And saw the silver thistle-seeds
Float wave-ward on a wind unfelt. . . .

I deemed the golden nymphs were gone. . . .
And then—I turned, and saw you rise
Nude as a nymph that flees the faun,
With anklets of the foam's white beads,
And Hellas in your halcyon eyes!

Fashion

Though my love display her limits,
    Though the longer dresses hide her
Knees from my enraptured gaze—
    I will never check nor chide her:

Though she wear them short and shorter
    There is always more to show;
And the dress that drapes her shoe tops,
    Leaves a vaster lot to know.

The Witch with Eyes of Amber

I met a witch with amber eyes
Who slowly sang a scarlet rune,
Shifting to an icy laughter
Like the laughter of the moon.

Red as a wanton's was her mouth,
And fair the breast she bade me take
With a word that clove and clung
Burning like a furnace-flake.

But from her bright and lifted bosom,
When I touched it with my hand,
Came the many-needled coldness
Of a glacier-taken land.

And, lo! the witch with eyes of amber
Vanished like a blown-out flame,
Leaving but the lichen-eaten
Stone that bore a blotted name.

On the Canyon-Side

Forgotten lies the world we knew,
One mile behind the looming hill;
And here, beside a laurel-darkened rill,
Slow-wandering, we have found
A fern-lost boulder large enough for two
That sit with arms enwound.

Upon your pale, delicious throat
Like a torn lace the shadows stir;
While, with a sharpened longing, I defer
The kiss that fain would fall;
And softly touch your yielded wrist, and note
How loud your pulses call.

Syringa-blossoms, frail and old,
Swept by the swiftly dying air,
Fall like a fragrant snow, and in your hair
Two poising petals rest;
And a great moth with wings of mottled gold
Pauses before your breast.

Now, while the world is far and dim,
Now, while the afternoon is new,
Reveal, I pray, the rapture that is you:
Hoard not the least caress,
Nor the last whiteness of the breast and limb,
From love made fetterless.

We Shall Meet

We shall meet
Once again
In the strange and latter summers,
And recall,
Like olden mummers,
An old play of love and pain.

I shall greet
You not with kisses
Of the days aforetime, knowing
These would fall
Vain as those of phantoms blowing
Nightward to the last abysses.

Faint perfume
Will attend you
Like a scrine-imprisoned myrrh;
And my dreaming
Heart where fallen autumns stir
Half their fallen light will lend you.

From the tomb
Love shall rise
Mutely, in a spectre's fashion,
To the seeming
Lamps for ever bleak and ashen
Of our necromantic eyes.

But no tear
Shall we weep,
Knowing tears are void and vain,
Like the scattered
Drops of rain
On a desert's iron sleep.

Chill and sere,
Like the grass
Flaffing in a field of snow,
We shall know that nothing mattered,
As we tell our faded woe
Ere we pass.

The Secret

Like a word
Of an archetypal tongue,
Never told,
Never sung;

All unstirred,
Like the corals of the deep
In their cold
And purple sleep;

Lost and far,
Like a forest-folded bloom
Lulled above
Its own perfume;

Like a star
In the nether darkness drowned,
Lies the love
We have not found.

Contradiction

I have calmed me with the thought of nothingness—
Who know that none shall evermore escape
From the world's dream and stand illusionless.

In fancy I have leaned from Lethe's edge—
Knowing the driven dust will pass again
When the tomb has broke its sealed and marble pledge.

And I have smiled at the idleness of love—
Who find the swords of your unforgotten beauty
Posted before, behind me, and above.

Alienage

Dear one, what do we here? . . .
Petal by petal falls the alien spring
In gardens where we pass ungarlanded,
And seek once more the doves and myrtles dead
In some retrieveless year;
And claim no leaf or garland for our own . . .
O, Paphos, and the moons of Paphos flown!
My golden dove, canst thou recall
Nights when delight was all,
And high desire could still outlive the dawn?
Hast thou forgot,
Here, in the grey, sad world that knows us not,
The years when we were nymph and centaur, drawn
To elder forests deep
That spring had turned to chrysolite and gold?
Hast thou forgot the tale of kisses told
By summer waters calm as sleep,
When Hesperean sunsets touched thy hair
From islands lost and fair?

Dear one, what do we here? . . .
Beyond the window-pane
The veils of shifting rain

Bedim the bitter world that is not ours;
And on dishevelled flowers
There falls a hueless twilight, brief and drear.
Give me thy lips again—
Let us forget the weariness and pain,
And the supreme disaster of our birth,
While in thy flesh my lingering
Slow kisses cleave and cling
And love alone hath verity or worth.
Ah, let me find, about thy bosom's fruit,
The fragile, vague perfume
Of unseen lilies crushed within the gloom
Of forests lone and old;
Ah, let me seek in leisured long pursuit
Amid thy harvest-colored hair,
For suns and summers of remembered gold;
And seal my lips on throat and bosom fair,
Till where my kisses fell, the phantom rose
Of Paphos blows.

Moments

From all the moments of our love,
What moment would I most recall?
That first mad kiss, that made you swoon
Upon the bedded leaves of fall?

That hour, when careless of the ferns
And blossoms crushed whereon we lay,
I found the fruits of my desire
Amid your garments' disarray?

That time upon the tiger-skin
When kiss by kiss my lips had set
A rosy girdle round your breast
And round your throat a carcanet?

That eve when sudden rapture was
The rainbow of a storm of tears,
And something in us rose and bloomed
That dies not with the barren years?

The dawn that found us wakeful still,
And lit the flushing window-pane—

Till I arose and drew the blind
And sought your waiting arms again?

Alas! I cannot bear to choose
Where all is infinitely dear:
From all our love, I would not lose
A smile, a pulse-beat or a tear!

Exchange

Sudden, familiar, unbesought,
Like the quick pulse of some recurrent pain,
Your beauty comes again
To roam the weary spaces of my thought.

I see the smiling phantom pass,
And wonder if my darker soul has flown
To haunt your dreams unknown,
Or linger like a shadow in your glass.

Metaphor

You are the stately sunset,
Departing with a hundred flames of amber
Beyond the pinnacles of autumn pine
And the low mountains
That bear the brief and vast Olympus of the clouds
Under a purpling zenith.
You are the stately sunset,
And after you
Silence will rear the moon-eclipsing night,
And a few spectral stars will gather,
Like wisps to lead the wandering gods astray
Into the black and boundless fen of all the gulfs.

The Wingless Archangels

Beyond the bourn of dreams, their fortunate sphere,
Golden and large in some rich galaxy,
Rolls upon ways prolonged of harmony;
And they, with wingless toil of many a year,
Climbing, have thought the ethereal heavens near—
Wise with the secrets of eternity,

And forcing truce with time . . . They deem them free
From change, and from the old, unchanging fear.

But on their immortality is blight—
Whose dream betraying deserts have undone:
They turn, where winds make chill the ashen light,
Blown as from space and bleak oblivion;
And mark the dim, portentous breath of night,
A black mist gathering on the silver sun.

A Valediction

Though the blown leaves arise and go,
The pines remain;
Though love and all his raptures pass,
Abideth pain.

Slowly I kiss thy muted mouth,
And turn in sorrow:
Perchance the closing earth will press
Thereon tomorrow.

Cocaigne

Our love hath found a secret land,
    A world from all the world apart,
And we may wander hand in hand
    E'en in the loud and whirling mart,
To meadows of a secret land.

We pass along the crowded ways:
    But still, with clinging kisses fond,
We loiter 'neath the myrtle-sprays,
    In green, Edenic peace beyond
The clangor of the crowded ways.

Never from one eternal tryst
    The miles have held our meeting hearts:
Our spirits cling, as love may list,
    And keep the embrace that never parts
In realms of one eternal tryst.

Forgotten Sorrow

A stranger grief than any grief by music told
Is mine: regret for unremembered loves, and faces
Veiled by the night of some unknown farewell, or places
Lost in the dusty ebb and lapse of kingdoms old
On the slow desert, rises vague and manifold
Within my heart at summer twilight. Through the spaces
Of all oblivion, voidly then my soul retraces
Her dead lives given to the marbles and the mould
In dim Palmyra, or some pink, enormous city
Whose falling columns now the boles of mightier trees
Support in far Siam. . . . All grievous love, and pity,
All loveliness unheld for long, and long estranged,
Appeals with voices, indistinguishably changed,
Like bells in deep Atlantis, tolled by summer seas.

Septembral

In silence now the purpling summer passes,
The swallows fly;
The failing river scantly glasses,
Where amber twilights wane,
Our dream-long kiss above the flow'rs that die . . .

Will love at last remain? . . .
Ever I pray to find—
(Though all the heavens be blind!)
The gold of love and summer in thy hair;
And breathe between thy shadowy breasts again,
In eves of autumn wind,
And flow'rs that failed upon a windless air.

Afterwards

There is a silence in the world
Since we have said farewell;
And beauty with an alien speech
An alien tale would tell.

There is a silence in the world,
Which is not peace nor quiet:
Ever I seek to flee therefrom,
And walk the ways of riot.

But when I hear the music moan
In rooms of thronging laughter,
A tongueless demon drives me forth,
And silence follows after.

The Barrier

In the desire of welded lips,
Of heart on prone tumultuous heart,
Abides no stronger thing than this
Dread love that keeps our lips apart.

Between us lies an ancient fear;
Before me, in thy troubled eyes,
A shadow flees as flees the nymph,
Tremulous with the faun's surprise.

Ever we meet—and hesitate.
We play before the sullen wall
Of love with careful words and light—
Lest the imperiled barrier fall.

Hard silence like a stifling hand
Withholds the word we fain would say;
Over us lies the dreamt caress
Transfixed with a dear dismay.

When shall the passion of the faun
Resistless in my heart arise,
And take the warm and trembling nymph
That flees within thy startled eyes?

The Funeral Urn

My heart is like some onyx urn
Upon whose cold and carven side
Antique symbolic serpents glide
In scrolls that wander and return;

Where orchid and where columbine
Intort their blooms ambiguously;
Where over some exotic tree
Clambers the grape's familiar vine.

How fair and strange the art thereof!
But—irony supreme—within,
The poisonous black dust of sin
And ashes from dark pyres of love.

Dolor of Dreams

The shadow of a sorrow haunts the light,
And sense of dreamt, forgotten tragedy—
Surviving phantom of a memory
Slain by the dawn with shades of yesternight.

Like the blue pallor of the daylight moon,
Most clearly seen within the enshadowed stream,
The wan waste face of some dead, tragic dream
Peers from the twilight places of the noon.

Till, half-bemazed, I am as one who stands
Upon the summit of a misty hill,
And hears remote, one moment loud or still,
The dolor in the bells of blinded lands.

Brumal

Life is a tale half-told,
Love is a broken song;
Beauty, besought so long,
Is a legend lost and old.

Winter and silence and woe
Have come, like the end of all:
Slowly the last leaves fall
At sunset over the snow.

Here, on the darkening wold,
In the bleak wind blown from space,
I recall thy fugitive grace,
And sigh for thy hair's lost gold.

Autumn Orchards

Walled with far azures of the wintering year,
Late autumn on a windless altar burns:
Splendid as rubies from Sabean urns,
A holocaust of hues is gathered here.

The pear-trees lift a Tyrian tinged with blood;
Strange purples brighten in the smouldering plums;
The fire-red gold of peach and cherry comes
To storm the bronzing borders of the wood.

Rich as the pyre of some Hesperian queen,
Feeding the ultimate sunset with sad fires,
Is this, where beauty with her doom conspires
To tell in flame what death and beauty mean.

O, loveliness grown tragical and dear!
My heart has taken from the torchful leaf
A swiftly soaring glory, and the grief
Of love is colored like the dying year.

Remembrance

Memory has in fee
A land where fallen suns
Illume the light and fragile bronze
Of autumn leaves unchangingly.
Memory has in fee
A land of fallen suns.

Memory knows the face
Of one who wanders there,
Tranquil and tall, for ever fair
With dreamful, slow, mysterious grace.
Memory knows her face,
Supremely pale and fair.

Memory sees the sky
Deep in her eyes alone;
And all the forest-bronze is flown,
Lost in her hair eternally:
Memory finds the sky
Deep in her eyes alone.

Memory takes her hand
Across the lonesome years—
And all the ancient stream of tears
Has ceased within an autumn land.
Memory takes her hand
Across forgotten tears.

Departure

Departing autumn trails
Her scarf of mist adown the morning vales;
Enmeshed like faery sequins in its fold,
Gleam the last leaves of gold.

Diversity

Within your voice the boughs of Eden sigh
In scented winds blown from the summer foam:
But in your gaze the lulling hills of home
Accept the silence of an autumn sky.

The Lemurienne

Pale girl with eyes of opalescent spar,
        Where cold, fantastic ciphers, dawn by dawn
Change, but are never solved, your soul lies far,—
        In some lost dreamland, like a sphinx withdrawn.

The End of Autumn

Spent autumn wanes; the leaf
Forsakes the vine, as from her coronal
The gems might fall,
Forgot by some mad empress in her grief.

Now, from the sycamores,
A ruinous and crumpled bronze is cast;
Grown sere at last,
The reeds lie broken on the river-shores.

Now, from the outland peaks,
The ghostly snows crawl downward on the blue;
Gone forth anew,
For huger suns the southering autumn seeks.

Decembral stars return
In long blue twilights to the eastern hill;
But, lost and still,
In high ravines her flameless embers burn.

Bleak with the winter's breath,
A wind comes down; fantastic skeletons
Of steel and bronze,
Creak the cold willows in a dance of death.

On Re-reading Baudelaire

Forgetting still what holier lilies bloom
Secure within the garden of lost years,
We water with the fitfulness of tears
Wan myrtles with an acrid sick perfume;
Lethean lotus, laurels of our doom,
Dark amarant with tall unswaying spears,
Await funereal autumn and its fears
In this grey land that sullen suns illume.

Ivy and rose and hellebore we twine.
Voluptuous as love, or keen as grief,
Some fleeing fragrance lures us in the gloom
To Paphian dells or vales of Proserpine. . . .
But all the flowers, with dark or pallid leaf,
Become at last a garland for the tomb.

Lemurienne

From dawn to dawn your eyes of graven spar
For ever change, with chill, forgotten runes;
But all the while your spirit lies afar,
A sphinx that peers on prediluvian moons.

You Are Not Beautiful

You are not beautiful; but, ah, too long
I sought, and found a slowly growing grace;
Till fairer now than beauty is your face,
And all your silence dearer than a song.

December

From the sad leaves withdrawn,
Remote, estranged and cold,
Forgetful autumn's gold
Alone abides in some December dawn.

Tearless and clear and chill
As eyes that have forgot
Far love, or find it not,
The pale bright heavens arch the barren hill.

Now, in this afternoon
Enchanted, blue and brief,
The year has lost its grief
In valleys mute below the spectral moon.

For here no mourning-dove
Laments the season flown:
On love that wanders lone
Falls the blue balm of silence from above.

For here no zephyr grieves
To tell the year's dead dream;
And down the pine-lulled stream
Lost memories drift and loiter with the leaves.

The Pagan

In amaranthine days ere time was born
My home was in some ocean-fronting land
Where idle sirens on the pearl-white sand
With laughters hailed the wheedling Triton's horn.

Adown the cliffs I saw red satyrs clamber,
To stare at emerald evening on the bay
Where floating sea-nymphs from the riven spray
Offered their swelling deltas fleeced with amber.

And once, when flowering laurel spiced the air,
Between the boughs I caught a dryad's hair
And all her yielded youth was mine to hold;

And after, when the breathless hour was done,
We stretched our glowing languor in the sun,
My face against her body's moss of gold.

A Meeting

When all the splendor wanes
Like a slow sunset from the changeful leaves,
And the grey time of rains

With hooded dawns and eves
Approaches, I shall come to you once more,
Some afternoon of sun and sunlit cloud
And knocking at your door
Await your soft and murmurous tread, scarce heard
For sudden pulses loud
By long desire and many memories stirred . . .
So you will come, and we shall meet again,
After the going-down of many days,
The death of many dreams;
Under the gracious heavens of your gaze
My heart shall lie as some autumnal land
Fulfilled with aureate light and azure haze,
The while we speak of themes
Familiar, or recall forgotten things—
Telling of autumn and the fallen flow'rs,
And the fled wings—
Lest love usurp our straitly guarded lips,
And the irrevocable word be said
That ends the wordless hours . . .

Unheard, like petals shed
In fields of poppy-bloom
The moments fall and turn to memories,
Though Love foresees
Here, in the sunlit room,
The ultimate night and silence of his doom.
But not too heavily the burden weighs,
While your sweet gaze
Lingers upon me like a tranquil light,
And all the murmured music of your voice
Becomes an echo for the songless days.
And heart and soul rejoice,
Knowing your presence for a little while,
But dare not tell
How love has made this hour ineffable,
And dare not tell the dearness of your smile.

Adventure

Let us leave the hateful town
With its stale, forgotten lies;
Far beneath renewing skies,

Where the piny slope goes down;
All with April love and laughter—
None to leer and none to frown—
We shall pass and follow after
Shattered lace of waters spun
On a steep and stony loom
Down the depths of laurel-gloom.
Finding there a world re-made
In the fern-embowered shade,
Weaving bright oblivion
Still from frailest blossom-trove,
We shall mix our wilding love
With the woodland and the sun.

Let us loiter, hand in hand,
Hearing but the heart's command,
Half our steps by kisses stayed,
Prove the spring-enchanted glade;
Breast to breast and limb to limb,
Seize our happiness and bind it—
Lose the pulse of time and find it—
Free as vagrant seraphim.
Ever leave regret and rue
To the dutiful and jealous
Fools that are not near to tell us
All the things we should not do.

Though the bedded ferns be broken,
And dishevelled blossoms lie
On the rumpled moss for token
Of the day's mad errantry—
Still the tacit pines will keep
Darkly in their sighing sleep
All the sweet and perilous story;
And the oaks and willows hoary
For unheeding ears will tell
Only things ineffable;
And the later eyes that look
On the pool-delaying brook,
Shall not see within its glass
Two that came to kiss and pass.

Transmutation

Slowly the sorrow of the fallen leaf
Turns to desire for some undreamt-of blossom;
So love's implacable and sullen grief
Dies on an alien bosom.

The Last Oblivion

Not while the woods are redolent with spring,
Or scentless immortelles of autumn blow,
Shall I evade your loveliness, or know
Surcease of love and love's remembering.

But haply wandering, worlds and cycles hence,
Through unforeseen fantastic avatars,
I shall forget you in the future stars,
And take of time an alien recompense.

Till in some strange and latter planet, wrought
From molten shards and meteor-dust of this,
My hand shall pluck an unsuspected bloom

That lifts again the scarlet of your kiss;
And I shall muse and loiter, knowing not
The love that perished like a lost perfume.

To the Chimera

Unknown chimera, take us, for we tire
Amid the known monotony of things!
Descend, and bearing sunward with bright wings
Our mournful weariness and sad desire,

Pause not to prove the opal shores untrod,
Below thee fading, and the fields of rose;
Till on thy horns of planished silver flows
The sanguine light of Edens lost to God.

There, for the weary sense insatiate,
Primeval sleep from towering scarlet blooms
Would fall in slow and infinite perfumes;

Or we could leave thy crystal wings elate,
Riding the pagan plain with knees that press
The golden flanks of some great centauress.

Immortelle

Her love is like an autumn flow'r
An immortelle with petals wide,
Risen beside the vine-wrought bow'r,
Whose red leaves, loosened hour by hour,
Pass on the airs of eventide. . . .

On some lost wind the loves that were
In the bleak night are blown away;
But the white memory of her
Endures amid the sigh and stir
Of all dead dreams of yesterday.

In Autumn

Erstwhile, for beauty's tattered gold,
    I have the forfeit tear,
    But now the orchard-lighting year
Has found a heart forlorn and cold.

Though poplars take the passing flame,
    And fling it on the windy skies,
    I listen, hushed with lone surmise,
To hear a half-remembered name.

Estrangement

I have forgot, who once had part
In autumn and in autumn's grief;
Still the red year illumes the leaf,
But not the silence of my heart.

When poplars take the passing fire
And fling it on the windy skies,
I listen, hushed with lone surmise,
In hope to hear a vanished lyre.

Bravely, on some autumnal morrow,
The topmost leaf shall flame and die;
But in my heart an alien sigh
Wakes only with an alien sorrow.

In vain the falling leaves caress
A lute among the roses lost;

And the frail touch of petals tossed
Will leave it mute and tremorless.

A Catch

O mouth by many kissed,
O heart that all might capture!
How art thou fain and mournful
For love that love has missed!—

For all clear weal and pain
Lost now to love for ever!—
Though kings may take their tribute
And reapers take the grain.

Consolation

Forget, forget, and be not sorrowful at all:
Ah, tend no more, in gardens of the terrene years,
This wormwood flowering tall with thy mellifluous tears.

Be glad: a fairer blossom blooms, chimerical,
A golden rose eloigned with vale on vale of blue
In realms beyond the sunset bourn of Xanadu.

Be glad: though here the skies are like a leaden wall;
For still in Saturn, from their isle septentrion,
The black swans fly to seek the jungles of the sun.

Forget, forget, and be not sorrowful at all!

The Temptation

In the close and clinging night,
When the rosy-bellied moon
Like a vestal in a swoon
By black hills was taken slowly;
When my prick was raised upright
With a hot, unwearied, holy
Lust for some tight-bottomed leman—
Siren, woman, witch or demon—
Then it was I heard a laughter,
Warm and clear, like amber melting
Through the heavy gloom, and after
Came a rain of blossoms pelting;

Perfume like an ecstasy
Swelling rose triumphantly,
And the darkness cleft with fire,
In a low-lit dawn revealed
Those whereof my flesh was fain—
Erycine and all her train,
Bodies bared for full desire,
Pacing on a sabbath field! . . .

Now, with hasty gaze, I know
All the cloven Hill has hidden—
Nymphs that rutting gods have ridden
Under suns of long ago;
Givers of a gift divine
Which the Fathers deemed malign;
They that tempted Antony,
Fair or sable succubi;
Vampires by the saints arointed,
Sanguine-lipped and purple coynted;
After whom, in lubric dances,
Now a stranger crew advances,
Tangled limbs and flanks revealing:—
Mountain-roaming oreads,
They whose pleasures icy-keen
Soon benumb the pulse of feeling;
Fountain-fresh limoniads,
All their lilied sex concealing
Under dripping fleeces green;
Golden-tailed, coquetting sphinxes,
Graceful, mad and silent minxes,
Fain for some enormous lover
Their unique behinds to cover;
Exile fays with childish bosoms,
And their undevirginate
Vulvas wrought like budding blossoms
Cool and small and delicate;
Mild and milky titanesses,
With their autumn-colored tresses,
Who would gently squat upon me
In the mode of centauresses;
Umber dryads fleet to shun me—
All are in a lovely rout
That rings me round and round about.

Some their shameless bottoms show
In a long and swelling row;
Some assail me with their pointed
Nipples keen as clitori—
Frantic perfume troublously
Crushed from out their breasts anointed;
Others with their ell-long hair
Seek my thrilling thighs to snare
And my moving body bind
With their amorous bottoms joined;
Some their lubric navels proffer—
Loins and bellies forward curving
Hard with avid lust unswerving;
One, a fringeless coynt would offer,
Veined and pale, that scarcely shows
Aught of all its folded rose;
One, with dim and shielded breast,
Coyly in the shadow lingers,
Golden thighs together pressed
For a stern and iron raping;
One, with deft lascivious fingers,
Holds the soft and coral chalice
Of her rounded vulva gaping
For the horizontal phallus.

Apologia

O gentlest love, I have not played
For you upon the lute of jade,
Nor on that fabulous bassoon
Wrought from the horns of minotaurs,
And set with subtly changing spars
And lucid metals of the moon—

The thing my childish fingers found
Cast on a god-frequented ground,
And unto whose compelling note
Sprang the brown dryad from her tree,
And palest vampires came to me
With limbs more sweet than trodden lote.

I have not made such melodies
As call the philtered sorceries;

But I will weave, some autumn day,
A song to make your beauty mine—
Wrought not with mystical design
And chords of passionate dismay.

For I will tell, with wonted words,
A tale of two that autumn birds
Had led beneath oblivious skies,
Who plucked the wilding asters rare,
And peered from grasses like your hair
To distance blue as your blue eyes.

Incognita

Haply I shall not know, as others know,
The face you have given to the fumbling sun,
That sculptor of chaotic night; and none
May share what loveliness the shadows show
To me, nor watch the curious cameo
Of your archaic brows against the moon—
A tarnished empress on a broad doubloon,
Flame-edged and glowing. Each must ever go
In the sealed world of his peculiar sense,
And this your beauty with diverse phantasms
People the swirl of all impermanence
For our diverse perception. . . . Virginal
You are, and vaguely loved, if loved at all,
For in the closest kiss are unknown chasms.

Enigma

Across thy face a glimmer passes—
Wrought by what far and hidden flame?
Say, is it loveliness, or love,
Or light of sunken moons remembered
From gardens none shall name?

There is a secret shadow clinging
Closely between thy lips of red:
Is it the grief of new desire?
Or half-forgotten darkness lulling
Sorrowful loves long dead?

Query

This doubtful love has slumbered long—
At most, a shadow-mobled flame,
The murmur of a muted song;
And scarce will tell its rightful name
Lest love should do our friendship wrong.

Fair comrade, have you found, as I,
A tremor in some troubling vein
When shoulders touch, the subtle sigh
That is not grief, that is not pain,
And vague delight in being nigh?

Have you, as I, the peril known
Of loitering where the leaves of fall,
Like tatters torn from dryads flown,
Have made, beneath the pines' black pall,
A secret, splendid bed and lone?

Sweet friend, would you my silence have—
A silence wrought of hushed desire?
Or speech wherein like some long wave
The riven deeps of love aspire?
Sweet friend, would you my silence have?

Can you, or I, a lover find,
And keep the tender friend that is?
With closing arms our friendship bind,
Affirm the hand-clasp with a kiss—
And lose not more than lovers find?

This doubtful love has slumbered long—
At most, a shadow-mobled flame,
The murmur of a muted song;
And scarce will tell its rightful name,
Lest love should do our friendship wrong.

Loss

Once, I could find you in my dreams;
Your swaying breasts were apples bright
In sombre sinful crofts of night;
You were the laughter-footed sprite
Who led me on by waning streams,

You were the nymph who called my name
From fountains of forlorn extremes.
But, ah, however far and fast
You fled, our lips would meet at last
In vales eloigned from time and shame.

Alas, I cannot find you now:
From alp to phantom alp in sleep
A phantom light they cannot keep
Goes outward to the oblivious deep,
And fades from my pursuing brow.
Lost in a wood of shadowy leaf,
Vain laughter dies, I know not how,
Remote, alone and unredeemed;
And I forget the dream I dreamed,
And sadden with evasive grief.

Concupiscence

As the fierce faun, on the cypress-bearded cape,
Desires the sea-girl, seen with billow-drifted
Hair the color of kelp and shadowy-rifted
Vulva that only knows the slow sea's rape,
And vainly stares, till the fair, unfondled nape
Goes down to ocean's coral-crofted valleys:
Then, in a daylong dream, he swings and dallies
Through the close gulfs about her swirling shape
And turns not when familiar dryads come
To tickle his bowed neck with sharpening tips
Of laughter-lifted bosoms, or to snare
His nodding yerd with loops of moon-warm hair:—
Thus, Lais, am I fain for masterdom
Upon thy flown unparted thighs and lips.

Maya

Fools of the world, who dream that dreams are true,
Believing still that life is what it seems,
And trustful that the world is more than dreams—
Free for a little, I have laughed at you—
Knowing all this a ghostly gossamer
In some eternal room of darkness spun;

A laughter of forgotten gods that were,
Echoing still in waste oblivion.

But once again, as others, I have lent
Myself to earthly ways and earthly walls:
Illusion of illusion, fantasy
Of doubtful phantoms, nevermore to be
When slumber on the last delirium falls
And lulls the tossing shadows turbulent.

Dead Love

Is it a dream, is it a memory—
 That, underneath some warmer moon of yore,
 We dreamt of love, we dreamt forevermore
To make of Love our immortality?

Alas, alas! for all the moons of old,
 And all the golden suns are blind with gloom . . .
 To thee, alone in some forgotten tomb,
The worm, with clinging kisses wan and cold.

Mocking my love, came long ago, thine eyes,
 That were the mirrors of mine own desire,
 Hold everlasting darkness; life and lust

Are shadows, in the lonely night that lies
 Mute on thy lips, and love's triumphant fire
 Is one for me with thy forgotten dust.

A Prayer

O vermeil mouth that I have kissed in vain!
O hair that was a golden web of pain,
Woven to hold my heart!—
Since you are lost, and Love is fled from me,
With you I fain would lose Love's memory,
And let my dream depart.

O arms, O bosom, white as foam or fire,
Made warm for my delight and my desire—
Return, return to me,
Or take with you the passion and the pain,
The lonely grief, the longing all in vain,
The dream, the memory.

Enchanted Mirrors

These are enchanted mirrors that I bring—
By daemons wrought from metals of the moon
To burnished forms of lune or plenilune.
Therein are faery faces vanishing,
And warm Pompeiian phantoms lovelier
Than mortal flesh or marble; and the gleam
Of suns that from Saturnia rose in dream
And sank on golden worlds that never were.

Therein you shall behold unshapen dooms,
And ghoul-astounding shadows of the tombs;
Oblivion, with eyes like poppy-buds,
Or love, with blossoms plucked in Devachan,
In stillness of the santal-pillared woods—
But nevermore the moiling world of man.

Minatory

Scorners of the Muse, beware!
She that you deny is queen
Of a thunder-girt demesne
In the worlds of Otherwhere;
Ships that ply on shadowy seas
Past the surging galaxies,
Bring the loot of heaven and hell
To her stellar citadel;
Powers benignant and malign
In her single service join;
Cherubim and seraphim
Wait upon her briefest whim;
Gods august you have not known
Gather to her awful throne,
Demons that you wot not of
Serve her with a fearful love;
Dim Summanus, lord of night,
Is her moiling minister,
Demogorgon toils for her
In the darkling Infinite.

Interrogation

Love, will you look with me
Upon the phosphor-litten labor of the Worm—
Time's minister, who toils for his appointed term,
And has for fee
All superannuate loves, and all the loves to be?

Love, can you see, as I,
The corpses, ghosts and demons mingled with the crowd?
The djinns that men have freed, grown turbulent and proud?
Alastor, Asmodai?
And all-unheeded envoys from the stars on high?

Know you the gulfs below,
Where darkling Erebus on Erebus is driven
Between the molecules—atom from atom riven,
And tossing to and fro,
Incessant, like the souls on Dante's wind of woe?

Know you the deeps above?
The terror and vertigo of those who gaze too long
Upon the crystal skies unclouded? Are you strong
With me to prove
Even in thought or dream the dreadful pits above?

Know you the gulfs within?
The larvae, the minotaurs of labyrinths undared?
The sombre foam of seas by cryptic sirens shared?
The pestilence and sin
Borne by the flapping shroud of liches met within?

Madrigal

Low-lidded eyes thou hast,
But all too beautiful for love to bear:
Fain would I kiss them fast
Like tranquil flowers closing
Tired with the burden of the sunset air.

Thy bosom's mootful white
Is softly curved, but fraught with poignant sorrow:
Thereon my lips reposing
In long and proved delight
A comfort from their present bane would borrow.

Sandalwood

Upon thy separate road
(Thou, who hast chosen the world's appointed way)
My songs shall be as the perfume of sandalwood
Borne by a secret wind from form-lost irretrievable islands,
Where the hibiscus bowers of our love,
And the palaces of roseate marble,
With all their vine-caught pillars,
Were dreamt, but never builded.
And through the clanging tumult of thy days,
A rumor of phantom chords,
Of dulcimers destroyed,
And lutes that might have been,
Shall call and cry to thee as the burden of my songs;
And thou shalt hear the spectral fountains fall,
Delicious as the laughter
Of ghosts of amorous women,
Of flowers that never were;
And winds that flee, exiguous and faint,
Like the sighs of long-dead lovers,
Through seedless gardens without place or name.
And thou shalt know
What immaterial myrtles, pale and sweet
As the breasts of love-worn queens,
Or flushed as with a maiden's glowing blood,
Were strewn to make
The forfeit couch where two shall never come;
And know
What topaz or what Tyrian-colored wines
The palm-entrellised grapes
Withhold in lost Cocaigne.

October

The blood of wounded love is on your leaves, October,
And in your seaward wind the sigh of love foredone:
Though I should fold them round me, cerement-like and sober,
In all your mist and rain is no oblivion,
Where memory clings the closer for the perished sun.
The blood of wounded love is on your leaves, October.

By you I am betrayed to all my memories,

Autumn, whose cleaving colors are a fallen sword!
Your distant vales are blue as Aidenn, yet no ease
I find therein, but pain against my coming stored:
Autumn, whose heart is one with all lost things adored,
By you I am betrayed to all my memories.

I would the mounded snow of mountains hyperborean
Were heaped upon your latest ember, quenching it!
In some tremendous world of ice, or world marmorean,
I would entomb for aye my fevers infinite:—
Yea, well it were to lie in frozen sleep unlit
Beneath the mounded snow of mountains hyperborean.

Ah, that my love and all your leaves, on Lethe drifting
Were borne, and cast upon the secret isles of sleep,
Where love and slumber are the same, and suns unlifting
And gods and men go down to quaff the dreamless deep:
Autumn, I would that thou and I were one in sleep,
With this my love and all your leaves on Lethe drifting.

The Envoys

None other saw them when they came
Across the many-clangored mart,
But in mine eyes and in my heart
They passed as might the pillared flame
Of lightning loosened on the tombs,
Or errant suns that wander by
To dawn on the Cimmerii.

Great monarchs, proud and cypress-tall,
With zones and crowns of argentry,
They were, who proffered royally
Full urns of pulsing gems to all:—
The blood-warm gems of lunar wombs,
Pale ores, and opals pavonine,
And beryls like to leopards' eyne.

Their eyes were lit with alien day,
Were filled of alien worlds; their feet
With starry splendors paved the street,
And silver dust of some bright way
Fell from their garments, with perfumes
More strange than breath of vernal gales
From Saturn's moly-cinctured vales.

What embassy were they, from suns
Of Algebar or Capricorn—
From planets of remoter morn
In flaming fields where Taurus runs—
Or haply come, immediate,
From out a four-dimensioned world
With the occlusive ether furled?

They strode upon the swooning pave,
They towered by the trembling spires,
Tall as apocalyptic fires
Above the peoples of the grave:
But, sightless and inveterate,
To Mammon vowed, the throng went by,
Charneled beneath an iron sky.

Yea, blinder than the steel and stone,
Men took not from their proffered store
One gift of all the gifts they bore,
But sued for gold to gods foreknown.
I, too, bemused, inebriate,
Amort with splendor, could but stand
And see them pass, with empty hand.

Ode

Your name is like the opening of a flow'r
The forest's brief and pensive-petalled rose,
Unfolding in a land of larch and pine,
Where shadowy snows
Loiter and sparkle secretly,
Asleep in many a forest-builded bow'r
Made sunless with the close and fragrant vine;
To vanish ere that sultry autumn hour
When the pale grapes are heavy with such wine
As fays of the north night drink
In elfin revelry,
Dancing beneath the ghostly, fluttered gold
Of birches, on some ice-worn ocean-brink,
Where the wide waters hold
Far out, the hue of sapphire-hearted skies
And your sweet eyes.

Un Couchant

Tombant au loin d'un ciel blessé,
Le couchant, sur l'étang de jais,
S'épand comme du sang fané.

Les ténèbres, par delà l'eau,
Nichent sans bruit dans le cypress
Avec le lourd et las corbeau.

Saisi du noir enchantement,
Un fier tombeau se fond dans l'ombre
Comme un fantôme, lentement.

Comme les goules, assouvis,
Les ifs, courbés sur l'ossuaire,
Sont paisibles et assoupis.

Le jour, un souvenir mourant,
S'égare dans le morne bois
Et se noie sous le noir étang.

. . . .

Tombant au loin d'un coeur blessé,
Sur l'eau du léthé mon amour
S'épand comme du sang fané.

A Sunset

Far-falling from a wounded heaven,
The sunset, on the pool of jet,
Is shed like faded blood.

The shadows of night, beyond the water,
Nest without noise in the cypress
With the tired and heavy raven.

Seized by a black enchantment,
A proud tomb dissolves in the shadow,
Like a phantom, slowly.

Like to sated ghouls,
The yew-trees, bowed above the ossuary,
Are drowsy and tranquil.

The day, a dying memory,
Wanders lost in the mournful wood,
And drowns beneath the black pool.

. . . .
Far-falling from a wounded heart,
My love, on the waters of Lethe,
Is shed like faded blood.

Un Madrigal

Mes rêves sont les loriots tards
Qui fuient les tristes brouillards,
Pour trouver, au ciel de ton âme,
L'été perdu et le dictame
De tous les floraisons fuyards.

Tout rêve est une fleur absente,
Mais son parfum à jamais monte
Vers les nuages de ton coeur,
Dans un air tiède et sans chaleur,
Taché d'automne et d'amarante.

Mes rêves sont des chants plus vieux,
Chantés par un soir nuageux,
Qui montent parmi les pétales
Des roses embaumées et pâles,
Tombant à tes volets ombreux.

A Madrigal

My dreams are belated orioles
That flee the mournful mists
To find, in the heaven of thy soul,
The lost summer and the balsam
Of all the fugitive flowerings.

My dreams are dying flowers,
But ever their fragrant lives
Mount toward the altar of thy heart
In a soft and heatless air
Where indolent clouds are born.

My dreams are olden songs
Sun on a clouded evening,
That mount among the petals
Of pale and perfumed roses
Falling at thy shadowy shutters.

The Saturnienne

Beneath the skies of Saturn, pale and many-mooned,
Her palace is;
Her wyvern-warded spires of celadon, enruned
With names benign and mightier names of malefice,
Illume with saffron phares
A marish by the black, lethargic seas lagooned;
Her dragon-holden stairs
Go down in coiling jet and gold on some unplumbed abyss.

Long as a leaping flame, exalted over all,
Across the sun
Her banners bear Aidennic blooms armorial
And beasts infernal on a field of ciclaton;
Amid her agate courts,
Like to a demon ichor, towering proud and tall,
A scarlet fountain spurts,
To fall upon parterres of dwale and deathly hebenon.

From out her amber windows, gazing languidly
On a weird land
Where conium and cannabis and upas-tree
Seem wrought in verdigris against the copper sand,
She sees and sees again
A trailing salt like leprous dragons from the sea
Far-crawled upon the fen;
And foam of monster-cloven gulfs beyond a fallow strand.

Or, looking from her turrets to the south and north,
She notes the gleam
Of molied mountains and of rivers pouring forth,
Clear as the dawn, to fail in fulvous rill and stream
The widening waste amid;
Or swell the fallen meres, abominable, swarth,
In green mirages hid,
To be the unquested grails of hell, of death and deathful dream.

Apostrophe

O world, thou art the form, the name, the symbol of my weariness:
But, older than thy drooling god, mine ennui had its prime abode
Potential in the fathomless, foreshaping yawn of night and flame.

O world, thou shalt abide and be, for some brief travail of the sun
The form and name of my distress, an image of the weariness
That shall survive thy kalpas done, the doom that is eternity.

Chansonette

Mon amour, la chair des roses
Se moule à la chair mortelle
Dans ta forme blanche et belle,
Qui recèle de fleurs closes . . .
Oh! la chair des blanches roses!

Que mes baisers lents demeurent
Sur tes seins et sur tes cuisses!
Dans l'obscur lieu des délices,
Qu'ils restent longtemps, et meurent
Que mes baisers en demeurent!

Il n'est pas de toi un pouce
Qui n'a sa propre caresse:
D'une subtile tendresse,
D'une passion jalouse,
J'ai connu de toi tout pouce.

La souvenance me monte,
Au plaisir elle s'allie:
Quand sous moi ton corps se plie,
Toute mémoire cuisante
Me mord encor et me monte.

Nous coucherons sur l'herbette
Par un soir d'étoiles douces . . .
Comme en un doux lit de mousses,
Je rendormirai ma tête
Dans ton giron sur l'herbette.

Idylle païenne

Je sais une terre ancienne,
Une terre où d'oiseaux perdus
Surnagent seuls dans l'eau païenne;
Où le vent est souvent si doux
Qu'il ne sème à la lame oisive
Les frêles fleurs des buissons verts

Qui poussent pardessus les mers
Du haut de la plage massive.

C'est un pays où les vieux dieux
Ne sont volés vers d'autres cieux;
Où des faméliques lamies
Nous leurrent au couvert caché;
Où des dryades endrmies
Gisent dans l'ombrage taché
D'un soleil d'or par la saulaie;
Où la sirène dans la baie
Du glauque golfe approfondi
Nage indolemment à midi.

Il n'est pas des châsses croulées,
Il n'est pas des lauriers cassés:
On trouve ici les jours passés
Et les nuits longuement coulées.
Pour nous, qui viendrons plus tardifs
A ses vallons, à ses massifs,
Ce pays reste impérissable,
Sommeillant chimériquement
Et baigné par l'enchantement
De sa jaune aube intarissable.

Idylle païenne

I know an ancient land,
Where the feignèd birds, long dreamt of us,
Float all alone in the pagan water;
Where the wind is oftentime so gentle
That it sows not to the idle wave
The frail flowers of the bushes green
That grow above the seas
From the height of the massive shore.

It is a land where the olden gods
Have flown not toward other skies;
Where famishing lamias
Allure us to their hidden covert;
Where drowsy dryads
Lie in the shade that is touched
By a golden sun through the willow-wood;
Where the siren in the bay

From the glaucous gulf profound
Swims indolently at full noon.

There are no crumbled shrines,
There are no broken laurel-trees:
Here one shall find the by-gone days
And the nights long flowed away.
For us, who come full tardily
Unto its vales, unto its groves,
This land remains imperishable,
Sleeping a sleep chimerical
And bathed by the enchantment
Of its never-failing yellow dawn.

Retrospect and Forecast

Retournez-toi, O Vie, pour voir de l'oeil frappé
Le sein qui t'a nourri, que la Mort ne déguise;
Maintenant dans ta bouche est la poussière exquise,
Puisée aux bas tombeaux. Tout ce de toi mangé,
Etait jadis au sein de la Mort allaité,
Tout servit d'alimenter la Mort, dans sa saison;
Les vermines au sol, l'étoile dans sa maison,
Ainsi que les goules, s'engraissent du passé.

Doit-il demeurer à jamais, affreux, immonde,
Cet alternat plus vieux que nul peut éviter?
Le Beau, faut-il s'enraciner en pourritures
Où la nuit dévore ses fleurs de flammes mûres?
La Vie, veut-elle, enfin, ne pas se dégoûter?
Ma Mort, veut-elle ne pas s'assouvir des mondes?

Sonnet lunaire

Une lune blêmie s'allume en mon royaume,
En mon ancien royaume, éloigné par les ans:
De ses nues, à travers des voiles découvrants,
Elle illumine un bois l'ancien Avril embaume.

Des vallons verdoyés erre le vieil arôme
De tous les prés en leurs premières floraisons;
Et l'autan a mêlé dans leur très simple encens
Les parfums magistraux de sandal et d'amome.

Nulle feuille n'a fui des bois du souvenir;
Là, nulle fleur n'épand une moindre petale;
La lune du passé, fabuleuse et fatale,

Est la même à jamais . . . Mais l'amour des vieux jours,
Magiquement, parfaitement, doit devenir
La face encor baisée de mon dernier amour.

Sonnet lunaire

A pale moon kindles in my kingdom,
In mine olden kingdom, eloigned by the years:
From her clouds, across uncovering veils,
She illumes a wood perfumed by olden April.

From valleys green there wanders the old aroma
Of all the meads in their first flowerings;
And the south-wind has mingled with their most simple incense
The magisterial perfumes of sandalwood and amomum.

No leaf has flown from the woods of memory,
And there, no flower sheds even one least petal;
The moon of the past, inevitable and fabulous,

Is the same forever . . . But the love of olden days,
Magically, perfectly, must needs become
The face again kissed of my final love.

À Mi-Chemin

Des rêves trop blafards,
Des chimères plus blêmes,
Des minaudiers blasphèmes,
Et des péchés cafards—

Tous sont les tiens, vieux lâche;
Tu n'as pas les cieux beaux,
Les tombeaux infernaux:
En limbes tu te cache.

Mais, avant que ton coeur
Ne perd l'espoir étrange,
Monte, monte le mur

Où sommeillent les anges;
Ou serre, en leurs abîmes,
Les succubes infimes.

À Mi-Chemin

The dreams that are over-dim,
The chimeras all too vague,
The lackadaisical blasphemies
And the hypocritical sins—

All, all are thine, old craven:
Thou knowest not the fairer heavens
Or the tombs infernal—
Thou hidest thyself in limbo.

But, ere thy heart
Shall lose the stranger hope,
Mount, mount the wall

Where drowse the angels;
Or clasp, in their abysms,
The lowliest succubi.

L'Abîme

Démons boudeurs
Passant parmi maussades fleurs;
L'upas fleuri
Qui couve un rivage flétri;
La tour d'ébène
Montant vers les nuées lointaines;
Soleils naissants,
Tout noirs, de marais phosphorescents;
Cités de fer,
Rouillées, perdues, dans une mer
D'un monde au loin;
Spectres d'encens ou de benzoin
En un coffret
Recélé d'un blafard palais;
Cornes de Pan,
Reêvés parmi les bois d'antan;
L'enfer de glace,
D'où, morfondu, le Satan passe
Aux puits de flamme:
—Ces, ces s'abîment dans mon ame.

Le Cauchemar

La puanteur des ondes croupissantes
Rompit mon rêve au sein des parades:
Dans des terrains poudreux et infinis,
Je m'enfousais sous des cendres pesantes.

Le poids de leurs nécropoles croulantes
M'opprimait tout le corps; des cieux noires
Planaient là-bas des soleils amortis
Entre luisaient sur des eaux pourrissantes.

Chanson de rêve

Les vents du renouveau
Penchent le blanc pavot
Et remuent le vert baumier,
La palme, et l'ébenier,
Dans l'île qui tu as rêvé
Mais qui tu n'as trouvé.

Là, toute fleur demeure:
L'azur plus tiède effleure
La cime à fleurs du magnolier;
Et là, le giroflier
Semé de boutons embaumés
Les gazons parfumés.

Quoiqu'elle soit plus loin,
Ses parfums de benjoin
Nous arrivent du chaud couchant:
Allons, au ciel dormant:
Ce soir, il nous sera facile
Devenir à cette île.

Le Cheveu

Quelquefois, lorsque j'ai trouvé
Un cheveu que ta tête aimée
Laisse à mon épaule embaumée,
Il est facile de rêver

Que ta tête encore se presse
Dessus mon coeur abandonné,

Et que je pouvais la donner
Des baisers vifs et des tendresses.

Éloignement

Que sert de ce désir qui me dévore?
Car vous êtes si loin! La rouge ardour
Ne coule pas au dèla de mon coeur,
L'amour dans mes veines étouffe encoure.

La flamme en moi brûle comme un bûcher
Se consumant solitaire et futile:
Quand vos serez à moi, foyer utile,
Chaud âtre, il servira de réchauffer

Nos corps et nos coeurs morfondus. Mes veines
Seront alors des citernaux ouverts
Parmi la sécheresse des deserts,

Où nous assouvirons nos soifs humaines.
—Vous êtes loin; nul a làché les eaux;
La feu n'a franchi des profonds brumaux.

Exotique

Ta bouche est le pareil d'une orchide incarnate,
D'où parfum et poison, inconnus, se leve
Aux lunes dans l'iris ou vert, ou se mele
Dans les charmilles d'est au pur matin qu'eclate.

Il auraut fallu voir, dans l'ile d'amarante,
Des couchants teints comme la flamme du l'encens,
Ou longs midis, chargés de senteurs qui montent,
Melées, sur lieues pourprées et sablon diamanté.

Tes seins, où le sang coule au marbre s'en fondus,
Tes reins de neige du tropique, et membres nus—
Ces, ces, par quoi desir et devenu divin,

Sont faits pour rêves dans un mystique palais,
Pour l'amour, et sommeil, et lentes voluptés,
Et mers d'été, qui moutonnent comme le vin.

La Méduse des cieux

Comme un cadavre froid qui sort de son tombeau,
La Lune rétrécie lève sa tête creuse,
Apportant la lueur mortelle et malheureuse
Que verse aux morts leur ciel comme un morne caveau.

Maintenant ses rayons ont blanchi des lieux sombres
En la pâleur d'un pays d'où la Vie s'enfuit;
Là, se traîne un ombrage au sépulcre qui luit,
Ainsi que des cadrans les désastreuses ombres.

A travers le terrain qui se glace et qui dort
Comme un monde que foule aux pieds la pâle Mort,
Une blancheur terreuse éternellement glisse:

Car le monde est gelé du blanc pouvoir des yeux
Remplis d'un froid silence et d'un dur maléfice—
Les yeux de la Méduse immortelle des cieux.

To George Sterling: A Valediction

I

Farewell, a late farewell! Tearless and unforgetting,
Alone, aloof, I twine
Cypress and golden rose, plucked at the chill sunsetting,
Laurel, amaracus, and dark December vine
Into a garland wove not too unworthily
For thee who seekest now an asphodel divine.
Though immaterial the leaf and blossom be,
Haply they shall outlinger these the seasons bring,
The seasons take, and tell of mortal monody
Through many a mortal spring.

II

Once more, farewell! Naught is to do, naught is to say,
Naught is to sing but sorrow!
For grievous is the night, and dolorous the day
In this one hell of all the damned we wander thorough.
Thou hast departed—and the dog and swine abide,
The fetid-fingered ghouls will delve, on many a morrow
In charnel, urn and grave: the sun shall lantern these,

Oblivious, till they too have faltered and have died,
And are no more than pestilential breath that flees
On air unwalled and wide.

III

Let ape and pig maintain their council and cabal:
In ashes gulfward hurled,
Thou art gone forth with all of loveliness, with all
Of glory long withdrawn from a desertless world.
Now let the loathlier vultures of the soul convene:
They have no wings to follow thee, whose flight is furled
Upon oblivion's nadir, or some lost demesne
Of the pagan dead, vaulted with perfume and with fire,
Where blossoms immarcescible in verspertine
Strange amber air suspire.

IV

Peace, peace! for grief and bitterness avails not ever,
And sorrow wrongs thy sleep:
Better it is to be as thou, who art forever
As part and parcel of the infinite fair deep—
Who dwellest now in mystery, with days hesternal
And time that is not time: we have no need to weep,
For woe may not befall, where thou in ways supernal
Hast found the perfect love that is oblivion,
The poppy-tender lips of her that reigns, eternal,
In realms not of the sun.

V

Peace, peace! Idle is our procrastinating praise,
Hollow the harps of laud;
And not necessitous the half-begrudgèd bays
To thee, whose song forecrowned thee for a lyric god,
Whose name shall linger strangely, in the sunset years,
As music from a more enchanted period—
An echo flown upon the changing hemispheres,
Re-shaped with breath of alien maiden, alien boy,
Re-sung in future cities, mixed with future tears,
And with remoter joy.

VI

From Aphrodite thou hast turned to Proserpine:
No treason hast thou done,
For neither goddess is a goddess more divine,
And verily, my brother, are the twain not one?
We too, as thou, with hushed desire and silent paean,
Beyond the risen dark, beyond the fallen sun,
Shall follow her, whose pallid breasts, on shores Lethean,
Are favorable phares to barges of the world;
And we shall find her there, even as the Cytherean,
In love and slumber furled.

After Armageddon

God walks lightly in the gardens of a cold, dark star,
Knowing not the dust that gathers in His garments' fold;
God signs Him with the clay, marks Him with the mould,
Walking in the fields unsunned of a sad, lost war,
In a star long cold.

God treads brightly where the bones of unknown things lie,
Pale with His splendor as the frost in a moon-bleached place;
God sees the tombs by the light of His face,
He shudders at the runes writ thereon, and His shadow on the sky
Shudders hugely in space.

God talks briefly with His armies of the tomb-born worm,
God holds parley with the grey worm and pale, avid moth:
Their mouths have eaten all, but the worm is wroth
With a dark hunger still, and he murmurs harm
With the murmuring moth.

God turns Him heavenward in haste from a death-dark star,
But His robes are assoilèd by the dust of unknown things dead;
The grey worm follows creeping, and the pale moth has fed
Couched in a secret golden fold of His broad-trained cimar
Like a doom unsaid.

Juvenilia

[Untitled]

A mother is a mother,
A son is a son,
And they love each other.

[Fragment 1]

III

I saw, as morning lit the sky, the temples gleam with red on high;
As blood they gleamed, the dawning light on old and grim sandstone.
In shadows black the darkness lay, behind the ruins stretch'd away;
In solitary majesty stood old Chittore alone.

IV

There I stood, a spell flung o'er me, gazing on the walls before me—
Broken stone and temples lonely, stately palace grim;
With its halls in desolation, forsaken by the Rajput nation—
Halls where footsteps echo, tho' no Rana walks within!

V

In marble courtyards old and lonely, tenanted by jackals only,
Stains of Rajpoot blood, and noble, lay upon the stones.
Beheld I, where some Moslem slain, a rusty sabre long had lain—
Grim remnant of Akbar, and the crashing Rajpoot thrones.

VI

Gone is famous Chitrung Mori, Khoumbhou is told in story,
Still the lofty Kherut stands, majestic, towering o'er.
Tho' Chitrung is forever gone, still his palace stands alone;
Unseen hands repelling, no Rana enters old Chittore.

VII

As I stood before that splendid tower, of a reign long-ended,
Strange were the thoughts, and weird, that flashed across my brain.
Who knows, but in yon zenana, of a long-forgotten Rana,
Strange scenes are enacted on a moonlit night again?

VIII

Who knows, but as the moon shall rise, again Pudmani's sacrifice,
Again great Akbar's whelming power o'erthrows the Rajpoot might!
As rises still the moon of red, and gleams on Kherut's lofty head—
What strange scenes are re-enacted, 'neath the covering night!

[Fragment 2]

III

Come with me, friend, and let the Dervish flout;
Come with me, for lo! the True Dawn is out;
And one moment of our time is past.
Let us sip—who knows—, this may be our last.
Come, let us go. Dead Ramadan is gone,
With all his want and fast—and now, the Dawn!
Come, my friend, for see, the red rose in bloom
O'er the white marble of a monarch's tomb;
And from the city's minaret I hear
The muezzin's song salute the waiting ear.

IV

One night I stood and saw the moon rise slow,
Lighting palace and mosque with silver glow;
Until each house in the uncertain light
Shone forth from its shadow of darkest night.
And so I stood, and watch'd her sink again,
Till darkness dropt o'er palace, house, and fane.
O, think thou, when she rises again to-night,
How many who have often seen her light
[. . .]

VI

Two days of Time my eye hath seen,
Two days of strange and varied mien.
Of one the face was bright and clear,
Of one the face was dark and drear.
And if thou seest thy darker day,
Think thou, it hath not come to stay;
The morrow's morn thou mayest see
The brighter one Time brings to thee.

And if this life be dark and drear,
Why not the next be bright and clear?
Who knows what we of earth shall see
When Time unveils futurity!

VII

Lo! I saw the sun hid in darkest night,
While moon and stars shone forth with ghostly light;
O, Allah, what a strange, unworthy sight
My startled eyes gazed on in wild affright!
And as I looked, the sun came out again,
And in his light shone over hill and plain;
Not for long the pale moon and stars had ta'en
The glorious light that now shone amain.
So I think that darkness may not conceal
For long the merit that Time must reveal.
Hidden brilliance shining forth again
More glory from obscurity hath ta'en!

IX

One eve I heard the muezzin cry
The Azân from his stand on high.
In meditation wrapt I stood,
And thought of all things bad and good.
One other muezzin I heard
Cry silently to each his Word;
His the cry of all joy and fear
His the Azân that all must hear.
I heard him calling forth to strife,
He, the muezzin men name Life.
And when he calleth out to thee
Take heed thou dost not turn, nor flee.

[Fragment 3]

VI

I saw the rising of a city great
Wherein Jumsheed in his glory once sate
And now within the royal palace hall
I saw the lizard and the spider crawl.

Where once had stood a jewell'd, golden throne
And all the glory of a king had shone,
Lo! the spider his silver web had cast
And a great marble slab had held it fast.
Who knows but on that stone Jumsheed had sate?
Strange are the vagaries of destiny and fate!
And as I stood the great palace walls before
The moon rose and in all her light shone o'er
And through the courts of that forgotten race
All the night she went seeking his last face.

[Fragment 4]

I

One thing at least is sure—our Time is short.
All else is naught but guess and vain report;
One day we think, one day we know and live—
The next, all things shall end for us—in what?

II

As sand upon a desert's face are blown
The sons of man to destinies unknown.
    Our fate is hidden by a darkened veil,
But this I think—that each shall find his Own.

III

Mayhap that Life and death, as Day and Night,
Alternate are.
Why not another Dawn for us—why not
A second day in wake of blackest night?

From Kamal

If you would know the course to happiness, the surest way,
List well my words: Heed not tomorrow, heed not yesterday.

[Fragment 5]

The die of olden deeds is cast
    Cast—and cast forever.
We cannot turn back the page of years,
    It is closed and sealed.
And all our hopes and all our fears
    Stand therein revealed.

Let them lie, and turn away,
    The die is cast, and cast forever.
What bodes the past to us to-day,
    The river is flowing ever and ever?
And all the thoughts and deeds of yore
    Have silent floated down the stream.
All that's past is forever o'er,
    'Tis but a bygone, shadowy dream.

The past is now behind us,
    The veiled future lies before.
Why should old thoughts bind us?
    Let them bind no more.
Life is passing, passing swift,
    We're floating towards an unseen shore.
Onward, onward we silent drift,
    Silent we meet what lies before.

And foolish man but reaps
    The fruits of his curiousity. [*sic*]
Alla knows and Alla decrees
    What is best for man.
With his eyes all things he sees,
    Far better than we ever can.

The shadows thicken on the blast,
    Evening draweth near.
Life's acts are nearly past,
    The end is cold and drear.
We've drained the cup and now 'tis empty,
    Still it's wine glows in our eyes.
Before us lieth eternity,
    Soon death will still our sighs.

Drink, drink while you may,
    Life is but a fleeting shadow.

Drink—drink and drink to-day,
    'Tis but a glimpse of El-Dorado.
Now the shadows thicken on the blast,
    The end is drawing nigh.
Soon we'll drink our last,
    Then plunge into the gulf—and say good-bye.

Think not of the past,
    For what is done is done forever.
[. . . ?]

[Fragment 6]

Heading for Chapter II

O'er Kyber's pass the Persians came,
    Where lay the Afghan, Ahmad Khan,
With clash of sword, and smoke, and flame.
    He dropt upon the caravan.
Where ride the peaks of Kyberee.
    Down they came to the Russian band
And sabres clashed, and swords flew free
    At Ahmad Khan's command.
                The Afghan Knife

Benares

I

I stood by the Ganges and watch'd the pilgrims come and go
Forth from the city's streets and fanes and all of India's land;
Stood on the ghauts and saw them coming, going, fast and slow,
Out of the streets, and plains, and jungle, and hot desert sand.

II

Of all races, and peoples, and castes, they came to the stream,
From all lands of the East, and some of the faraway West;
There by the Ganges I saw them, under the burning beam
Of Melia's sun—king and beggar, the worst and the best.

III

And lo! I saw the blind *Facquir* stand by the Rajah's side;
Each stood, judg'd not by rank and power, but acts and deeds.
All men came with their sins to stand the Ganges stream beside,
To bathe in its holy waters—his and his brother's needs.

IV

Down by the ghauts I saw them come, out from the tribes of man,
Out of the cities, and jungles, and deserts of the East.
Turban of white, and turban of red, as the river ran,
I beheld,—each by his brother's side—the great and the least.

V

The temples of sandstone shimmer'd in haze of sultry heat;
The river gleams, as gleams a glittering Orient blade.
Out on the ghats the people came the holy stream to meet.
I saw the 'Rajah's palanteen, the priest within his shade.

VI

A Sudra and a Brahmin stood upon the steps of stone,
A thousand tongues I heard from every Orient land;
And o'er me stole the subtle spell of mystic ages gone—
A thousand years, Benares, past [*sic*] me by at thy command!

VII

A thousand years flashed past on Genii wings as there I stood,
The scales of modern sight and sound had silent slid away;
And I a pilgrim was, amid the mingled bad and good—
A suppliant and a pilgrim in Benares on that day!

VIII

Benares! a thousand pictures spring into life at thought
Myriad images of all its life and mystery
How many palaces and people, long, ah long forgot—
That mystic word may bring in recollection unto me!

IX

Before my eye of thought again in silence there appears
Great Siva's golden temple standing high above the street.
The burning ghat, in smoke and fame and wet with final tears
The Monkey temple and the Ganges bank where many meet!

X

In thought again I floated down great Ganga's ceaseless stream,
And saw the palaces stand out in light of silent moon
And Aurungzebe's pale minaret in that silvery gleam
A fairy shaft of light that paled and faded all too soon!

XI

Thus lay the ghats in glorious light of India's dawn
May silent lie beside the eternal, ceaseless river.
And then in starlit shadow when sultry day is gone
As they have lain for countless years, and shall lie forever.

The End

The Prayer Rug

I

Out of the past thou comest, rug of Persian loom,
And calm thou lyest in the still and silent room.
Who was thy weaver, O Rug of Memories,
And whose were the knees that prest thee long ago?
Who was he who prayed with upraised eyes,
Whose the passionate voice that murmured low?

II

What strange and marvellous tales, I wonder, couldst thou tell
Of great warriors, saints, and souls dragged down to hell;
Of Princes, Sultans, Shahs and Viziers strong,
Poets who prayed to Allah on bended knee;
Beautiful women, with laughter and song,
Many tales, I think, couldst thou tell to me.

III

If thou couldst speak, and sweep aside the Web of Years,
What wondrous tales of joys, and hates, and loves and fears
Thou mightest tell; of great armies marching forth
With brave array of flashing spear and blade;
Of mighty battles that shook the very earth,
And kings and shahs that, kneeling on thee, prayed.

IV

Rug of thousand memories, woven long ago,
Many the marvellous tales that thou mayest know;
Rug of countless years, prest by myriad knees,
Sultans, Kings, have, praying, knelt upon thee.
How many strange and marvellous tales of thee,
I wonder, couldst thou tell to me.

The Rubaiyat of Seyyid

I

Within the Great Bazaar I walk'd one Day,
And as I went I heard a dervise say:
"Think, Brother, there is but one Life to live:—
Therefore waste not our little Time Today."

II

To-day we live, To-morrow we may die;
Spend not your Time in unavailing Sigh.
Why mourn because of misspent Yesterday?
Let not this Day pass you unheeded by."

III

Lo! the Past has left us, fleeing away
Unto the Dusk of long-dead Yesterday;
And deep-veiled To-morrow is not yet—
"Therefore waste not our little Time Today."

IV

If in the Book of Time there be a Blot
On the white Page against thee, mourn it not.
The Black Word is written, and the closed Page
May not turn back again. Leave it forgot.

[. . .]

XVII

Where is the Tomb of Kaikobad the Great,
Or the Palace where Sultan Mahmud sate?
Go ask of the Spider and the Jackal,
And say with me, "O Allah, this is Fate!"

XVIII

Think, ye who stand within this great Bazaar
Men call the World, how Allah from afar,
Guides our Kismet with his great steadfast Hand,
Appointing to each One his destined Star!

XIX

The Books of Wisdom I have studied o'er,
And might still study them forevermore,
But that all they taught me was little else
Than that which I had known ten times before!

XX

So all the Books my Hand hath flung aside,
And I, within a Shiraz garden bide:
One Petal of a fallen Rose shall teach
Me more than many other things beside.

XXI

All earthly Wisdom known to Man I found
Within my Shiraz garden's leafy Bound;
Flowery symbols of Earthly Sight and Sound
In each Rose and Hyacinth growing 'round.

XXII

As the Moon rose list'ning to the Nightingale,
I stood and watch'd till the Stars grew pale.
Ah, how many Secrets may the Stars know,
That we know not, who stand without the Veil!

XXIII

Stand here and watch the petals falling 'round
And think we too must lie upon the ground
Perhaps tomorrow, as silent as they—
Lie still and pale and utter not a Sound.

XXIV

For each Red Rose that silent falleth now,
Another shall yet grow upon the Bough;
A thousand Roses each Day fall to Earth,
Tomorrow shall a thousand more endow.

Sunrise

A faint, golden light,
Small, yet bright,
Comes out of the cold, gray morning,
Advancing slowly from the East
Brighter and brighter it grows, the darkness scorning,
And driving before it the cold, gray morning.

And following it old Sol in all his glory,
Celebrated of old in many a story.
Higher and higher he goes,
And the breeze of the morning blows,
And the tiding cometh to every city and farm and house and prison:
"Awake! Awake! the sun hath risen!"

The Skull

Here before me thou dost ly, [*sic*]
Once the home of a human mind
O didst thou fear to die,
In thy earthly passions blind?
For thy occupant I breath a sigh,
I wonder what he found.

What things did thy eye
Behold? And what was the sound,
Or sounds that thy ear heard?
Where is the lowly mound,
Under which thy body lies?
Or is the earthly sherd
Scattered beyond the ken of human eyes?

What wert thou in life?
Didst thou sin in thy errors blind?
Didst thou mix in earth's strife,
O house of a human mind?
Who wert thou, and what thy name,
What thy station, in our world?
Wert thou known to fame,
Hast thou a lofty flag unfurled?
Was there on thee the breath of shame?
If so, was thine the blame?

The Orient

Fertile plains and burning sands
In a dream I once did see;
Cities and rivers and caravans
Appeared to me;
High walls and higher domes,
Bazaars and narrow ways,
Where the leper, the outcast roams,
And the filthy beggar stays.

All of this I did behold,
In my disordered dream.
Mosques and minarets of gold,
That in the sunlight gleam.
And faraway the burning sands,
The scattered groups of trees,
The camel trains and caravans,
Bathed in the sultry breeze.

The river winding thru the plain
Gleams silvery in the bright sunlight.
Beside it rises a stately fane,
Awful in its massive hight.
And faraway the city sounds

As I stand there and meditate
Upon the boundless bounds
Of destiny and fate;

Of empires that long have passed away,
Of the Persians and the golden caliphate,
And think that on this day
I stand where they once stood and say, "It is fate."
Oh where is the might of Tamerlane,
And were doth Babylon stand?
Their power will never live again,
They are buried in the shifting sand.

Hark! Across the palm-dotted plain
Above the cities' noise and din,
Faint, faint, sounding again and again,
Cometh the shrill cry of the muezzin.
Broken, broken is my dream,
Faded in the past forever away
And yet many a theme
It might suggest, and many a lay.

Time

O who can stem its tide,
And who can turn its hand?
Who thru it can backward slide
Who can evade its command?
It hath no respect for race or pride
Each must go at time's demand.

Fortune, and rank, each must go
With the poor and the unknown;
The high and the low,
Each time doth own;
The great and pompous show
Is one with the pain and the groan.

The king and the beggar are the same
And one are rich and poor.
One to time are shame and fame,
And one are gentleman and boor.
Nothing to it is a mighty name;
The end of all is sure.

To an Eastern City

Proud city of the Orient thou art,
Known of old.
Dear art thou to many a passing foreign heart
Dearer than gold.
Of the East thou art the mart
Where strange things are sold.

On the desert's edge thou dost stand,
Between it and a stream.
By the burning winds thou'rt fann'd
Scorched by the sun's hot beam.
Beyond thee the burning sand
Before thee the rippling stream.

In thy dirty, narrow streets of old
The slave trade goeth on.
Here man by man is sold
Till all are gone.
Here human flesh is bartered for gold,
Father, brother and son.

Proud city of the Orient thou art,
Dear to many a passing foreign heart.

Fortune

Fickle, fickle fortune,
Fickle, fickle fortune:
Dance to my tune,
Favor me but once.
Upon the sage who woos thee
Thou wilt not smile.
The dunce who should lose thee
Thou takest for awhile.
To thy ever-changing heart
He hath a thousand paths
But the wise man's art
Cannot win thee, fickle lass.
Canst thou favor him but once,
And bestow a simple smile?
Throw away the dunce,
And leave him to another's guile.

He is but a simpleton,
Not worth thy while.

The Ocean

The mighty ocean roars
In his solitude.
He dashes his waves on many shores
In angry mood.
He roars, he foams and dashes,
He flings his waves about.
The white sea-foam he lashes
In reel and rout.

He flings the surf on many a shore,
And crashes 'mid the rocks.
The surf he flings behind, the surf before,
Man's bravery he mocks.
The sea his anger doth send forth
In shape of raging wave.
His anger he sends o'er the earth,
Naught can save.

Yet he is good when quiet,
And when he is still.
But when the raging waves do riot
They will kill.
The Ocean old is like all men,
One time calm and smooth,
Another time he is not, and then
We know the calmness was a ruse.

Allah

Om

In the spotless snow of mountains and the green of grassy plains,
In the blazing heat of summer and the coming of the rains
Ye may see him in the forests and each green and growing thing—
In the tinted leaves of autumn and the flowers of the spring.
In the peace of summer evenings and the twinkling of the stars
Out beyond in space unmeasured to the universe's bars.
In the arid sand of deserts and the sapphire of the sea,

In the crashing of the breakers and the breeze that bloweth free.
[Illegible] ye where ye list something shall there his show or presence speak.
Earth and sea and sky do it proclaim. What need for ye to seek?

Arab Song

Over the scorching sands I ride,
Sands before and on every side,
Beneath an iron and cloudless sky
Where moves a pitiless sun on high.
Never a palm or a sign of green
Breaks the desolate, dismal scene.

But oh, Beloved, if thou mightst ride
Across the desert at my side,
'Twould be as that garden of the rose
Thro' which the stream of Bendemeer flows!

Arabian Love-Song

I come from the heart of the desert,
Drawn by thy beauty's fame.
And I stand beneath thy lattice-window,
And call upon thy name.
I love thee more than words can tell,
Thy beauty is a skein,
That subtly hath entangled me,
And made my heart all thine.

I love thee, I love thee,
With a passion that naught but death can cool,
The flame in my heart will grant me no rest,
For the sight of thy beauty is fuel.
I faint in the flash of thy glance,
And naught but thy kiss can revive me.
Thy eye is as a burning lance,
Piercing far into eternity.

There's a flame that's consuming my heart
'Tis fiercer than the fires of hell.
And naught but thy love's sweet art
Can release me from the torments fell.

Love me,—but deign to love me,
And my happiness will be complete

I swear by the heavens above me,
That I love the sod beneath thy feet!
And the moon and the stars thou seest,
Shall attest my oath.
And the God that in Heaven is
To do so will be nothing loath.

I love thee with a burning flame,
That even death shall never cool!
For in paradise we'll surely meet,
And defy the destroyer cruel.
Open thy chamber-window, sweet,
And open the door of thy heart.
And I'll teach thee the love that shall never die
With all a lover's artless art!

[. . .]

On thy threshold's open door:

"Relic of departed splendor,
Speak, I do conjure thee,
Of the stately days of yore.
Tear aside the veil of Eternity,
And answer me as I spoke."
And this did the Temple make reply,
Thus the desert silence broke,
With preliminary sigh:

"Mortal, I will break my stillness.
At thy command I'll tell.
And if from truth I do digress,
May I fry in hell.
Seven hundred years I've stood,
Here in this desert town.
Much I've seen bad and good
Much of smile and frown.

Bedouin Song

Across the hot sands, towards fertile lands
On our swinging camels we forward fly
On a heaven of lead, on the sands of red
Shines the sun, as it goes on high.
O camels go, to waters that flow,

Where the green palms wave in the breeze.
Forward, forward fly, passing swiftly by,
Till we see the waters and trees.

Sing, sing, each step shall bring
Us nearer to our journey's end.
Across hot sands, towards fertile lands,
Till red into green doth blend.
Brothers, brothers sing as we go, towards waters that flow,
And palms whose branches wave on high.
Camels trotting, camels swaying, each step bringing
Us to our haven of rest more nigh.

They gleam, they gleam, 'neath the sun's bright beam,
And the waters like silver glow.
And green branches move in the fronded grove
With the zephyrs that come and go.
The journey is done, our course is run,
And we lie 'neath the grateful shade.
Brothers sleep, in slumbers deep,
And dream of some faithful Arab maid.

The City of the Djinn

I saw within the shadow of a Dream
Some city of the Djinn in Eastern seas,
Before whose walls the jewell'd waters gleam,
As gems upon the brow of Orient mysteries;
Upon whose emerald minarets there shines
First rays of th' glorious morning sun.
At night the red moon her shimmering signs
Throws on them in silver glory one by one.
I saw the palaces in silence lie,
No life within their golden, jewelled room;
No ships upon the seas that rippled by
No shape of man or beast—and all was gloom.

In treasure-rooms I saw, before the walls
All gems of mystic Eastern land and sea.
And flung within the silent magic halls
The precious pearls of Ind and Araby.
In pillar'd rooms that tower'd dark and tall
There shone in gloom the silks of far Cathay
Gold flung there by Genii hands ere Adam's fall—

Diamonds and emeralds in silence lay.
And o'er it all there seem'd a magic spell
That bound the palaces in silent chain
How long, how long no man may know or tell—
How long that spell upon the place had lain.

Passing the pillared rooms at last I came
To one in which there lay a couch of gold.
And on it one whose fabled, ancient fame
I oft had heard in olden story told.
In robes of silk, with beard of white he lay,
As one who holdeth might and kingly pow'r.
And on his finger shone and gleam'd away
The ring of Empire through each passing hour.
In troubled sleep I heard him softly sigh,
Repining for his long-gone kingly might
And through the hours that pass'd so slowly by
His signet gleam'd into the shadowy night.

And so I stood the silent room within,
Beside the couch of gold whereon he lay—
He who was once the Sultan of the Djinn
And on his hand the ring that holdeth sway.
And I thought of Solomon's by-gone might
And the magic pillars of Chilminar,
Builded by Jan ben Jan in a single night—
Of the Djinn who followed the Ring afar.
And still the magic signet gleamed away
Into the night and fell the walls upon.
And so I saw it shine with steady ray—
The signet ring of mighty Solomon.

The Desert

Mile on mile of burning sand,
Mile on mile of a desolate land;
A palm tree here and there,
Green, refreshing, fair.
A brazen sky above,
A brazen earth below
What here for man to love?
What here for man to sow?

* * *

A train of camels faraway,
Sweltering under the midday
Sun; dark-faced he men who ride
Upon them. The tide
Of fierce passions ebb and flow
On their swarthy countenances.
Sons of the desert, they who ride
The light gleams on their lances.

Nearer and nearer come they,
Until they pass away.
My eyes follow them as they go,
They are neither friend nor foe.
Smaller and smaller they seem,
As faraway they ride;
Like creatures in a dream,
Like the ebbing tide.

The desert swallows and envelops them,
Shaggy camels and dark-faced men.
Thou shalt never see these more,
They are gone, and gone before.
From this life they pass away
Dark the tide that ebbs and flows
Or the light of the dying day;
They were neither friends nor foes.

The silence once more surrounds them,
The desert once more hounds them.
Boundless, boundless are its bounds,
Devoid of sights, devoid of sounds.
Massive, great, sublime,
Endless, never-ending,
Out of space and out of time,
With eternities forever blinding.

A Dream of Vathek

Dramatis Personae

Vathek Azrael, the angel of Death
Mahomet Al Borak
Slaves, attendants, friends, etc, etc.

Act I

Scene I. A palm grove in the gardens of the palace of the caliphate. Vathek, in his royal robes, reclines on a couch under the shade of the trees. Several attendants stand nearby, and two choruses of Caucasian slave girls lull him to sleep with their songs.

First Chorus: Sleep, sleep,
Be thy slumber deep.
We strew thee with the flowers of our song.
They were striped from Eastern bowers,
May they make thy slumbers long.
Sleep, sleep,
Be thy slumbers deep.

Second Chorus: Sleep thou, o our lord,
And pleasant be thy dreams.
Let the sword
Be absent. Let the beams
Of the bright sun shine
Upon thee.
Let them be forever thine,
When we sing to thee.

First Chorus: May flowers deck thy slumbers,
As these we strew upon thy bed.
Let the measured numbers
Of our song steal upon thee. Led
By them thou wilt go
Straightway to the land of dreams.
There thou wilt meet no foe
Save the bright sunbeams.
Sleep, sleep,
And be thy slumber deep.
We strew thee with opiate flowers,
Stript from trees in idle hours.
Sleep, sleep,

And be thy slumber deep.

Second Chorus: Sleep, but not forever.
Be thy dreams like the river,
Swift flowing to the seas.
And as we strew thee with these,
Flowers, flowers,
Songs conceived in idle hours,
Let thy mind slowly drift,
Thru the golden rift,
Into the land of dreams,
Where naught is but that which seems.
Sleep, and be thy slumbers pleasant:
Let joys in them be present.
Let griefs steal away
Like the light of the dying day.
Sleep, but not forever.
Awake another time.
Let naught sever
Thee from our clime.
Sleep, sleep,
And be thy slumbers deep.

First Chorus: Let sleep upon thee steal,
Let it stay.
Sleep till thou canst not feel,
The influence of the noisy day.
We strew thee with the flowers of our idle song.
They were conceived in idle hours,
May they make thy slumbers long.
Sleep, sleep,
And be thy slumbers deep. (The caliph sleeps.)

The scene suddenly fades away, as Vathek's mind is filled with a dream. It changes to the desert. The caliph finds himself standing in a lowly spot, beneath the shadows of three solitary palms. It is night. The stars and the crescent moon shine forth with unusual brilliancy. The sands are bathed in ghostly silver. Silence prevails everywhere. Vathek stands silhouetted against the horizon, and meditates, speaking aloud.

Vathek: Strange and silent is the scene.
Nature sleeps profoundly. Man
Can never slumber as deep. How
Still the night is. There is

No sound to break the monotony.
  And why, I wonder,
  Am I here in this spot?
  What can be the mission?
  (As he speaks the last words a voice from the empty air speaks to him.

  Voice: Mortal man, thou art here,
Called hither by Allah.
Sufficient that it is his will.
Wait and watch. Much is yet
To come. Watch well. (The voice ceases.)

  Vathek: I am much astonished.
How is it that I hear,
Yet do not behold the speaker?

  Voice: Seek not to know.
  Vathek: Who art thou?
  Voice: What thou must not know.
  Vathek: Why should I not?
  Voice: It is the will of Allah.
Seek to know no more.

  Vathek: Art thou angel or friend?
  Voice: I will tell thee naught. I am called.
I go.
(Vathek stands wrapt in meditation.)

  Vathek: It is strange. Was it friend or angel
That spoke to me so mysteriously?
I should like to know.
  (He remains silent for some time. Suddenly the air is filled with radiance, and Al Borak appears. The camel alights beside him.

  Al Borak: Mount and ride with me.
I take thee to the seventh heaven.
Mahomet would speak with thee.
Come, make haste.

  Vathek: Wonder upon wonder appears to me,
I must be enchanted by the fiends.
First, I hear a voice speaking from the empty air,
Then Al Borak appears to take me to heaven
  To speak with Mahomet.
  What can it mean? I have forebodings.
But I will mount and ride,

Ride, whate'er betide.

Al Borak: Make haste, o evil caliph.
The night wanes swiftly.

Vathek: Why callest thou me evil? (Mounts.
Al Borak: That you shall soon know.
Vathek: Tell me now, I pray.
Al Borak: As you insist, I will. Thou hast
Disobeyed the prophet of God,
Thou hast been licentious in thy actions,
And lazy in thy morals and religion.
However, it is not too late to repent.
Mahomet calls thee to heaven
that he may warn thee ere the
Time is past, and repentance will
Arrive too late to avail thee.

Vathek: I might have known that it was so.
He calls me to threaten me, does he?
I will wait. There are others besides the prophet.

Al Borak: What sayest thou?
Vathek: I said that Mahomet was not all.
Al Borak: But he is more than you.
Vathek (aside): Perhaps.
Al Borak: Haste, we must go. The moon and the stars wane,
And I must return you here before cock-crow.
(They are off, shooting up into the sky, and disappearing from sight.

Scene III [*sic*]. The seventh heaven. Mahomet is discovered seated upon a throne. Allah is not present, but a radiance in the distance, emanating from him shows where he is. Azrael, the Angel of Death stands on the right hand of Mahomet. Israfel, on the left, sings a song. A number of other angels join in with him. There are two choruses, each supplanting the other in turns.

Israfel: Let the universe ring
With thy praises;
Let the planets sing
As they rotate in dizzy mazes.
Let all rejoice
In thee;
Let all take voice
With me.

First Chorus: Sing, sing,

Let thy praises ring.
Sing them thru the universe,
Sing in verse.
Hail, hail,
O mighty prophet.
We sing without fail
And let
Our voices ring loud and full
In thy praise.

Second Chorus: Hail, all hail to thee.
We sing our best for thee to hear.
We rejoice, and we
Hope to reach thy ear.
Our voices ring,
O mighty king;
We let them ring anew.
Let them bring
Sound to thy ear, too.

Israfel: I sing in praise of thee,
And hope that thou wilt hear me.
My voice is weak, I know,
But let it reach thy ear.
Thy soul is white as snow,
I pray thee hear.

First Chorus: The sun hath risen as of old,
Could it rise if thou wast not there?
Would it not be over-bold
To do?
Would not it fall back again,
Pale and cold with shame?
If not, 'twere a brazen thing,
That Allah's hand would smite to earth.
Therefore, let us sing,
And loud shall be our mirth.

Second Chorus: The stars and moon in thy praise unite.
They know thou art their overlord.
Well may they fear thy might,
The path of thy flaming sword.

Israfel: Prophet of the worlds art thou,
Dominion dost thou hold

Beneath the hand of Allah.
Dominion shalt thou hold
Till the sun is cold
And the stars grow old
And the leaves of the Book of Life unfold.
Thou art overlord and king
Let thy praises ring,
Let them bring
Sound to thy ears, o king.
Angels, sing,
And sing forevermore.
Sing till thy tongues are sore
And Allah the door
Of heaven opens.
Sing till o'er
The planets and the stars,
The sound of thy voices forms a web
Of everlasting music.
Sing till Venus and Mars
With love of our lord grow sick.
Sing till the twinkling stars
Strive to mimic.
Hail, o king,
Of thee we sing;
Let thy praises ring
Forevermore.
Amen.

First Chorus: The stars shine as they have shone before,
As they shall shine forevermore,
Till the last page of the Book is turned,
And worlds and men are burned
In the fires of Allah's wrath.
'Tis but the aftermath
Of the evil deeds of men.
We sing, we sing till then,
And forever after
The coming of that disaster.
Mahomet thou art our master,
Of thee we sing the praises.
Thou shalt endure for all eternity,
As the sun rotates in his mazes,
So thou shalt live.

Thy life is like unto a ring,
The ring of which we sing.
Let the music of our voices bring
Sweet things to thy ear, o king.

Second Chorus: The blazing sun endures
Till the coming of the end.
Still he goeth on his endless tours,
Still he goeth till the end.
He shall go till the wrath that Allah sends
When worlds shall meet their ends.
Thou shalt live till then,
Till the sons of men
Are in hell and heaven;
Thou shalt live forever after,
Thy life the sleep of the Seven.

Israfel: My soul with rapture thrills
As I sing thy praises.
My voice thru the vault of heaven shrills,
And many an echo raises.
I pray that thou hear my humble song,
That thou accept my words.
May my voice ring loud and long,
And clash like the flashing swords.
Thou, o my master, art the overlord,
Holding dominion under Allah's hand.
Thou rulest by mandate and sword,
Thou rulest all the land.
May the thunder be less loud
Than my voice.
May the blackening cloud
Be less—

Mahomet: Cease, I hear sounds from without.
Al Borak and the false vice-regent come.
(The caliph enters.)

Vathek: Hail to thee, great prophet.
Thou art greater than the praises
Of the angels seem to imply.
I waited without and heard them
Ere entering. They cannot express thy
Greatness, which is second only to that of the protector.
All hail to thee!

Mahomet: If thy heart were as sincere as thy words
Would seem to imply,
I should not have called thee here,
But my all-seeing eye hath beheld
Thy iniquity.

Vathek: O prophet of Allah, I fail to understand.
Mahomet: Add not another lie to thy multitudinous sins.
There are plenty already, so thou needst not
Commit another. All must be written down
To thy account in the judgment book. If
Thou wilt forswear thy iniquity there is yet
Time a-plenty, in which thou mayest cause
The good to over-balance the bad.

Vathek: Overlord, I do not understand. What meanest
Thou by "my iniquity?"

Mahomet: Cease, ere I grow angry at thee.
Tell me more falsehoods, or I will let
The thunder-bolts of my wrath descend upon
Thy wicked head.

Vathek: I understand that false reports of my conduct
Have reached thy ears. Believe them not,
For they are lies designed by those who
Hate me, to injure me in thy estimation.

Mahomet: If thou wilt not swear upon thy soul
That thou wilt tell me the truth,
I will throw thee to the fiends of Eblis.

Vathek: I swear.
Mahomet: Now tell me what thou hast done.
Spare not thyself, for the salvation of thy
Soul dependeth upon the truth or falsity
Of what thou sayest. If thou tellest
Not the truth, I will give thee ten minutes
Of hell to show thee the reward thou
Wilt gain if thou persisteth in thy
Iniquity on earth. Speak!

Vathek: I have ruled my kingdom wisely, and have
Encouraged the true religion. I have not been
Licentious, or—

Mahomet: Beware! Thou speakest falsely.
Vathek (sadly). Prophet of Allah, whose lying tongue hath pois-
Ened [*sic*] thy ear against me? Who hath breathed
Perjury, and instilled hate of me into thy mind?

Mahomet: I, with my own eyes have beheld thy iniquity.
Vathek: Then my fate is sealed.
Mahomet: Nay, not so. There is yet time. I promised
That thou shouldst have ten minutes of hell
As a warning. Fiends!
(Ten Afrites enter and, surrounding Vathek, roast him on a spit of flames for some time. He endures the torture without a sound. Mahomet and the angels look on in silence.
Mahomet: It is enough. He has had a sufficient foretaste.
Go.
(Exit fiends.
Now, false vice-regent, what thinkest thou?

Vathek: That I will repent, and cease my wickedness.
Mahomet: Those are the first sincere words that thou hast
Spoken since entering here. I know not how
Long thy repentance will last.

Vathek: It will last longer than thou thinkest.
Mahomet: I sincerely hope so.
Azrael: Vice-regent, take my advice and adhere to thy
Spoken word. The tortures thou hast felt
Are naught to those thou wilt feel if thy
Wickedness continues. But there are still pages
Of thy life that are blank. Take care that
What is written upon them is to thy credit.
Make sure that they are not black, like
The pages that have gone before. Beware!
Thou mayest yet enter paradise.

Vathek: I take thy advice well to heart, and will
Remember it. It is a text to which I
Will adhere the rest of my days.

Azrael: Thy days are many, o caliph. I, who know
The hour of each man's death, will tell thee that.
But take care that these days are well-filled.

Israfel: Caliph, thou shouldst remember the words of the
Angel of Death. He speaketh truly.

Vathek: I will, sweet singer.
Mahomet: Thou hast received a warning of what will
Overtake thee if thy future life is as the past.
I hope that thou wilt live as a good Moslem
Should till the end of thy days; I desire that
Thou, of all the caliphs, should enter paradise.
I have a special fondness for thee, in spite of all
Thy faults. They are many, so beware that
They do not drag thy soul down to hell.

Vathek: Thy words, o prophet of Allah, are music to my
Ears. I will live in accordance with them.
My footsteps trend according to the dictates
Of the musician. And they will now trend
Upward. Farewell!
(Exit Vathek.

Scene IV. The palm grove in the gardens of the palace of the caliphate. Vathek still sleeping.

First Chorus: Sleep on, sleep on,
Vice-regent of the prophet.
Awake not, awake not,
Until the coming of sunset.
It is yet noon,
Sleep, sleep.
Night will come too soon,
Be thy slumbers deep.
Soft and low, soft and low,
Restful to thy pillow.
To and fro, to and fro,
We go, we go,
Like the rhy[th]mic billow.
Sleep, sleep,
Be thy slumbers deep.
Thou wilt wake too soon.
Sleep on
Softly, softly croon,
Sleep is a boon,
Sleep that ends too soon;
Sleep on.

Second Chorus: The zephyrs stir,
The palm-fronds move.

They whirr, they whirr,
Sleep on, o love.
The sun shines down,
It cannot reach thee.
Do not frown
If we teach thee
Our burning love.
We would that it might softly fan thy brow,
So that thou might more sweetly slumber.
Softly we swing, to and fro,
In rhy[th]mic measured number.
Sleep on, sleep on till night.
Be thy sleep calm and deep
Be the noisy world hid from thy sight.
Sleep, sleep,
And be thy slumbers deep.
(Vathek awakes.

Vathek: What? Is it but a dream that thus
Hath troubled me? It was so real that I
Mistook it for reality. What, slaves, art thou
Still here? How long have I slept.

Slave: Ten minutes, o vice-regent of the prophet.
Vathek: Can it be that such a troublesome vision was
Crowded into such a small space of time?
Well, it is sufficient for me to know that 'twas
But a disordered dream. But I shall not sleep
Again. Mayhap another such vision could come to
Me. Besides it is time for the divan to be called.
Ho, slaves, escort me to the throne-room.
(To himself.)
The dream shall trouble me but little. It maketh
No change in the routine of my life.
(Exit Vathek.)

The End.

A Dream of Zanoni

Once, while Zanoni slept,
He dreamt a dream, and his memory kept
It, and he told it to a friend;
And this is the dream, from beginning to end:

He was the caliph (so he dreamed)
And to him he seemed
To be reclining on a couch of down,
Clothed in a robe and costly gown;
In his hand a sceptre, and on his head a crown.
Before him stretched the vast throne-room,
Sight and shadow, shine and gloom.
On a dais stood the throne
(And in his dream it seemed it was his own.)
Fever racked his limbs, and his breast
Knew no relief or blessed rest.
The caliph (or Zanoni) groaned in his pain
To his slaves he said: "How long have I lain?"
"Three days, O shadow of Allah," said they,
["Thou] wert wounded in the fray."
"Oh God!" he groaned, "must I forever lie,
"On this couch until I die?
"Shall I never lift sword again
"Or sacifice in sacred fane?
Cursed be my birth and power,
Cursed be the unhappy hour
In which I was born,
To wear this sceptre and this crown of thorns!"
The caliph groaned again and sought to rise;
Burning hot his face and eyes,
He sought to rise in vain;
Back he sank, and his fevered brain
Wandered off into fantastic dreams,
Dreams, yet not dreams: only that which seems.
His spirit flickered and seemed to go,
Close in the grasp of Death, its foe.
Zanoni woke in a shower of sweat,
Half doubting whether he was alive yet.
"Tis a strange dream," quoth he
"But its moral I plainly see.
Great power can never bring happiness to me."

Eblis Repentant

I am fallen, fallen far,
    Downward like a fleeing star.
Gone is all my heavenly power,

Cast away in one fateful hour.
The curse of Alla is on my head,
There to stay forevermore.
And he who once by God was led,
Is now led,—nevermore.
Tho' all the treasures of earth are mine,
What are they to me?
Of purer and rarer design
Are treasures of the Tooba Tree.
Genii obey me, fly at my word,
Unlock the doors to jewels untold.
O! would that mine ears had never heard
The clink of earthly gold.
Cursed be the hour in which I fell
Down to these regions of fire and hell,
Cursed be the hour in which I swore
That I should not bow to man.
I was happy in God's presence before,
Now on my head is the eternal ban.

Yet why should I bow to a creature of clay,
I, who am of ether[e]al spirit made?
Why should I the mandate obey,
Fall down at Alla's irade?
I, who stood in rank the nearest
To the lord of earth and sky?
I, who was to him the dearest,
The favorite above all—?
I fell, I fell, from my high state,
Fallen must I be forevermore.
Dragged to hell by a pride innate.
A pride that I shall loose—nevermore.

Eternally cursed, eternally damned,
Tho' all the earth-treasures are at my command,
Fallen—tho the Genii of fire fly at my word
Tho' mine is Suleyman's wonderful sword.
Fallen—tho' mine are the treasures of Jan ben Jan
And the secets unknown to earthly man.
There are jewels more bright than the jewels of earth,
And friends more faithful than the slaves of fire:
But on my head is Alla's curse,
And against me Alla's ire.

A fallen angel, prince of angels—I,
    Fallen from my home—the sky,
Exiled here forever and all time
    Till the dead awake and the end is nigh.
Fall'n is my pride—its head is low,
    And despair is in my eye;
Tho' once ye could not say 'twas so,—
    When to Allah I was nigh.

The wine of life is glowing clear
    Drink, drink, while ye may.
Death is cold and life is dear,
    Drink, drink, to-day.
A fleeting moment's all we have,
    Use it well, use it well.
Life to us Alla gave,
    Soon will sound our funeral knell.

'Tis His to give and His to take,
    A trying of our souls.
'Tis for us alone to make,
    Eblis sets the snares and shoals.
A test, a trying of the gold,
    In the crucible of pain.
And when man hath grown old,
    In the grave he's lain.

Let us drink the cup we're given,
    Bitter, sweet, as it may be.
In death there is a hell or heaven,
    Punishment, or reward, for all eternity.
Sweeter still the paradise,
    That we hope to gain.
Tho' tis hid from mortal eyes,
    We shall reach it—thru a world of pain.

From the Persian

I read upon a gate in letters bold:
"Let he who giveth Dross expect not gold."

From the Persian

I

Out of the Great Bazaar there came a cry
From one who sought to know the Reason Why,
And hastening near I heard the stern Reply:
"Seek as thou wilt, O man, thou shalt not find
The Great Answer. Better to be resigned
Than to seek that which thou mayest not find."

II

Often I think of One who died,
A Friend, whose bed I stood beside
And as he went his Voice I heard
Speak unto me a final Word.
"When I am dead, friend, bury me
Beneath some green, and leafy tree.
That o'er my grave the grass may grow—
All flesh is grass—Ah, be it so!"

III

A dim, and scarce distinguished whisper I heard
That mine own Ear hath kindled into flaming Word.

From the Persian

I stood amid the ruins of a city great
Where once Jumsheed in his glory sate
And musing o'er some forgotten tomb,
I said, "O Allah, this is fate!"

Each summer wind that passes o'er the plain
May lift the dust of Kaikhosru again
Who knows but 'neath this ancient slab of stone
Jumsheed of olden fable long hath lain?

Where is the tomb of Kaikobad the Great?
Or the palace where Sultan Mahmud sate?
Ask ye of the spider and the jackal,
And say with me, "O Allah, this is fate!"

Think, ye who stand within this great Bazaar

Men call the World, how Allah from afar
Guides our Kismet with his steadfast Hand
Appointing to each one his destined star!

Haroun Al-Raschid

He is gone, and gone forever,
  Yet his goodly fame still stays.
Naught its golden web can sever
  Naught can quench its blaze.
Centuries have rolled away,
And many a year hath passed
Since his day.
But until the last
His memory shall stay
And naught his name can blast.

Golden and goodly was his time
  Down thru the ages its echo hath come.
Known is it, and famed, in every clime,
  In many a song it hath been sung.
And in our time, to-day,
  Still it doth endure.
Ne'er shall it pass away:
His fame is safe and sure.

The Inscription

Upon a famous Sultan's tomb some hand had written, "Where?"
But vainly sought I an answer—, no other word was there.

Jewel of the Orient

Amid palm groves and almond trees,
Stirred in the summer breeze,
Beside a winding stream,
Glittering in the midday beam,
Between high walls of stone,
With clinging vines o'ergrown,
With glittering domes and spires,
Seeking the higher airs,
Standeth the palace of the caliphate,
With its courts and archéd gate.

In the trees the bulbul sings,
And faraway the still air brings
A louder, strident sound:
The voice of the servant of Mahound,
Calling the hour of midday prayer;
And ringing thru the still air,
It cometh to the startled ear,
Commanding all who may hear.
And long, and long it rings,
Until all living things
Seem vibrant with its stirring notes.
And suddenly it ceaseth. But the echo still floats,
And sounds in and about the groves.
And as it further roves,
It dies, and dies away
Like unto the fading day.
And with the last, low note,
A boat adown the stream doth float,
Bearing gay-clothed occupants.
And their fervid luxuriance
With the fertile groves doth blend,
Both to the same and the perfect end;
Both to adorn, and both to please,
One the clothes, the other the trees;
One, the people by whom they are worn,
The other, the landscape to adorn.
And which the most useful is?
And the truth ye could not miss
If ye said they were the same,
Different only in the name.
And thru the shade, the boat,
With languid sail upraised, doth float,
Over the silent-moving stream,
Over the waters silv'ry pale.
A light shallop floating on the stream
It is. Nearer and nearer it sails,
Now in shadow, now in beam,
Now when the sunshine fails
To penetrate. Nearer, till thou can see,
Its gay-gown[e]d occupants.
Rich-robed they seem to thee,
Clothed in all luxuriance.

Nearer—nearer the shallop advances,
Nearer sails the boat.
And now thou canst see the continuances
Of they who in it float.

They lie on cushions rare,
On couches of silk and down.
Above them the silent air,
Devoid of all sound.
Two are men and one a woman.
One of these men is Haroun Al-Raschid,
The other, a eunuch. The lady, scarce human,
In her beauty, is—let her name be whispered 'mid
Lilies in bloom. Amina, the caliph's daughter,
The Jewel of the Orient.
Many a prince had sought her,
Many on winning her were bent.
[. . . ?]

Jewel of the Orient

In Bagdad, capital of the caliphate,
'Mid palm groves and trees,
With many an orchid gate,
Standeth the palace. Buried in these,
The almonds, palms, and brushes;
Terraced down to the river's bank,
Where the Tigris rushes,
And the reeds grow thick and rank.
Here the sun shines thru the fronds,
In vari[e]gated lattice design,
Here stand the pink almonds,
And roses red as wine.
The tall dates wave over all,
And lordly stands the cedar of Lebanon;
The bamboo groweth tall, singeth
And the bulbul singeth on,
The branch of a sandalwood tree.
The river rushes in between,
Flowing to the sea,
Here discerned, there unseen.
Lordly stand the palace towers,
And the open orchid gates.

In the garden's [*sic*] stand the bowers,
Filled with perfume that elates.
The sky above is blue,
And silver the winding river.
The bright beams shine thru,
The lattice work, gleaming ever.
A zephyr stirs in the greenery,
The branches move up and down.
And looking yonder you may see
Their shadows dance and frown.
Far[a]way gleam the white stone walls
Of mighty Bagdad, the minaret o'er all.
And here the shadow deepest falls,
Like a black funeral pall.
Adown the stream cometh a boat,
With upraised, listless sail,
Adown the river it doth float,
[. . .]

Kismet

As sand upon a desert's face are blown
The sons of man to destinies unknown.
Whate'er thy fate that fate will come to thee,
Whatever is thine thou yet will surely see.

Beside a loom within some far off land
A weaver sits to guide it with his hand.
Uncounted and unseen the centuries flee
To merge at last in time's eternal sea,
And still the weaver sits but what design.

Mohammed

Mule-driver, dreamer, prophet, he, low-born,
Amid the peoples rose and told his dream
Who unbelieving carelessly did deem
Him madman, and his story laughed to scorn,
All but a few, who faithful and forlorn
Did by him stand, though desperate did seem
For weary years his cause. At last, supreme
His star on fortune rose and shone. Uptorn
And shattered thrones and empires marked his way—

A whirlwind he that desolation spread
And death did breathe till mighty nations low
The awe-struck, astounded lay.
Dreamer and statesman then he upward led
Them, and to ends still higher did point the way.

The Muezzin

At setting of the sun I hear his call
Float on the still air from minaret to city wall—
High o'er palace and bazaar,
Echoing from roof to roof, near and far;
Weird and mournful—reaching everywhere,
To the canopied market place; the beggar's lair,
The Prince's palace, and the merchant's stall—
To each comes the muezzin's call.

Hark! ye true believers, let each lay aside his work
Upon your knees, O faithful, do not shirk.
Hearest thou the muezzin's echoing call,
From mosque and minaret to city wall?

There is another muezzin called Life,
Who resideth in this world of war and strife;
To each man comes his call—
To win or fail—to do or fall.
And be sure that when it comes to thee,
Thou dost not shirk, nor turn, nor flee.

Ode from the Persian

Tho they bring me gold of Bokhara and gems of Samarkand
And costly silks from foreign lands across the desert sand,—
Diamonds from Golconda and pearls of Bokreen's strand,
[. . .]

Odes of Alnaschar

I

Ah! my Best Belovèd, all words to tell
Of thy beauty would be inadequate.
All terms that are known to me could not spell
One letter of it, nor Heaven and Hell

Furnish a word the image to create.
Countless tongues I search'd, some word to find,
And all the works of each great mastermind
I could not find the word I sought to know
In any tongue, or book, nor high and low.
Therefore, I think that when He made thee, love
He took all words down here and up above,
And cast them into thy faultless form and face,
Thy beauty, Best Belovèd, and thy grace!

II

I met a dervise on the way to Ispahan,
And greeting gave to him. "Tell me, O fellow-man
What hast thou found?" I said. "Hast thou a key to ope
The door of Heaven wide. Ah, tell me, then, thy hope."
"Long, long have I searched," the dervish then made reply
"Long have I sought the Answer to the Where and Why.
In many a land, and e'en to the Seventh Sea
And this I tell thee now. I know no more than thee."

III

How many fools their lives have vainly vex'd,
In such a Search, on such a vain pretext!
Why waste thy precious time, and vex thy mind
In bare search for the key no man may find?

Omar's Philosophy

I

Many have failed and few have won,
    Their names are writ in the Book of Fame
Countless the myriad deeds they've done,
    Deeds of goodness and deeds of shame.

II

There are countless others, forgotten, unnamed,
    Who sank to the dust from whence they rose;
Down to the grave, unsung, unfamed,
    Devoid of friends, devoid of foes.

III

There are names that high are writ
On the pillars of the Hall of Fame,
Whose dark, dank tombs still are lit
By the lamps of shame and fame.

IV

There are names that lead the rest
In the lists of that Book above;
But if ye cannot call me blest,
Write me in the Book of Love.

V

I care not for shame or fame
Nor if I be writen in that Book above.
And what to me is a mighty name,
If I be written in the Book of Love.

The Palace of the Jinn

I saw, within the shadow of a dream
An island of the Jinn in seas afar
About whose strands the lonely waters gleam
And foam-tipped waves like argent jewels are.
Those seas no mariner hath e'er essayed
No daring lone white sail e'er ventured o'er.
Upon that isle no bird its flight e'er stayed
No shape of man or beast is on its shore.
Yet high above the shimmering citrine beach
Between it and the atlantean peaks
That auspulating, skyward reach,
A palace great man's presence seeming speaks.
I saw it wonderful and vast uprise
Of gold the dome and battlements and wall
With towers that pierced the clear cerulean skies,
How aureately coruscant was all.
How gorgeous with the moonday tropic sun!
What mortal hand such fabric might uprear?
Nay, not of man. By Afrit hands alone
'Twas built, I said; no work of man is here.

And now in my fantastic dream I went
Along a pathway up the shelving sand
And slope till with white marble steps it blent.
Far, far above the dazzling yellow strand
These towards the palace wearily
Whose shut and shining gates I reached at last.
And scarce had I paused when they oped silently.
And into a spacious court I passed.
[. . .]

The Prayer Rug

How calm, O Rug of Persian loom
Thou lyest in the silent room
Thou woven dream of Eastern days
In cloth and colors rich and rare
Whereon a vagrant sunbeam plays
And writes its golden fancy fair

Who long ago with patient care
Thy pattern wove in Ispahan?
Who first upon thee knelt in prayer
What turbaned, swart Mohammedan?

O Rug, if speech were gift of thine
What wondrous tales thou mightst unfold
What priceless treasure then were mine
In chronicles and stories old.

What solemn prayers hast thou heard,
How many knees thy woof have prest?
Some Shah, perhaps, with fervent word
His empire's hopes to God confessed.
Their shadows pass in long review
These alien men of days long gone
Men come and go, the old is new
Yet love and hate, fear, hope, go on.

The sultans pass, empires decay,
Where now in Mahmud's golden throne?
Yet thou, O Rug, have seen his day,
His triumphs and his fame have known.

Dumb relic of the gorgeous East,
Thou lyest here, but why and where?

The kings, the captain, great or least
That knelt on thee in earnest prayer.
The poet's dream, love's blissful tale
Within some scented garden told
Viziers crafty, women frail
Merchants cunning, warriors bold.

Their shadows come, their shadows flit,
Yet they are dust, their names forgot.

The Prince and the Peri

I

In that fair land where the Tigris flows,
'Mid groves of palms and gardens of rose,
    Where the fair sun shines alway,
Dwelt the young prince, Feramorz,
And shine the sun as bright as could be,
It could not shine upon one more fair than he;
    Or if it shine forever and ever,
    To the brink of Eternity.

His cheeks are moons, his eyes are stars,
Brighter than Venus and Mars.
    And brighter still the brain behind
The fair, broad brow, its bars.
And search ye ever and ever,
For all time, ye could never
    Find a form more handsome than his,
Nay, not if ye searched forever.

And is not that mouth Love's bow,
Where the shadows flicker and flicker, and go?
Shadows of mirth and a cheerful mind,
May ye ne'er flicker low!
Well may thy father be proud of thee,
And thou of him. For he,
The peerless Haroun Al-Raschid,
Is, and thou the child of destiny.

His only son, born to a throne,
Heir to a kingdom thou'rt never to own,
A kingdom forgotten in Peristan's bowers,

Carelessly away from thee thrown.
How few would a kingdom throw away,
Like a valueless bauble, a day in May?
Yet fairer the kingdom thou gainest,
A land that forever shall stay.
Peristan's bowers are thy abode,
And the path of love was thy road.
From that path you ne'er could stray,
With love as thy staff and goad.

Happy the days of thy infancy,
Happy were they, and free.
Yet happier still the days that followed,
And happy the days yet to be.
For he who hath drunk of Youth's fountain,
Can never know grief or pain.
For he shall live forever, and ever,
In the bowers of Peristan.

II

Pale shines the moon o'er the Green Sea,*
O'er the Deep of Eternity;
    Pale the glimmer like a death-torch,
Pale in its shimmering greenery.
The dim stars twinkle on high
Twinkle like a lover's passing sigh.
Soon they'll fade and pass away,—
Fade and say good-bye.

Silver the shimmer on Ormuz' shore,
Black once, now black no more.
And the beetling cliffs stand forth,
With huge shadows cast before.
What is that? A spangled gleam on high,
White against the spangled sky.
And passing o'er with flutter of wings,
Out of the heaven of Eternity.

It flitteth forth, it flitteth back again,
Back beyond our feeble ken;
A fairy creature she who flyeth o'er,

*The Persian Gulf.

Not of the sons and daughters of men.
Soon she'll vanish in faraway space,
Gone before us, gone before our face.
She flyeth fast, she flyeth far,
A daughter of a recreant race.

Let us take wings and fly behind,
Faster than the fast south wind,
With the beckoning North star as our guide,—
Lone guide of human-kind.
Fly! fly, beneath the blue vault far above.
Fly o'er plain and fronded grove.
Fly, midway 'tween heaven and earth,
Fly with the speed of Eagle and dove.

And as we go on the wings of the breeze,
Far above deserts and moonlit seas;
Bright North star our beckoning guide,
O'er hot sands, rivers and greeneries.
Far beneath us the Tigris' flow,
Flowing southward as we go.
High above us heaven's vault,
With all its starry gleam and show.

III

Flies the peri far ahead,
From her bright wings radiance shed.
The bright north star is her guide too,
Yet by other stars she's led—
Bright twin stars that gleam,
Shine like the sun's bright beam.
By them the peri's beckoned and led,
O'er desert and forest and stream.

Eyes that might twinkle by Alla's throne,
Eyes that might be the houris' own,
    Wonder ye that the peri was led
By the bright North star alone?
Feramorz, their fame has flown,
On the fragrant breezes blown,
    To those bowers of Peristan
Suspended in midair—alone!

The bright full moon is rising slow

O'er the gardens silvered below.
And 'mid the flowers, on a ray of light,
The peri has flown, their secrets to know.
"Is Feramorz here?" to them she says,
Lighting mid the flow'ry maze.
"He is, he is," the blossoms reply,
"Under the moon's pale blaze.

"At night he's wont to wander here,
Along the Tigris' stream so clear.
And over yonder, under the palms
He is; you're sure to find him there."
"And there I go," was the peri's reply,
"There I go, if he is nigh."
So off she flew, on her ray of light,
Passing many a floweret by.

Soon the bright stream glimmered near,
With the moonlight on its waters clear.
And the palm trees whispering soft,
Said, "He is here, he is here."
And 'mid them, standing near the stream,
She saw Him, like an angel in a dream,
Down to earth from heaven cast,
On a bright moonbeam.

Quatrain

I once the pilgrimage to Mecca made
And saw her in all holiness arrayed;
Yet in the lonely desert I as near
To Allah was, as in the Kaaba's shade!

Quatrains

Think not of the past,
For what is done is done forever;
The die of olden deeds is cast,—
Cast—and cast forever.

We cannot turn back the pages of years.
It is closed and sealed;
And all our hopes and all our fears
Stand therein revealed.

Let them lie and turn away,
    The die is cast—and cast forever.
Think not of them today—
    The river is flowing ever and ever.

And all the thoughts and deeds of yore
    Have silent floated down the stream
All that's past is forever o'er.
    'Tis but memory's shadowy dream.

Quatrains

The Snare

In his path the hunters set
A snare for the mighty beast of prey
And the fisherman dips his net
Deep in the waters of the bay.

And so hath Eblis placed a snare
In every human way.
So that he may trap the biters there
With the might of Juggurnath.

Song

Over the desert I forward ride,
With sand at my heels and sand at my side.
And the the sun beats steadily down.
As forward I go, bound by bound.

But even this were heaven with thee,
Tho surely 'tis hell alone for me.
The sands would blossom, as forward we ride,
And the air would cool—with thee at my side.

Quatrains on Jewels

The Diamond

O diamond glittering and clear,
    Thou art a precious tear
Imprisoned in resplendency
    For all eternity.

The Pearl

Thou hold'st the secrets of the sea, o pearl:
Its brooding sadness and its mystery
Its argent foam and lustrous swirl
Of sounding surf are all in thee.

The Turquoise

O turquoise from far Orient lands,
Brought hither o'er the burning sands,
Reflection still in thee there lies,
Of Persia's calm, untroubled skies.

The Ruby

Within thy fervid heart there glows
O ruby red as fire
Hot passion and desire
Such as no other jewel knows.

The Opal

[. . .]

Rubaiyat

I

I sought in wingèd flight from star to star
That place where the sources of wisdom are
In all lands, from Araby to Cathay
I searched; long, long was the search, and far.

II

Yet all in vain: I could not hope to find
That which has baffled many a learnéd mind;
Still lay unraveled the knot of human fate,
The secret that I might not hope to find.

III

Yet I think that when the Veil is flung aside,
And I, Saiyid Abdulla, step inside,

Life's mystery shall be revealed
And I shall know why man has lived and died.

IV

And so I am content, and calmly wait
The unravelling of the skein of fate.
All that is mine will surely come to me.
Kismet cometh to all men soon or late.

V

[. . .]

Rubaiyat

I

Some talk of paradise and some of Hell,
Of pleasure and of torments dire they tell.
And some of sleep eternal speak to us;
But this I think—that all shall yet be well.

II

Whate'er thy fate that fate will come to thee,
Whate'er is thine thou yet will surely see.
The thing is written, and the Hand moves on
To write of other things than Thou or Me.

III

Our fate is hidden, with a darkened Veil
That hides from us the things beyond the Pale.
Wait awhile and You and I shall yet find
The destin'd Fate—our Kismet will not fail.

IV

When evening cometh, and the caravan
Sets out from Bagdad or from Ispahann
Across the desert to the future Realm
Make haste—for we shall find the Fate of Man!

Rubaiyat of Saiyed

I

I stood in the forsaken market-place
Of an old and long-forgotten ancient race;
Before the palace of some great Sultan
As the pale moon was seeking his lost face.

II

But think ye, that tomorrow I may be
As much forgotten and unmourned as he.
I, myself, in this mighty universe,
Am but a pebble in a boundless sea!

III

[. . .]

The Seekers

There are sons of earth who seek to fly,
    Up to those worlds beyond our ken;
There are sons of earth who fear to die,
    Who search for the secrets unknown to men.
But vain is their search, and bare,
    For death comes to them just the same,
And he who seeks to tread the air
    Is known but to name and fame.

Impious are they who seek to know,
    The secrets held by Alla alone.
Whose restless spirits flit to and fro,
    Seeking to reach His wonderful throne.
Bare is the search for them, and vain,
    Death cometh all too soon.
Empty is their earthly gain,
    Death their only boon.

Let them seek for all time,
    Yet those secrets they shall never learn.
Let them seek in every clime,
    Still their restless spirits yearn.
Let years pass unnumbered by,

Into the gulf of Time;
Still they yearn, and still they sigh
For those secrets grand, sublime.

The wisdom which Alla holds alone,
Is forbidden to the sons of men.
To them it can never be known,
Tho' they seek and seek again.

Some Maxims from the Persian

I

As drops the quiet night from tired, departing day,
So drops the End of Life, and Death to his own sway;
To-morrow we shall know no more than yesterday.

II

Though Allah—who is just—forgive the Scar and Stain of Sin,
Still remaineth—and forever—the Memory within.

III

Though thou sinnest in secret, and think that thy act is not known,
Beware of the Stain that remaineth—the Stain forever thy own.
Beware—for he who soweth shall surely reap what his Hand hath sown.

Stamboul

Gate of the Orient, set
On a golden shore
Beyond thee the sea of jet*
And the sea of blue before.
Key of the Eastern lands,
Their bolts and bars art thou
What country can give thee commands,
To whom but thy master shalt thou bow?
Nay. 'Tis not theirs to demand,
Not theirs to command.

None but thy master shalt thou obey,
None can order thee but he.

* The Black sea.

Let the others storm and let them say
What they please of thee.
Gate of the East thou art,
Key and bolt and lock,
Its master and its mart.
Who will dare to mock?
The sultan is thy master,
Come fortune or disaster.
To none shalt thou bow but he:
He rules thee and commands thee.

Suleyman Jan ben Jan

In the midst of the Seven Seas he lyeth
    On a couch of gold.
For the days of yore in his dreams he sigheth,
    For he hath grown old.
On his finger sparkles and gleameth
    The ring that holdeth power.
Thru the darkness it softly beameth,
    Lighting each passing hour.

In his robes of silk he reclineth,
    And his beard is long and white.
In his fevered dreams he pineth
    For his bygone might.
And ever and ever gleameth
    Into the shadowy night,
The ring which man deemeth
    To give him Suleyman's might.

The Temple

Here it hath stood for long ages,
A stately Moslem fane,
Rear'd in the time of the sages,
Who long in the dust have lain;
They who erected it are gone,
But their work still stands.
It shall stand till Eternity's dawn,
A monument to human hands.

Around it the lonely plain
With ne'er an Arab in sight.
Alone it stands—a stately fane,
Shimmering in the noonday light.
Sand—sand—red, and burning hot,
Stretching as far as the eye can see.
Green, waving palms—a welcome blot
In the red monotony.

It stands on the site of a forgotten town,
The last relic of man's habitation.
They who peopled it have gone down,
As a dead and bygone nation.
Alone standeth the mosque and its minaret,
Still as they stood of old.
Around it the city's ruins set,
'Mid a sea of reddish gold.

Few are the scattered stones that lie,
Portions of a fallen wall;
Even walls must sometimes die,
Even they cannot slight death's call.
Tow'ring above the shattered remnants,
Like a sentinel at his post,
With well-preserved, yet time-worn countenance,—
Stands the fane—a pale ghost.

Ghost of a glory that is gone,—
Ghost of a time that is no more.
When breaketh Eternity's dawn,
It shall be reborn, and not before.
Pale ghost, thou standeth,
As those stood of yore;
Then before you One demandeth
[. . .]

The World

Life is but a fleeting shadow,
    Passing swift away.
'Tis a glimpse of El Dorado,
    Lost another day.
The hours run fleetly by,
    Like an ever-rushing stream.

'Tis but a flickering sigh,
    And broken in our dream.

What you see to-day
    Will be gone to-morrow.
So enjoy it while you may
    And think not of sorrow.
That will come all too-soon, [*sic*]
    So be happy while you may.
For Life is but a passing boon,
    Coming swift, then swift away.

Thy hours that pass so swiftly by,
    Forming an ever-rushing river,
Flow into the sea of eternity,
    And then are lost forever.
A moment, a day of this is ours,
    Then, like a breath, it's gone.
And we who sojourned in life's bowers,
    Have vanished away, till another dawn.

Let us be happy while we may,
    "Now" is the watchword of life.
To-morrow we shall pass away,
    Beyond this vale of peace and strife.
"Oh! fools that after some to-morrow stray,"
    Think not of the future years.
Think but of to-day,
    "Now", is the key-word of the spheres.

Fools ye are that seek to rend
    The veil from future happenings,
And behold with awe-struck eyes the end
    Of all living, breathing things.
Leave the future as it lies,
    Seek not to peer within.
It's [*sic*] secrets were not made for mortal eyes
    To gaze upon and revel in.

Alla guards and alla [*sic*] keeps
    The reins of destiny.

Youth and Age

A young man stood on the threshold of life,
And looked thru the open door.
But he saw not the pain and the strife,
He saw but the golden shore.
He saw the joys of the earth,
And knew not the sorrow that lay beneath.
He heard the laughter and the mirth,
But saw not the blade within the sheath.

Said he, "Joy and happiness lie before me,
Once I have reached manhood's golden shore.
Naught but the sky will be above me,
When once I have passed thru this door."
His heart was filled with the joy of life,
As with gay and eager step he went within.
He knew not the pain and the strife
And the travail of the sons of men.

He was filled with joy and happiness,
And imbued with the hope of youth.
All of its fears and all of its hopes he did possess,
With the love of life and the love of truth.
Ambition was his, and the hope of success,
With the courage to bear and to strive.
A love for Allah he did profess,
And a hate for the evil Dive.

Years passed by, and the youth grew old,
And his illusions flew away.
He knew the dross that covers the gold,
And the night that hides the day.
He saw the sword within the sheath
And the tears below the laughter.
He knew the sorrow that hides beneath,
And the pain that cometh after.

He was a saddened and a wiser man,
For all things lay revealed before.
He had attained the hights above which none can
Go higher. He heard the sullen roar
Of the multitude far below.
He smiled sadly to think that they
Might never conquer their foe,

And speed higher and away.

In his heart there was no joy,
For he knew life's mockery.
He sighed for the days when he was a boy,
And knew naught of eternity.
"But," said he, "my pain will soon be o'er,
And life's troubles far below.
Soon shall I stand on another shore,
Where my soul can meet no foe."

Zuleika

An Oriental Song

The last red rays of the sun are glowing
    On minaret and wall.
Slowly they sink, so slowly going
    And the shadows spread o'er all.
And loudly thru the stillness rings
    The muezzin's call to prayer;
I sink, and think of other things,
    Of Heaven, and all that is there.

Yet, into my brain there stealeth,
    Slowly, sweet thoughts of you;
And my heart in secret kneeleth
    To thee, as many others do.
My brain is a chamber haunted
    By the image of thy face;
'Tis a holy shrine, enchanted,
    Because *thou* art in that place.

But welcome the ghost that haunts me,
    The image of thee, my sweet;
Dear is the face that enchants me
    And the eyes that have brought me to thy feet.
Where are the waters that can quench
    My quenchless love for thee?
Where is the earthly power or strength
    That can part thou and me?

Asia

She stands uncertain of her destiny
This ancient and far-spanning continent
O'er whom the nations of the Occident
Long years have fought and striven for mastery.
Not yet within the book of history
Is written her last page, for here are pent
Titanic forces in the Orient.

And seed, O mighty destinies
Call ye in turn the nations of the west
Think ye this great and fruitful teeming land
Not to be reckoned with in future days?—
This land where long ago with pomp ablaze
Empires upsprang and flourished, of which stand
The ruins yet have splendors to attest?

Aurungzeb's Mosque

Where ceaseless Gunga ripples by
I saw the minarets uprise;
O'er Benares, towering high
They gleam beneath the sultry sky,
Where that great seething city lies.

Tall, slender, tapering, they stand
Above the teeming sandstone ghaut
Where people bathe, and barges land—
Built by great Aurungzeb's command
Still it standeth, and he is naught!

The Mughals and the Sultans go
The Rajah's and the Nizam's die.
And Aurungzeb is lying low
Where Kistnok's stream doth ceaseless flow,
While his great mosque is tow'ring high.

The Burning Ghauts

I

Black loom the Ghauts against the evening sky,
In columns dark I watch the smoke arise.

Red flare the flames of fagots, leaping high—
Red flare the flames o'er yon dark sacrifice.

II

Down to the Burning Ghauts I see them bear
A priest, revered in all this earthly life.
Down on the Ghauts I see the torches flare—
Silence and flames, and end of human strife.

III

Watch that procession wending, mournful, slow,
Dark against the red and setting sun.
On the black pyre they lay the Rajah low,
Silent, impassive—for his work is done.

IV

High leap the flames above the looming pyre,
The shades of Indian night are falling fast.
High leap the flames—then sinks the fagot fire,
Dying slow—all things must end at last.

V

[. . .]

The Burning-Ghauts at Benares

Dark loom the ghauts against the stream and sky;
    The smoke doth rise and wind in columns grey;
Red flare the flames of fagots, leaping high,
    Then smoulder down, as dies the darkling day.

Now wendeth a procession, mournful, slow,
    Sharp-lined athwart the sun that sets in red;
Upon the pyre they lay the Raja low,
    Impassive, mute—this is his final bed.

Swift leap the crimson flames above the pyre,
    As shades of India's night are falling fast;
On high they leap—then sinks the fagot fire,
    And dieth slow. All things must end at last.

Dawn

I

Lo! the Sun hath leaped,—a flaming sword above the horizon,
Driving before him pale moon and stars—the Phantom Dawn is gone;
And o'er the Desert's vast expanse the morning light hath spread—
The Sun hath leaped from blackest Night—a flaming Sword of red!

II

I saw the glorious light flame on the distant minaret
Of some great king whose Sun of Life forevermore is set.
I saw it gleam from street to street—the glorious light of Dawn,
And over desert and city spread until the fiery day was gone.

III

The desert's sand was flushed with gleam of fiery morning sun,
And still it gleamed and shone until the flaming day was done.
Watching by the marble place where red roses were in bloom,
I saw it light the peacock's feathers—on a Moghul's tomb!

Delhi

Once I sat where flows the Jumna stream
  With Delhi's worn and battered walls beside;
Where flocked the minarets with fiery gleam,
  And palaces where men have loved and died.

A strange and glorious scene it was I saw,
  From city wall to highest spire,
And to the palace, whence India's law
  Went forth, from Akbar to Alamgire;

Where ruled the Moghuls in all their pow'r,
  And once did stand the Peacock Throne;
Where gleamed the glorious gem of Kohinoor,
  And treasure ran from every zone;

Whose princes reigned three hundred years
  O'er India, with an iron hand;
Through splendor great, and blood, and tears,
  And conquerors from a foreign land.

Delhi! city of barbaric wealth and Moslem power

Thy sunlight flashing on each fane;
Each minaret gleaming like the Kohinoor—
Thy palaces redolent of pleasure and of pain.

More dazzling e'en than them
Are the memories that 'round thee throng—
The barbaric pearl and gold of yesterday—
The Moghul emperors who reigned so long;

The wars of Aurungzebe and Alamgire,
The Afghans, and the Britons from beyond the sea—
Each memory like a flashing spire,
Redolent of peace and war—and thee.

A Dream of India

With dull, tired eyes and drowsy, wearied mind,
I closed and laid the heavy book aside,
That of far, strange, and storied India told,
Its race, its customs alien and old,
And for a space to muse within the chair reclined.
Soon Slumber came upon a darkened tide,
And Morpheus with poppy chains to bind
And lead me captive forth o'er sea and land,
On unseen wings as swift as morning light.
Afar I flew within the purple night,
Till sudden paled the stars—a phantom band,
And crimson dawn came like a rose full-blown.
Then Day, at once to his full stature grown,
Upstrode, and spread his glitt'ring armies wide
O'er tawny sands that now beneath me lay,
Thro' which a sluggish river wound away
To jungles vast and deep where night did bide,
In coverts from the light secure. Now on
I flew, nor slackened in my rapid flight,
Till over marble domes and min'rets bright,
That sparkling in the fervid eastern sun,
Did mark a city of the Orient proud,
I paused and hung. Then in the market-place
I lit, to mingle with the swarthy crowd,
Where jostled men of varied dress and race,
And in strange tongues did roar the traffic loud.
Here cheek by jowl the priest and outcaste walked,
And haughty Thakurs swaggeringly stalked;

Here desert men on swinging camels rode
With antique matchlocks o'er their shoulders swung,
And fierce-eyed Afghans from their high abode,
In sheepskin cloaks, pushed thro' the surging throng.
Now on the pavement clanged the iron staff
Of some gaunt, scant-clothed fakir, wild of face
To whom the throng respectfully gave place,
And 'fore whose coming dance-girls ceased to laugh.
Close at his heels a money-lender stout
Came leisurely, and serpent-charmers strolled,
With hooded cobras twined their necks about,
Whose twitching tails the Hindu boys, o'erbold,
With deftness pulled. Then quick the crowd gave way
To warning shouts from men in brave array,
Who room demanded for a Rajput queen.
Soon came her gorgeous, glitt'ring palanquin
Of velvet purple-blue and gold brocade,
Upborne by white-robed servitors. And now
Some veiled Mussulmani wife or maid
Stole past, or Hindu girl with o'er her brow
A scarlet sari drawn. Such was the throng
That, brilliant-costumed, filled the market-place
Thro' which I walked, and then a street along,
Or shops, where each within his tiny space
The merchants silent sat their goods among
And here all things were bought, all things were sold,
And work of craftsmen added to the din
And tumultuous surge of trade that rolled
With glare of hues the great bazaar within.

Now by that ceaseless human current borne
I went the narrow, seething street adown
To where, its carven gateway open thrown,
A massive temple stood on high. Deep worn
Its granite threshold was by countless feet,
That through long centuries had entered there.
I went within and through a court to where
Great brazen Vishnu on his lofty seat,
With face and eyes inscrutable, serene,
That saw not, gazed upon the busy scene,
As thronging worshippers before him passed
And at his feet their floral off'rings cast.
Their supplication with unhearing ears

He seemed to list, as one whose thought and gaze
Are on far things and other scenes or days.
Incarnate spirit of the Eastern years
Embodied Time, whose calm and scornful eyes
Naught may perturb, naught startle or surprise,
Great Vishnu seemed, and I for one brief space
A futile pigmy. Quickly passed the thought
And saw I but a brazen image wrought
By artists' craft—a sculptured form and face.

Then in my dream I once again took flight—
And like an arrow thro the light
I sped, till far from habitat of men
In Himalayan fastnesses supreme
I came to earth upon a mountain head.
A dizzy pinnacle: Here one might deem
He overlooked the world, for wide outspread
The hills and plains extended to the south—
Towards a receded, dim horizon line.
How terrible the sight—and how divine—
The sky-aspiring peaks, inspired, lone
Snow mantled and devoid of life or growth
Seemed high, and Winter's everlasing throne;
From which he held an undisturbèd sway—
And over all the spell of Silence lay—
Illimitable and inviolate.

The Ganges

Adown the ceaseless Ganges tide
    Where Gaya looms, at dusk I go;
Adown the stream I softly glide
    With Gungas' great, eternal flow.

Upon the bank the city looms,
    Dark athwart the evening haze;
The setting sun my red illumes,
    And strikes yon fane with dying rays.

Through that great banyan's leaves I see
    The Indian moon in silence rise;
While Gaya lies in mystery,
    I watch with calm and peaceful eyes.

Still float I down the Ganges stream,
In shadow and in sil'vry light;
And watch the city all a-gleam
Through the peace of India's night.

Alchemy

The rain poured down in torrents fast
The heavy storm clouds rolled;
But suddenly the sun broke through
And turned the rain to gold.

And so, perhaps, it may befall
Some sad day of thy years,
Black sorrow's clouds shall sudden break,
Joy turn to gold thy tears.

The Book of Years

Past time and space there is a Book of Years
Wherein are writ our loves and joys and tears,
A hand moves ever on our fate to trace,
And time and change may not those words erase.
And therein you and I shall some day read
Each thought of ours, each fateful word and deed.
Therefore do naught that will not please thy eye,
When read within that book beyond the sky.

Courage

On a disparate, despairing field,
A man plunged into the fight,
With his good sword shining bright.
Before him his foe reeled,
And fell away, like fruit before the blight.

His comrades turned, at his call,
And rallying, fought like men.
Down they back their foes then,
Drop them one and all
Like imprison'd swine in a pen.

And so they won the victory that day,
By the bravery of one man.
Great was his deed, greater than

Words can tell. Far more than my lay
Ever could or ever can.

There was another man, discouraged,
Enfeebled in the battle of life.
His heart with despair was rife,
And temptations about him raged,
Assailing him with great din and strife.

But he rallied and won,
In spite of all that against him lay,
And stood on the conquer'd field that day,
With a good work done
That ne'er could pass away.

The Days of Time

Two days of Time my eye hath seen,
Two days of strange and varied mien.
Of one the face was dark and drear,
Of one the face was bright and clear.
And though thou seest the darker day,
Know thou it hath not come to stay;
Tomorrow's morn thou mayest see
The brighter one Time brings to thee.

The Departed City

I stood 'mid the ruins of a city great,
And mused on the vagaries of destiny and fate.
Here, where I stand, a city once stood,
With all its mingled bad and good.
Here dwelt man and all his glory,
Here men were born, and here men grew hoary.
In this empty hall wherein I stand,
A king did issue his command.
There stood a palace, stately and tall,
Yonder, once was the city wall.
Where, now, is all this glittering pomp and show?
All—All, in the dust is laid low.

A Dream

Once while I slept a vision came to me
And said: "I come from lands that are faraway,
I come to you o'er land and sea.
My home is where the dawn of day
First hath its birth. From golden lands
I have flown to you. Follow me."
I arose. Away we flew o'er sea and sands,
O'er forest and plain and sea.

'Twas night; below us calm and silent lay
The wide expanse of mother earth.
Enshrouded in darkness it stretched away,
Where the day first hath its birth,
To the golden orient of the sun,
That far land where night and day
And all the things that in them lie,
Meet, and are mingled into one.

All was silent as thus we flew,
No sound the stillness broke.
Out of the east a zephyr blew,
And then the Vision, turning, spoke:
"All is peaceful now, the earth is still,
All men in slumber are lain.
But soon o'er forest, and plain and hill
Will ring their voices, again and again.

"The spirit of war is in the land,
Tho' darkness hath quelled it now.
On yonder hills that silent stand
Soon all will be bustle and show.
An army lieth encamped there—
A mighty force, the invader's flower
Who soon shall rend the silent air
With shouts as forth they ride in power.

"In a few short hours, where all is quiet now,
The earth shall quake with the tread of feet,
The sun shall glitter on pomp and show,
And the ground shall shake where armies meet.
Yonder they sleep—the pale monlight
Glitters on the sentinel's spear.

Tho now 'tis a calm and peaceful sight—
'Twill not be for long, for war is here."

I looked—and saw the gleam of steel,
The silent forms 'gainst the moon out-lined.
I felt the things that men can feel
When memory brings strange things to mind,
I thought of the countless wars of men,
And wondered why such things should be.
Why should things be now as they were when
The earth was in its infancy?

Sadly I mused as thus we hung
Above that ominous, silent scene.
Concealed by the veil that night had flung
In mercy, to hide where war had been.
Why, I mused, should man thus fight
And quarrel with his brother?
Had not centuries brought us light
To see and judge and love each other?

"Why," I said to the vision,
"Why should these things be?
How can they be beneath the sun,
When so many ages have rolled by into eternity?"
"They are," said the vision, shaking its head,
For Man is still deaf and blind.
Till he can learn by peace to be led
Still to war he'll be inclined.

"Yet I think that a time will surely come
When things shall be better than they now are.
When man no more shall be deaf and dumb,
When vanished and fled is the spirit of war.
Surely 'twill come, so let us pray
To hasten its coming from afar.
So soon may the clouds be rolled away
And disclose peace's shining star."

Fear

He who would fear
Must all hope lose.
Deaf to its voice will be his ear,

From him all hope will ooze.

Nothing will he ever attain,
Who holds fear of any kind.
Useless will be his brain,
Useless his mind.

Ye brave, who do not fear,
Will gain life's laurels and rejoice.
To hope's words your ear
Will listen, and speedily make its choice.

The Fear of Death

Mortal man, why do ye fear
    The coming of the end?
Why is life to ye so dear,
    Why do ye seek the torn to mend?
Why is death to ye so drear,
    Death that is a heaven-send?

Know ye not that ye must die
    Like they that went before?
Why at death's coming do you sigh
    And shrink till all is o'er?
Why seek ye to pass it by,
    To drive it from thy door?

Submit ye must whate'er betide,
    Shrink ye then no more.
Soon ye shall wonder why ye sighed
    And why ye wept before.
And ye shall know that they lied
    Who said that death was sore.

The Feast

Mighty and great was the king,
Stern and severe his rule;
Thru the land his name did ring,
On the lips of sage and fool.
Many, ah many are the years
That silently have rolled away,
Like dim, uncertain, passing fears

Since his day.

Great, oh great, was his pomp and pride
Great his wealth and great his throne.
On the necks of the mighty he did ride,
His rule was iron, and his heart was stone.
Yet wise was he, and he knew all;
Knowledge was his, and ancient lore.
He knew the pride that goeth before a fall,
And ere it was too late, forbore.

High was his name in the land;
From border to border it rung;
From fertile plain to burning sand,
It rang, and hung on every tongue.
At last there came a certain day,
Memorable in the annals of all time,
And which, tho' it long hath past [*sic*] away,
Is known in every clime.

It was the king's birthday,
A time for feasting and mirth.
(Because, the legends say)
It was the anniversary of his birth.
Great, o great was the feast
At the court of the king.
And even the least
Made the rafters ring.

In the midst of the figs and wine,
The king rose up and said:
"Good friends of mine,
Well have ye been fed,
And great is your merriment.
But remember what I say:
All is heaven sent
And all may pass away."

Hate and Love

Love came, and with its art
Beautified a trusting heart.
Into it the sunshine came,
In its chambers wrote its name.

Love stayed for a little while,
Gay and light, and free from Guile.
Happy days were these,
Lightsome, free, and gay,
Passing unperceived away.

Hate came and drove out love,
Love escaped and flew away;
Hate was not a gentle dove:
Drear and dark that day.
The sunshine no more came,
No more in those chambers wrote its name;
Hate dwelt forever in the heart
Cheating it with foul and lying art.

Dread and dark the days,
Presenting no light unto the gaze;
Passing slowly with leaden hours,
Dark; forbidding, devoid of flowers.
No hope of change was there,
All was ugly and not fair;
No hope till all was passed away,
No hope but the dawning of a better day.

Hope

Some despair and some hope,
Some are cheerful and some mope.
But I would choose,
If choice were given me,
The thing that once attained you cannot lose,
Till time unveils eternity.

The Land o' Dreams

There is a land twixt space and time,
Thy country of dreams;
It is an unknown clime,
Where nothing is, only that which seems.
Its people are shades of the past,
In the past they only exist.
They cannot, cannot last,
For they are only mist.

And yet I have visited the land,
And found it pleasant to sojourn.
Fertile soil and desert sound,
And many other things I did learn
It was made of. In short you could find there
All that ever was and ever could be.
There was solid soil and empty air,
And all things that should be.

And in this land I met
Many whom I once did know.
They were happy there—and yet—
And yet—when I left they would not go.
And so I left them there and came away,
Back to this sorrowful vale of tears.
Ah! When shall come that day,
When I shall brush aside the web of years.

The land of dreams hath faded into air;
'Twas but a vain deceiving,
A mirage, a vision fair,
Which, when coming, is leaving.
Oh! happy that happy land,
Where the people are only mist,
Where there is fertile plain and desert sand,
When naught doth exist.

And many and many a time
Since my first visit there,
Have I entered that happy clime,
And beheld its visions fair.
And ne'er again shall it fade away;
It shall always exit for me,
One day, and every day,
And for thee.

The Leveler

For name or fame
Death hath no respect.
What to him is fame or shame,
The fall'n, or the erect?

The peasant and the prince are one,

And one the nameless and the named.
All things that lie beneath the sun,
Yield to the arrows that death hath aimed.

But the fame of he who was good
Hath lived after he was dust.
Nothing ever will, or ever could
Cover his name with rust.

Shame, too, may endure,
But who for it hath mourned?
They who yield to its lure
Will find their names with thorns adorned.

Love

What is love ye say?
A thing that man cannot define,
A thought that flies away,
A passion that is blind.
Love is oft delusion,
The lust of a pretty face.
A fond illusion,
A passion low and base.
Of love there are two kinds,
The love of the human form,
And the love of minds.
The first is but a passing storm,
The last a thing that stays,
Beautifying the brain wherein it dwells.
The first was but a blaze
Dying out with the wedding bells.
The last, o reader mine,
Shall endure forever.
It is a thread so fine
That no knife can sever.

The Lure of Gold

For a paltry sum of gold
Many a man his soul hath sold,
And lived forevermore accurst,
Till his soul its fetters burst,

And its lonely way did wend
To tortures which have no end.

Beware of his fate
And ere it is too late
Forbear. Thou wilt find it best.
My mind will better rest,
If thou doest only what is right.
And when thy soul from men's sight
Has passed, thou wilt find
That there are no fetters to bind,
And drag thee down to hell,
And its torments fell.

As we sow, so shall we reap,
And the reaper must keep, [*sic*]
The fruit of what he hath sown
And fear not that thou wilt be alone
If thou sowest good seed:
Its fruit thou mayest sometime need.

Mercy

They are not many,
They who possess this virtue
In the highest degree.
They are few,
Those who pretend
To have it, are many.
They would not lend
Their strength to help a bitter enemy.
But he who is truly merciful
Would aid his direst foe in his extremity.
His cup of revenge would be full,
For he would have heaped
Coals of fire on his foe's head.
His would be the truest revenge,
Fuller than if his enemy had bled.

* * *

Aid thine enemy if he need thy help,
And forgive him if he transgress.
'Twill be a better revenge,
Far better than thou canst guess.

The Moon

Out of the darkness she glideth,
Casting her light o'er the earth.
On the wings of the night she rideth,
'Twas the night that 'gan her birth.
Her silver glory is cast o'er all,
The silent woods and hills.
It is a ghastly pall,
Covering streams and rippling rills.

Out of the skies she wingeth,
And higher and higher she goes.
Light to all things she bringeth,
Trees and earth, and friends and foes.
Into the skies she smileth,
When cometh the glorious dawn
When she goes no man thinketh,
He only knows she is gone.

He knows she shall come again,
In all her glory another night.
He shall see her then,
In all her silver light.
And she shall come until the End,
When worlds and men shall be no more;
And o'er the earth her light shall send,
Till nations meet on the sable shore.

Perseverance

He who has the gift of striving,
Never discouraged, never despairing,
Hath the true secret of living,
Living, and forever daring.

Perseverance is a sword
That use can only sharpen.
It is a word
To which all men should harken.

It is a divine gift,
For he who owns it success will surely achieve.
From the mire it can lift

Him, and will never desert or cleave.

If ye have it not, get it,
And use it as thy scimitar.
As it is a jewel, too, set it,
Near thee, not afar.

'Twill be thy sword and shield,
Thy corselet and thy javelin.
Where is the foe but who must yield,
And acknowledge thee to be a man?

Poem [?]

Up this wo[. . .]
And over this wo[. . .]
Never sit down with a rip in your [gown,]
But paddle your own canoe.

I have no wife to bother my life,
No lover to prove untrue,
Its all day long with a laugh and a song
Paddle your own canoe.

One is company and two is none,
I have no sorrow to make me blue,
Its all night long, with a cigar and a song
And I paddle my own canoe.

Up and down, and down and up I go
First here, then there, and thru.
But I never sit down with a rip in my gown,
But I paddle my own canoe.

I have no strife to mix up my life,
And neither have you.
So let us sit down, in the club up town
And paddle our own canoe.

Resignation

Whate'er may be my destined lot or fate,
Whate'er the future life, I calmly wait;
What use to fret or fear—the end of man
Unchanging is, and cometh soon or late!

The River

From its distant mountain source
Cold as ice and pure as snow
Runs the river here its course
Swiftly to the plains below.
Flowing ______ the canyon walls
Thickly clad with oak and pine
Past each hill that steeply falls
Like a blade the stream doth shine
Twisting, turning ever, free
Winding now then flowing straight,
Always onward to the sea
Never doth it hesitate.
From this hilltop watch with me
Gazing down where 'neath our feet
Far below the stream we see
Gleaming through the haze of heat
[. . .]

The River of Life

Winding—winding to the sea,
Ever on, goeth the river free.
Here he bends, and there he goes,
Here he stops, and there he flows.
Onward—to the sea
Goeth the stream so blithe and free.

And so floweth the River of life,
Onward thru peace and strife,
Here it turns and there it goes,
Here it stops, and there it flows.
Onward—to the ocean of eternity,
Goeth the river of life so blithe and free.

Sea-Lure

Oh! magic luring of the sea,
Whose myriad voices call to me,
With lapping whisper of the waves
The pensive tide that rippling laves
A gentle beach, or sullen roar

Of billows on a stubborn shore;
The hissing spray, the murmuring tide
Into my dreams and visions glide.
Or whispering the voices speak
O'er with the tones of waves that wreak
Their foaming rage imperiously,
Fore'er they call unto the sea.

The Sea-Shell

I put the sea-shell to mine ear,
And in its chambers seemed to hear
Faint echoes of the ocean's roar,
Long-treasured from a distant shore.

Thus in the chambers of the brain,
May echo like some haunting strain
A voice heard many years ago
Whose living tones we may not know.

Silence

'Tis a gift that few possess,
Yet 'tis worth more than gold.
Than gold ye should not value it less,
Ye who the precious gift hold.

Well can silence serve thee,
Tho thou may thinkest it not so.
To deeds of bravery it can nerve thee,
Ye who have learned your thoughts not to show.

Cherish the gift if thou hast it,
And keep it forever and a day.
Keep it—and cast it
Not heedless away.

Solitude

Long, long I sought for solitude,
For peace and rest, in dale and wood.
But fruitless was the search for me—
From my own self I could not flee.

And if the lesson well we heed—

The lesson by our failure taught
Another time we may succeed
Success from our defeat be wrought.

Summer Idleness

Come with me and let us go
Up the path that windeth slow
'Mid the oaks that high o'erhead
Gnarled and mossy branches spread
'Mid the laurel and the pine
'Neath the wild grape's clinging vine.
Up the rocky, steep ravine,
Where the willows rear their screen.
In its shady sheltered nook
Where the tiny, purling brook
Doth its secrets low confide
To the bending bracken fern—
Secrets that we two may learn
If from life's turmoil set free,
From its noise and bustle fled
We may wander, fancy led,
Listen to the bird and bee
Sing and hum their melodies
Hear the faintly sighing breeze
In the solemn pines and feel
Nature's magic 'ver us steal—
Magic that doth soothe and heal.

To the Best Beloved

Let he who will search through every land,
From China to Japan to India's strand,
O'er mountains and seas, and desert sand;
Yet in all his searching he will not find
A magnet half so strong as a woman.

The World

The world is a world of ups and downs,
A world of smiles and frowns.
The sunshine followed the rain,
And pleasures cometh in the tracks of pain.

There's joy that succeeded sorrow,
Tho cloudy today 'twill be sunny tomorrow.

Spring cometh in the path of Winter,
And spring into summer doth enter.
Dawn cometh after night,
And darkness gives place to light.
So don't worry my dear,
If thy life be drear,
For 'tis a long lane that hath no turning:
Thy grief is only a school for learning,
To appreciate the joy that cometh after pain,
And value more greatly the sunshine after rain.

And all the grief and all the sorrow
We shall forget in the bright tomorrow.
We shall wonder why we cried
And laugh where once we sighed.
When cometh the happy day
When grief and pain shall pass away.

[Fragment 7]

Wavy—wavy grow their lines,
    The wind sighs in the trees.
Now silence reigns again supreme,
    The breeze drops down once more;
Still stays the silver gleam,
    Shining the whole land o'er.

Higher goeth the golden sphere,
    The shadows shorten slow;
The light is there, the light is here,
    The light is high and low
Hour after hour passes away,
    The moon sinks slowly down.
Soon cometh the day,
    Banishing night's silver frown.

CPSIA information can be obtained
at www.ICGtesting.com
Printed in the USA
BVHW040803210420
R10767800001B/R107678PG577227BVX1B/1